The Guide to Workforce Planning

Allys Watson

Dedication

This book is dedicated to my granddaughter Z, an exceptional human being whose love of music and youthful outlook on life have been a profound source of inspiration. Her ability to interpret and experience the world through music has provided me with invaluable insights, encouraging me to approach the serious topic of human resources-workforce planning with creativity and vibrancy. Her passion and remarkable perspective have motivated me to infuse this work with depth and energy, ensuring that its important themes are not only discussed but truly brought to life.

Acknowledgment

I would like to extend my deepest gratitude to everyone who contributed to the creation of this book. My heartfelt thanks go to my colleagues and mentors in the field of human resources and workforce strategy, whose wisdom and encouragement have shaped my thinking and inspired many of the ideas presented here. I am indebted to the many organizational leaders and HR professionals who generously shared their stories, challenges, and triumphs; your experiences have brought real-world depth and vibrancy to these pages.

I am especially grateful to my family for their unwavering support and patience throughout this journey, and for reminding me of the importance of balance and perspective. Special thanks to my granddaughter Z, whose creativity and zest for life continue to inspire me every day. Finally, to my readers—thank you for your curiosity and commitment to shaping the future of workforce planning. May this book serve as both a guide and an inspiration as you chart your own path forward.

Preface

Imagine stepping into a grand concert hall just as the first notes of a symphony begin to swell—every instrument, every player finely tuned, poised in perfect harmony to create something far greater than the sum of its parts. This is the essence of strategic workforce planning: an artful orchestration of human potential, every talent and skill aligned with the rhythm and vision of a dynamic organisation. In a world where change is the only constant and business landscapes ripple unpredictably like an ocean tempest, mastering this orchestration becomes both a necessity and a craft. Welcome to "Workforce Planning: Mastering Strategic Planning for Tomorrow's Talent Needs," a journey into transforming the abstract, often intimidating arena of workforce strategy into a vivid, accessible, and actionable masterpiece.

If you are an organisational leader, an HR professional like me, or a business strategist, this book is a compass and a canvas. It serves not only to guide you through the labyrinth of forecasting, risk assessment, and talent segmentation, but also to embolden you to envision a future where your workforce thrives amid uncertainty. The pages ahead are infused with the pulse of real-world stories— industry leaders grappling with disruption, HR teams navigating technological revolutions, visionary strategists weaving agile cultures—all brought to life to illuminate the roadmap you can craft within your own organisation.

At its heart, this book is a celebration of human capital as the most nuanced and powerful asset a company can steward, like a conductor who listens to each instrument's voice, balances crescendos, and anticipates shifts in tempo, workforce planning requires acute sensitivity to the signals of the market, the evolution of technology, the cultural undercurrents within organisations, and above all, the aspirations and capabilities of people. This balance is art and science, inspiration and analysis. It is the work of leaders who see beyond immediate staffing needs and grasp the vivid mosaic of future possibilities—those who can look across the stage of business and anticipate the roles their talent will play in tomorrow's narrative.

Throughout this book, you will encounter themes that resonate deeply with that vision. Strategic alignment is the spine of the narrative—it reaffirms that workforce planning is not an isolated HR function but a fundamental business imperative. When talent strategies synchronize with overarching goals, the entire organisation moves with deliberate purpose and unmatched momentum. Forecasting, then, emerges as an indispensable tool, not merely a guess at what lies ahead but a sophisticated dialogue with data, emerging trends, and risk scenarios that challenge and expand traditional thinking. Agility and resilience become your mantra, teaching you to meld a workforce that flexes gracefully in the face of disruption, evolving demand, and shifting technologies. Leadership and culture are revealed not as distant abstractions but as the very lifeblood of sustainable change, channelling the energy and creativity of individuals into a symphony of collective success. Finally, technology integration—through AI and data analytics—empowers this whole endeavour with unprecedented predictive power and insight, turning uncertainty into opportunity.

Yet, this book is not a dry manual nor a jargon-laden textbook. Instead, imagine it as a vibrant tapestry woven from vigorous metaphors, compelling case studies, and practical frameworks, designed to illuminate complex concepts with the warmth of storytelling. It invites you to reflect, to challenge assumptions, and to engage actively with tools and insights that transform ideas into action. Each chapter unfolds with pacing that mimics the ebb and flow of a well-composed melody—sometimes stirring and robust, other times thoughtful and deliberate—but always moving you toward a crescendo of understanding.

Why, you may wonder, focus so intently on workforce planning in times when change accelerates like never before? Because the future of business depends fundamentally on the ability to anticipate talent needs with precision and creativity. The organisations that flourish will be those that treat their workforce not as a static resource to be managed but as a dynamic ecosystem to be nurtured, aligned, and propelled forward with intention. The gig economy, remote work paradigms, and continuous learning imperatives—these are not fleeting trends but elements of a new world order in the employment landscape, requiring leaders who are both visionary and pragmatic.

This volume is a call to action for every leader ready to step up and become a maestro of their workforce's future. It is an invitation to mindfulness and mastery, to move beyond reactive firefighting toward proactive design of talent architectures that can absorb shocks, seize opportunities, and compose a future brimming with innovation and resilience. The Planning you will develop through these pages is not rigid or formulaic but a living, breathing strategy—flexible yet anchored in strategic foresight; robust yet adaptable; deeply human yet powered by technology.

As you turn these pages, I encourage you to think of yourself as more than a reader. You are an architect of possibility, a visionary planner whose decisions today will shape the successes of tomorrow. Whether you lead a multinational corporation or a growing startup, whether you are an HR professional looking to elevate your strategic impact or a business strategist seeking new pathways to growth, this book offers you a lens—the knowledge and tools to see clearly through the fog of complexity and the inspiration to act decisively and creatively.

May this book serve as your guide, your challenge, and your companion on the journey of mastering workforce strategy. Together, let us tune the instruments, raise the baton, and conduct a symphony of human potential that resonates across the concert hall of tomorrow's business world—transforming uncertainty into harmony, and dreams into enduring success.

Welcome to "Workforce Planning." The orchestra is waiting.

Contents

Dedication iii

Acknowledgment iv

Preface...v

Introduction..1

The Symphony Begins: Understanding Workforce Planning..........3

    Workforce Planning Defined 3

    The Orchestra Metaphor 10

    Strategic Alignment Basics... 17

Reading the Market: Environmental and Business Scanning 26

    External Market Trends 26

    Internal Business Factors 35

    Competitive Intelligence 43

    Regulatory and Social Changes 51

Forecasting the Future: Talent Demand and Supply....................59

    Quantitative Forecasting Methods 59

    Qualitative Insights 67

    Balancing Demand and Supply..................................... 76

Navigating Risks: Identifying and Mitigating Workforce Challenges 84

    Types of Workforce Risks 84

    Risk Assessment Techniques.. 91

    Mitigation Strategies.. 98

Building Workforce Resilience................................... 104

Segmenting Talent: Understanding Workforce Diversity and Needs...115

Demographic Analysis.. 115

Skill and Competency Mapping................................ 123

Tailoring Strategies for Segments............................ 142

Data and Technology: Tools for Strategic Planning...................152

Workforce Analytics Fundamentals 152

AI and Predictive Modelling...................................... 156

Leadership's Baton: Driving Workforce Strategy 177

Leadership Roles in Workforce Planning................... 177

Communicating the Vision 185

Change Management Essentials 191

Building Agility: Creating a Flexible Workforce 207

Cross-Training and Skill Development 207

Flexible Work Arrangements..................................... 214

Continuous Learning Cultures 221

Metrics for Agility 228

Measuring Success: Metrics and KPIs for Workforce Planning .236

Identifying Relevant KPIs.. 236

Data Collection and Analysis.................................... 242

Continuous Improvement Processes.......................... 249

Embedding Strategy: Implementation and Communication........258

Developing Implementation Roadmaps...................... 258

Stakeholder Engagement 266

Transparent Communication Strategies...................... 275

Feedback and Adjustment Cycles............................... 282

Embracing the Future: Trends Shaping Workforce Planning......289

Remote and Hybrid Workforces.................................. 289

Automation and AI Impact 298

Demographic and Social Shifts................................... 305

The Final Movement: Crafting Your Workforce Planning..........314

Framework Overview 314

Action Planning Tools 321

Sustaining Momentum 330

Workforce Planning Information Gathering Form 340

Section 1: Organisational Context 340

Section 2: Current Workforce Profile 340

Section 3: Workforce Planning Objectives................. 341

Section 4: Risk Assessment and Scenario Planning ... 341

Section 5: Tools, Resources, and Communication 341

Section 6: Continuous Improvement and Learning 341

Section 7: Additional Notes 342

About The Author 343

Introduction

Imagine the pulse and precision of an orchestra—each musician tuned in, not just to their own notes, but to the shifting rhythm of the whole ensemble. Workforce Planning sets itself apart from the crowd by handing leaders the conductor's baton and unveiling its proprietary Harmony Model: a step-by-step framework blending real-time analytics with the irreplaceable intuition of human insight. While other workforce planning books offer theory, Workforce Planning gets your team playing in sync, transforming abstract strategy into a living, breathing performance.

What makes the Harmony Model so distinctive? It charts a clear pathway: from mapping your current talent with detailed skills matrices—like a score charting every instrument's role—to orchestrating seamless succession planning that ensures no vital player is ever left out of tune. By weaving in predictive analytics, you'll anticipate talent gaps before they appear, allowing your organisation to respond with agility rather than scrambling to catch up. Picture a scenario where, as business needs shift, you already know which rising stars are ready to step up, and which skillsets need nurturing—because your Harmony dashboard revealed it in real time.

Packed with vibrant case studies and actionable steps, Workforce Planning doesn't just narrate best practice; it invites you to join the symphony. You'll leave with practical tools—succession pipelines, dynamic skills inventories, forecasting dashboards—not just concepts.

Whether you're an HR professional (like myself) or a business leader, this is your backstage pass to conducting a resilient, adaptive workforce, finely tuned for whatever the market's next crescendo brings.

With its lively metaphors and sensory storytelling, Workforce Planning transforms workforce planning from a dry exercise into a captivating art form—helping you compose a future-ready organisation where every individual is part of a harmonious whole.

Allys

ALLYS WATSON
CAHRI MPRS NCFM

AHRI
Australian
HR Institute
Certified
Practitioner HR
CPHR

The Symphony Begins: Understanding Workforce Planning

Workforce Planning Defined

In the dynamic symphony of organisational success, workforce planning emerges as the melodic foundation upon which every harmonious business achievement is composed. At its essence, workforce planning is the strategic process by which an organisation anticipates future talent needs and orchestrates the acquisition, development, and deployment of human capital to meet those demands with precision and timeliness. This crucial function transcends the mere filling of vacancies or reactive hiring; it is a forward-looking discipline that aligns talent strategies meticulously with the overarching ambitions and evolving realities of the business landscape. To grasp workforce planning is to understand how it transforms uncertainty into opportunity, knitting together the art of prediction with the science of optimization, enabling organisations to navigate change with agility and foresight.

The fundamental premise of workforce planning is deceptively simple yet profoundly impactful: an organisation must understand not only who it employs today but also who it will need tomorrow, and how to get from point A to point B with economy, swiftness, and strategic insight. This forward gaze requires a deep examination of current workforce capabilities, an astute analysis of external and internal business drivers, and an ongoing dialogue between talent considerations and corporate objectives. It is this seamless integration between human capital and business strategy that defines the maturity and readiness of an organisation. Without it, companies risk stumbling into talent shortages, skill mismatches, and missed market opportunities, much like an orchestra attempting to perform without sheet music or rehearsal—a discordant cacophony where potential solos are lost in chaos.

To appreciate the pivotal role workforce planning plays, we must first situate it amidst the broader strategic management framework. The completeness of any business strategy hinges on knowledge—not only of markets and products but of the people who drive innovation, serve customers, and perpetuate the brand's ethos. Workforce planning operates at this nexus, a bridge that connects human potential with the pursuit of competitive advantage. It serves as a lens through which an organisation views both its present capabilities and its future aspirations, rendering visible the gaps between where it currently stands and where it aims to be. In a world characterized by accelerating technological disruption, shifting demographics, and volatile economic conditions, workforce planning becomes an indispensable compass, guiding leaders through the fogs of uncertainty toward clear, actionable insight.

The Guide to Workforce Planning

Central to workforce planning is the concept of strategic alignment, an orchestra conductor's blend of vision, timing, and adaptability that ensures all players move in concert toward a shared goal. This means talent decisions cannot be siloed or relegated to operational checklists; instead, they are integral components of a living, breathing strategy ecosystem. This ecosystem accounts for a complex array of variables: impending retirements, emerging skill requirements, potential leadership vacuums, and fluctuating market demands. It contemplates the cascading effects of external forces—such as globalization, regulatory changes, and technological innovation—while remaining deeply attuned to internal cultural dynamics and employee aspirations. By weaving these disparate strands into a coherent plan, organisations harness workforce planning as a dynamic tool for resilience, innovation, and sustained growth.

Moreover, workforce planning is inherently a discipline of anticipation rather than reaction. While many organisations remain trapped in a cycle of filling immediate vacancies—akin to patching leaks in a ship—true workforce planning imagines the tides that will strike tomorrow, fortifying the vessel before the storms arrive. This proactive stance is achieved through meticulous environmental scanning and scenario analysis, which enable organisations to peer beyond the horizon and prepare for multiple eventualities. It shifts the mindset from being overwhelmed by the uncontrollable flux of the labour market to exercising influence over one's talent destiny by shaping recruitment pipelines, nurturing critical skills, and cultivating adaptable roles. Such foresight transforms workforce planning from a back-office function to a strategic vanguard, a creative act that mobilizes the firm's most valuable asset—its people—to seize emerging opportunities rather than succumb to disruptions.

This elevated conceptualization of workforce planning also underscores its multifaceted scope. It is not a task handled solely by human resources departments but a collaborative endeavour that involves leadership at all levels. Executives provide the vision and business context, line managers offer granular knowledge of operational demands, and HR professionals translate these insights into strategic talent architectures and metrics. This interplay demands not only technical competence but also emotional intelligence and persuasive communication, as workforce planners champion the cause of human capital as a vital contributor to business outcomes. By integrating these diverse perspectives, workforce planning generates a rich tapestry of insights that informs decision-making, drives accountability, and fosters a culture of continuous talent evolution.

An additional dimension to consider is the evolving nature of the workforce itself, which has grown exponentially more complex and fluid. Traditional models of workforce planning, steeped in steady-state assumptions and linear career trajectories, no longer suffice in a terrain sculpted by gig economies, remote work, and accelerated automation. Modern workforce planning must incorporate agility and resilience, preparing the organisation to pivot and respond as skills demands shift, new roles emerge, or unexpected challenges arise. This requires sensitive calibration of workforce segmentation, where different talent pools—permanent employees, contingent workers, freelancers, and digital collaborators—are managed with tailored strategies that reflect their distinct contributions and risks. Through this inclusive lens, workforce planning acknowledges that the organisation's human capital ecosystem is diverse and dynamic, deserving of nuanced stewardship.

Importantly, workforce planning derives its potency from data-driven insight, yet it remains rooted in artful interpretation and strategic judgment. Quantitative analyses—such as predictive modelling, trend extrapolation, and skills inventory mapping—provide the essential scaffolding for informed decisions. However, these tools gain meaning only in the hands of practitioners who contextualize numbers within the intricate realities of their organisations. The interpretative layer adds texture, weighing qualitative factors such as cultural fit, leadership potential, and employee engagement, which are less tangible but equally vital. This melding of analytics and intuition elevates workforce planning into a discipline that is both rigorous and human-centered, embracing complexity without succumbing to paralysis.

The benefits of robust workforce planning ripple throughout the organisation. With clear Planning for future talent needs, companies can reduce costly workforce gaps, streamline recruitment efforts, and accelerate onboarding processes. Additionally, it promotes internal mobility by identifying skill-development opportunities that align with career aspirations and business demands, thereby enhancing employee retention and engagement. By anticipating workforce risks—whether arising from demographic shifts, competitive labour markets, or changing regulatory frameworks—organisations can devise contingency plans that mitigate impact and sustain productivity. Ultimately, workforce planning catalyses a virtuous cycle where strategic foresight fuels talent readiness, which in turn enables superior business performance, competitive differentiation, and value creation.

To illustrate workforce planning's transformative potential, one need only observe companies that have embraced it as an operational imperative. For instance, forward-thinking technology firms invest heavily in analysing emerging skill trends, partnering with educational institutions, and designing flexible talent models that accommodate rapid innovation cycles. Manufacturing giants, faced with an aging workforce, leverage detailed succession plans and targeted reskilling initiatives to preserve institutional knowledge and maintain operational continuity. Retail organisations harness data analytics to forecast seasonal demand fluctuations, deploying agile labour strategies that balance fixed staffing with temporary contingents. Across industries, the common thread lies in workforce planning's capacity to convert complex challenges into executable strategies that anticipate, rather than react to, talent demands.

At its core, workforce planning is an organisational mindset—a commitment to viewing people not as mere resources to be managed but as pivotal contributors to a shared vision. It invites leaders to adopt the role of conductors, thoughtfully guiding the nuances of recruitment, development, and retention to create a symphony of performance that resonates with purpose and precision. In doing so, it bridges the abstract realm of strategic intent with the concrete realities of day-to-day workforce execution. This harmony between vision and action, between numbers and narratives, defines workforce planning's unique and indispensable role in securing an organisation's future.

Thus, workforce planning stands as both an art and a science, embodying a forward-thinking discipline that empowers organisations to shape their futures rather than be shaped by external forces. By fostering alignment between talent and enterprise goals, adopting a proactive stance imbued with data-rich insights, and embracing agility amid complexity, workforce planning lays the foundation for sustainable success. It enables organisations not just to survive in a volatile world but to thrive with confidence, creativity, and coherence. For leaders and strategists alike, mastering workforce planning is mastering the craft of organisational stewardship—it is the Planning upon which tomorrow's talent needs are met, and business aspirations realized.

The Orchestra Metaphor

Imagine stepping into a grand concert hall, the air vibrating with anticipation. At the centre stands the conductor, poised to awaken a symphony of sounds from a diverse congregation of skilled musicians. Each musician holds an instrument uniquely crafted, producing a distinct voice—strings, woodwinds, brass, and percussion weaving a complex tapestry of melodies and harmonies. This is no ordinary gathering; it is an intricate dance of coordination, timing, and expression, all converging into a singular, magnificent performance. The metaphor of an orchestra offers a powerful lens through which to understand the nuanced art of workforce alignment in organisations. Just as a conductor unites varied musical voices into harmonious crescendos and subtle diminuendos, so too must organisational leaders orchestrate their human capital to meet strategic objectives, crafting a composition that resonates with both internal purpose and external demand.

The Guide to Workforce Planning

At first glance, the orchestra may appear a paragon of effortless unity, but beneath the surface lies a profound complexity that mirrors the challenges faced in workforce planning. Each section of the orchestra—violinists, cellists, flutists, trumpeters—possesses distinct roles, skill sets, and tempos. The conductor's baton does not simply command; it interprets a carefully crafted score, anticipating how the interplay of instruments must evolve in real time to create cohesion. Similarly, workforce planning demands leaders who can interpret the organisational strategy as a dynamic score, carefully tuning roles, competencies, and capacities to harmonize with shifting market rhythms. It is not enough to have talented individuals; their contributions must coalesce with precision, respecting timing, sequence, and the subtle energy that fluency in collaboration brings.

The beauty of the orchestra also lies in its capacity to embrace diversity while ensuring unity. No two musicians play the exact same note in the same way; even repeated sections breathe with variations of expression, reflecting individual artistry within collective discipline. In the modern workplace, this serves as a vital reminder that workforce alignment is less about uniformity and more about synergy. Leaders must cultivate an environment where diverse talents and perspectives are not merely tolerated but strategically woven into the fabric of enterprise objectives. Crafting a symphony from a multitude of voices requires acute awareness of everyone's strengths and limitations, alongside a clear understanding of the ensemble's ultimate purpose. Herein lies the core of strategic workforce planning—it is an art of balancing individuality with cohesion, spontaneity with structure.

Moreover, the orchestra's performance is defined not only by the present interplay of sound but by the unseen preparations: rigorous rehearsals, tuning, and meticulous attention to detail. The musicians hone their skills over years, but the conductor's role in synchronizing these skills is pivotal for success. This preparation parallels the foundational work necessary in workforce strategy. Foresight, environmental scanning, and meticulous talent forecasting lay the groundwork to anticipate future challenges and opportunities. It is through such anticipatory actions that organisations avoid discordant moments—where talent mismatches or misaligned objectives create strategic cacophony. Organisational resilience emerges from this advanced preparation, much like an orchestra's grace under pressure stems from trust, rehearsal, and shared vision.

The conductor's subtle gestures—sometimes barely perceptible—guide transitions, modulating tempo, volume, and even emotional tone, evoking a reaction from the ensemble that propels the music forward. Such nuanced leadership is emblematic of the strategic stewardship necessary in workforce planning. Leaders are tasked not only with setting direction but with sensing organisational mood, culture, and latent potential, adapting fluidly to the evolving environment. Workforce strategy is far from static; it requires adaptive leadership attuned to market fluctuations, technological advancements, and employee aspirations. The analogy deepens when considering that even the best musicians cannot thrive under a rigid or disconnected conductor—the human element, empathy, and situational awareness become as crucial as technical skill. In workforce terms, this equates to leaders who foster engagement, champion inclusivity, and maintain open channels of communication, transforming strategy into lived experience.

Delving deeper, an orchestra's complexity reveals insights into the necessity of balance across multiple dimensions—short-term improvisation interlaced with long-term planning, recognition of technical expertise balanced with emotional expressiveness, and the orchestration of diverse instruments to produce a unified output. Workforce planning also navigates this multidimensional terrain, requiring a comprehensive perspective that integrates immediate operational demands with future growth trajectories. The strategic imperative is to cultivate talent pipelines that not only fill vacancies but also nurture capabilities aligned with envisioned business transformations. This means being vigilant for emerging skill trends, disruptive technologies, and evolving customer needs that shape the organisational 'score' in unforeseen ways. Like an orchestra prepared to adapt mid-performance, workforce planning must remain flexible, enabling rapid recalibration without losing sight of core themes.

An additional layer of the orchestra metaphor lies in the role of the sheet music—or, in organisational parlance, the strategic plan. The musical score is a painstakingly developed plan, crafted with intent and symbolism, yet open to interpretation. It prescribes the notes but invites artistry in execution. Similarly, workforce planning frameworks provide guidelines and metrics, but the real mastery lies in interpreting them through the lens of context, culture, and human dynamics. Strategic alignment, therefore, is not a rigid mandate but a living, breathing roadmap that evolves as organisational priorities shift. This dynamic interplay between structure and creativity challenges leaders to think beyond static spreadsheets and rigid forecasts, embracing the fluid nature of human capital development as an ongoing performance.

From this vantage point, the interplay between the orchestra's sections underscores the interdependencies within organisational roles. The violas may subtly underpin the melody, the percussion punctuates rhythm and momentum, while the woodwinds weave nuanced counterpoints. Each path, while individually significant, derives power from synergy and timing. In workforce terms, this highlights the importance of cross-functional collaboration and integrated talent management systems. It is insufficient for departments to work in isolation; rather, they must operate as interlocking gears, attuned to one another's tempos and cadences. Workforce planners must facilitate these connections, breaking down silos to foster innovation and agile response. When departments sing from the same sheet, the organisation resonates as a cohesive whole—a symphony designed to captivate its audience: customers, stakeholders, and society.

While the orchestra metaphor is powerful, it also illuminates potential pitfalls. Excessive rigidity within an ensemble can stifle creativity, rendering the music mechanical and lifeless. Correspondingly, an overly prescriptive workforce plan can suffocate innovation and employee autonomy. Conversely, too much improvisation may breed chaos, highlighting the need for disciplined frameworks that enable freedom within boundaries. Thus, the art of workforce alignment demands a delicate equilibrium—one where structure supports agility and where human ingenuity is harnessed toward strategic intent. The conductor's challenge in striking this balance serves as a vivid reminder that workforce planning is not a mechanical process but a dynamic art, requiring constant recalibration and emotional intelligence.

Further enriching this metaphor, consider the audience's role in an orchestral performance. Their response—whether rapt attention, enthusiastic applause, or reflective silence—influences the emotional energy enveloping the musicians. Similarly, the external environment—customers, competitors, regulators—acts as a responsive audience to organisational labour. Workforce planning must therefore incorporate market feedback and societal expectations, attuning talent strategies to create value not in isolation but as part of a larger ecosystem. The responsiveness to this 'audience' signals the difference between static HR functions and vibrant, strategic human capital management that propels sustainable growth and innovation.

Ultimately, the orchestra metaphor distils the essence of workforce alignment as an exercise in harmony, foresight, and adaptive coordination. It encapsulates the profound truth that an organisation's success derives not solely from individual brilliance but from the orchestration of diverse talents into a unified, purposeful whole. Like a masterful symphony, workforce planning demands intentionality, empathy, and vision—qualities that breathe life into strategic objectives and transform abstract plans into tangible achievements. As leaders embrace this metaphor, they embark on a journey that transcends conventional management, positioning themselves as conductors of human potential, inspiring their organisations to perform at the highest level of excellence and innovation. This opening image sets the stage for a deeper dive into the fundamentals of strategic workforce planning, framing it as not merely an administrative necessity but a vital, creative act central to tomorrow's business success.

Strategic Alignment Basics

In the vast symphony of organisational success, where every instrument must master its parts to create a harmonious composition, strategic alignment serves as the conductor's baton, guiding each note and rhythm with intent and clarity. At the heart of workforce planning lies this essential concept: the deliberate and thoughtful synchronization of the human capital strategy with the overarching business objectives. This is not a perfunctory exercise in concurrency; instead, it is a dynamic, forward-looking process, steeped in understanding that talent resources are the very lifeblood for achieving strategic ambitions amid an ever-changing market landscape. Strategic alignment represents the bridge between the sometimes-abstract visions of organisational leaders and the tangible, day-to-day reality of workforces mobilized to bring those visions to life. It requires leaders to move beyond siloed thinking that isolates personnel management as an operational necessity and embrace it instead as a core driver of competitive advantage, innovation, and resilience.

To fully grasp the essence of strategic alignment in workforce planning, one must first appreciate the evolving context in which modern organisations operate. Markets no longer reward only scale or cost efficiencies alone; they increasingly value agility, creative problem-solving, and adaptability. Business goals now often read like promises to stakeholders—customers, investors, communities—pledges to respond swiftly to shifts in technology, consumer behaviour, regulatory environments, and global disruptions. In this ecosystem, workforce strategies incapable of anticipating and evolving alongside these goals represent underlying risks, not just missed opportunities. Strategic alignment, then, becomes a safeguard against these risks by establishing an intentional, systematic process through which workforce capabilities—skills, cultures, capacities—are meticulously calibrated to support both current operations and future growth trajectories. It transforms workforce management from a reactive practice into a proactive, predictive discipline, one that enables organisations not only to meet demand but to shape that demand through skilled and motivated human resources poised to lead change.

The foundational principle here is that business strategies and workforce strategies must be conceived as two inseparable facets of the same strategic coin. This means leaders must first articulate clear, measurable business objectives—whether it's launching new product lines, entering markets shaped by emerging technologies, scaling rapidly in response to consumer demand, or pioneering sustainable practices. These objectives set the stage, defining what success looks like over the short, medium, and long term. Once these goals are crystallized, workforce planners translate them into talent imperatives: the number and type of roles needed, the competencies required, the cultural attributes essential to navigate complexity, and the organisational structures that ensure agility and collaboration. The alignment finds fluid continuity here; it is a process of iterative refinement, where changes in business focus directly inform talent acquisition, development, and deployment strategies, and where workforce data feedback continuously informs strategic decision-making about business investments and priorities.

A crucial, often overlooked nuance is that strategic alignment isn't merely about matching workforce numbers to expected demand; rather, it's about tuning the entire workforce ecosystem. This includes understanding the quality and diversity of skills, the adaptability and learning capacity of employees, and the alignment of incentives and leadership behaviours with the strategic vision. For example, if a company's business goal centres on innovation and market disruption, the workforce plan must prioritize recruiting creative thinkers, investing in continuous learning platforms, encouraging cross-functional collaboration, and fostering an organisational culture that tolerates experimentation and embraces failure as a learning signal. Alternatively, a business focusing on operational excellence and scale may place greater emphasis on standardized processes, efficiency training, and lean staffing models balanced with sufficient redundancy to ensure reliability. Thus, strategic alignment is nuanced and context-sensitive—it requires deep insight into the organisation's unique DNA and the environments in which it competes.

Moreover, strategic alignment is not a static achievement but a living process. Business goals evolve under the weight of external pressures such as technological breakthroughs, geopolitical shifts, regulatory changes, consumer trends, and competitive moves. The workforce strategy must remain fluid, continuously re-examined and recalibrated to ensure ongoing relevance and efficacy. Notably, rapid advancements in data analytics and artificial intelligence have empowered organisations to enhance this agility, enabling real-time talent demand forecasting and scenario planning that better anticipate future workforce needs. Yet, technology alone cannot achieve strategic alignment. It demands leadership commitment—a mindset that values foresight, transparency, and the deliberate integration of workforce planning into core business strategy discussions. Leaders must champion this integration at the executive level, embedding workforce considerations into boardroom dialogues, operational plans, and financial forecasting, advocating consistently for the human dimension as a strategic asset rather than a cost centre.

At the practical level, organisations striving for strategic alignment often begin by establishing governance frameworks to synchronize planning cycles and decision-making. This means HR, business units, finance, and strategy teams collaborate in joint planning sessions to align assumptions, define workforce-related key performance indicators, and agree on reporting mechanisms. These multi-stakeholder processes leverage diverse perspectives and facilitate shared ownership of workforce outcomes, which is vital given the intricate dependencies between talent availability, skills development, and business execution speed. For example, supply chain disruptions that may delay product launches need immediate workforce adjustments; without alignment and coordination, such responsiveness is impossible. Instead, through integrated workforce planning, organisations gain visibility into where they can stretch capabilities, where skills gaps exist, and how to prioritize talent investments that will deliver the greatest strategic return.

Consider also the role of communication in cementing strategic alignment. A workforce plan disconnected from the broader organisational narrative risks being ignored or misunderstood. Hence, clear storytelling that links workforce initiatives to business outcomes is fundamental. This narrative must permeate all levels of the organisation—from C-suite executives commissioning strategic reviews to frontline managers who implement staffing changes—to ensure everyone understands how their efforts contribute to the collective ambition. Engaging employees in this strategic storyline instils a sense of purpose and fosters agility, empowering teams to make workforce decisions aligned with greater organisational goals rather than local convenience or short-term fixes. Moreover, embedding alignment in the organisational culture creates a feedback-rich environment where suggestions and insights flow upward, allowing workforce plans to evolve in concert with both frontline realities and executive vision.

Equally important is recognizing that strategic alignment encompasses not only internal considerations but external factors as well. The talent marketplace is influenced by broader economic, social, and technological shifts. Successful organisations extend strategic alignment outward, engaging with educational institutions, workforce development agencies, and professional networks to anticipate talent pipeline dynamics and skill shortages well before they impact operations. This external focus allows for more strategic talent partnerships, targeted upskilling programs, and sourcing strategies that anticipate labour market fluctuations. Organisations that master this proactive stance gain first-mover advantage in accessing emerging talent pools, particularly in industries undergoing rapid digitization or disruption. Thus, strategic alignment positions workforce planning as an outward-looking discipline, integrating market intelligence with internal strategy to create a cohesive and resilient talent ecosystem.

Achieving strategic alignment also involves a delicate balancing act between short-term operational responsiveness and long-term talent sustainability. Organisations often face immediate pressures—urgent hiring needs due to turnover, project demands, or unplanned vacancies—that tempt a focus on quick fixes. However, a purely reactive approach jeopardizes long-term success by ignoring developmental pipelines, succession planning, and cultural cohesion essential to sustaining competitive advantage over decades. The most effective workforce plans, therefore, incorporate a dual horizon: addressing acute demands while simultaneously nurturing future-ready capabilities. This duality requires robust scenario planning and forecasting capabilities that allow decision-makers to envision multiple futures and prepare contingencies. For instance, a technology firm anticipating automation trends might immediately hire talent in artificial intelligence while simultaneously investing in educational partnerships to build talent pipelines for emerging roles a decade away. By linking these layers through strategic alignment, organisations ensure that workforce investments are not ad hoc but part of a coherent narrative linking talent supply with evolving business imperatives.

The benefits of such disciplined alignment are profound. Organisations that successfully align workforce strategies with business goals experience greater operational efficiency, faster innovation cycles, and enhanced employee engagement. Employees understand how their roles contribute to larger objectives, giving them clarity and motivation, which reduces turnover and builds a stronger employer brand. On the leadership side, aligned workforce plans translate into data-driven confidence in decision-making, enabling prioritization of initiatives with the highest strategic payoffs while minimizing reactive firefighting. This calibrated approach produces agility not by chance but by design, enabling organisations to pivot quickly in the face of disruptions without sacrificing continuity or morale. Importantly, in an era where human capital increasingly defines market differentiation, strategic alignment emerges as the linchpin for harnessing talent not as a resource to be expended but as a source of innovation, engagement, and sustainable growth.

In weaving together the threads of business strategy and workforce capability through strategic alignment, organisations compose a living plan that harmonizes intent with execution, vision with reality. This Planning requires ongoing attention, investment, and cultural embedding. It challenges leaders to deepen their understanding of human capital beyond counts and costs, to embrace their roles as orchestrators of talent ecosystems, and to see workforce planning as a grand, strategic art form that directs the symphony of organisational success toward ever-evolving horizons. Through strategic alignment, workforce planning transcends its traditional boundaries to become a pivotal instrument in crafting futures—not merely responding to them—a paradigm shift that separates thriving enterprises from those struggling for relevance in an unpredictable world. As such, mastering strategic alignment represents the foundational step for any organisation determined to lead boldly, innovate relentlessly, and cultivate talent ecosystems tuned perfectly to the cadence of tomorrow's business realities.

Reading the Market: Environmental and Business Scanning

External Market Trends

When we peer beyond the walls of our organisations and venture into the bustling marketplaces where industries converge, evolve, and sometimes fracture, we find ourselves immersed in a complex ecosystem steeped in perpetual flux. The external market trends act as both the weather and the tide by which the delicate vessel of workforce planning manoeuvres, compelling us to attune our senses to the subtle shifts and roaring storms that shape talent demand. It is in this vast expanse where the interplay of economic currents and industry whispers craft a narrative that must be understood—not as cold data points, but as living signals that anticipate the rhythms of human capital needs, the very lifeblood of any enterprise intent on thriving amidst uncertainty.

To grasp the monumental weight of external market trends is to embrace a panoramic perspective that extends beyond the immediate operational horizon. Industries rarely evolve in isolation. They resonate with the wider economic environment—booms sow wildflowers of hiring surges, recessions summon the shadow of contraction and recalibration. Within this intricate dynamism, the talent marketplace mirrors the broader economic choreography, sometimes leading, sometimes following, but always entwined in a dance that determines whether organisations will glide forward with confidence or stumble amid unforeseen challenges.

Consider, for instance, the technology sector, a vibrant stage where rapid innovation and competitive fervour dictate relentless transformation. Here, workforce demands oscillate like a symphony's crescendo and decrescendo, driven not merely by the advent of new coding languages or software breakthroughs, but by broader economic impulses and shifting consumer behaviours. When the global economy pulses with vigour, ventures mushroom swiftly, eager to seize untapped markets, itching to onboard the freshest minds proficient in artificial intelligence, machine learning, or cybersecurity. Conversely, when economic tremors surface, hiring freezes tighten their grip, and the strategic emphasis pivots toward nurturing existing talent, reskilling, and optimizing workforce flexibility. This illustrates a critical insight: industries act as barometers for economic health, and their labour needs morph in tandem, rendering workforce planning a perpetual exercise in anticipation shaped by the ebb and flow of external forces.

Turning our gaze to the economic indicators themselves reveals a reservoir of intelligence waiting to be harnessed. Metrics such as unemployment rates, gross domestic product growth, consumer confidence indexes, and sector-specific benchmarks are not static figures; they are vivid signals pulsating with meaning for workforce strategists. A rising unemployment rate in the broader economy, for example, can foreshadow an increase in available talent pools, potentially easing recruitment pressures in some domains while intensifying competition in others, particularly where specialized skills are scarce. Similarly, GDP expansion signals growing business activity, often accompanied by increased hiring but also by heightened competition for elite talent as companies jostle for market share. Interpreting these economic signposts requires more than cursory glances—it demands nuanced analysis, contextualized understanding, and forecasting models that elevate raw data into actionable foresight.

Moreover, it is vital to explore the effect of global economic shifts on localized workforce planning decisions. In our interconnected world, supply chains stretch across continents, geopolitical developments ripple through financial markets, and capital flows fluctuate with dizzying speed. A technology company headquartered in San Francisco might feel the ripple effects of manufacturing slowdowns in Southeast Asia or shifts in trade policies enacted thousands of miles away. Such disruptions often cascade into workforce implications, evidenced in sudden requirements for alternative sourcing strategies, adjustments in role priorities, or fluctuations in talent acquisition costs. The challenge for workforce planners is to build resilience into their frameworks, cultivating an agile mindset that pivots effortlessly as external tides change, ensuring the organisation maintains not just survival but thrives on adaptive strength.

Industry-specific trends further colour the texture of talent demand, often with profound implications. Take healthcare, where demographic shifts such as an aging population spark surges in demand for nurses, therapists, and specialized medical professionals. Parallel to demographic factors, technological advancements such as telemedicine and AI diagnostics reshape skill requirements, creating a landscape where traditional roles evolve at breakneck speed while new positions emerge from the fertile ground of innovation. These dual dynamic challenges require workforce architects to decode signals within their particular industry ecosystem, engaging with professional bodies, attending to legislative changes, and continuously scanning the horizon for emerging patterns that will redefine the contours of work. Without this vigilant gaze, organisations risk crafting workforce strategies misaligned with the real future rather than the faded echoes of the past.

Environmental factors, often overlooked in mainstream discussions, play an increasingly pivotal role in shaping workforce needs. Climate change implications ripple through industries—from agriculture adapting to shifting weather cycles to energy sectors transitioning to renewables—each generating waves of demand for new skills and novel roles. The rise of environmental, social, and governance (ESG) criteria further propels organisations to reconsider their talent composition, elevating executives, analysts, and frontline workers proficient in sustainability practices and regulatory compliance. Such macro trends are not peripheral; they are central pillars reshaping the foundation upon which workforce strategies must be erected. Ignoring these forces risks obsolescence, while engaging deeply pays dividends in competitive advantage and societal contribution.

Layered within this intricate theatre is the formidable influence of technological disruption. Digital transformation sweeps across sectors like a relentless storm, wielding both promise and peril. The rise of automation and artificial intelligence reshapes entire job families, amplifying some while eroding others. Talent demand pivots toward roles incorporating sophisticated technological fluency, strategic agility, and creativity, demanding planners anticipate not just the volume of talent needed, but its qualitative evolution. This shift challenges traditional workforce planning paradigms, inviting greater integration of predictive analytics, scenario modelling, and real-time market intelligence. Workforce architects must evolve into market futurists, attuned to emerging capabilities and prepared to orchestrate transitions that are as seamless as they are visionary.

The Guide to Workforce Planning

At the confluence of these forces lies the critical recognition that external market trends are not mere background noise—they are active currents that must be engaged with intention and insight. Strategic workforce planning demands a dynamic approach anchored by continuous environmental scanning and interpretation. This involves constructing a multidimensional radar capable of detecting not only the obvious signals but also subtler tremors beneath the surface. Regular engagement with industry reports, economic forecasts, market intelligence platforms, and expert networks becomes imperative. However, gathering this information is but the first step; the transformative power lies in integrating these insights into cohesive workforce forecasts that align tightly with organisational strategy.

Bringing the organisational context into this interplay reveals further nuance essential for meaningful workforce planning. No two organisations respond identically to external market trends; their history, culture, financial health, strategic priorities, and risk appetite shape how external forces manifest internally. For example, a start-up with aggressive growth projections may respond to booming market trends by ramping up hiring rapidly, leveraging venture funding, and an entrepreneurial mindset. Conversely, an established multinational might adopt a more cautious stance, focusing on talent development and retention amidst industry expansion, mindful of legacy systems and stakeholder expectations.

Understanding these organisational filters is crucial for workforce strategists, enabling tailored responses that marry outside-in awareness with inside-out realities.

The integration of external market trend analysis into workforce planning cycles demands deliberate structures and processes. Organisations that excel in this regard often embed cross-functional teams tasked with horizon scanning, forecasting, and translating findings into actionable workforce interventions. These teams engage regularly with business leaders, human resources, finance, and operations, ensuring that labour market insights inform budgeting, recruitment, learning and development, and succession planning. The resulting plans are not static documents but living plans, continually refined as new data emerges and market contexts evolve. This iterative rhythm fosters organisational agility, empowering leaders to recalibrate workforce investments proactively rather than reactively.

A particularly illuminating example surfaces when examining the manufacturing industry's navigation through globalization and automation trends. As supply chains became increasingly complex and volatile, manufacturers confronted pressing questions about the nature and location of their workforce. Rising trade tensions and geopolitical shifts prompted relocation strategies, influencing talent pools and skill deployment. Automation introduced a paradigm shift, demanding reskilling and redefining job roles. Organisations that succeeded in aligning workforce strategies with these external movements—by investing in workforce analytics and scenario planning—were able to sculpt workforces resilient enough to absorb disruption and flexible enough to exploit new market opportunities. Their experience underscores the profound impact that meticulous external trend analysis has on sustaining competitive advantage.

Furthermore, the labour market itself—a component of the external environment—is constantly evolving in structure and accessibility. Trends such as the gig economy, remote work proliferation, and demographic shifts in workforce participation redefine how organisations attract, engage, and retain talent. Market analyses must extend beyond traditional employment models, anticipating new patterns of worker preference, talent mobility, and contract typologies. These emerging dynamics compel organisations to rethink their workforce architecture, crafting flexible models that accommodate fluctuating talent demands without compromising culture or productivity. Workforce planning that overlooks such shifts risks structural mismatch and lost opportunities.

At a more granular level, regional economic conditions and industry clusters offer fertile ground for workforce planners to refine their projections. Localized economic booms can create intense competition for talent, inflating salaries and causing turnover risks.

Conversely, regions grappling with economic stagnation might present an abundant talent reservoir, but with caveats linked to skill gaps or misalignment with organisational needs. Effective workforce planning incorporates this geographical intelligence, aligning recruitment and development strategies with regional realities. Transcending one-size-fits-all approaches, this granularity instils precision and adaptability in workforce design.

The art of decoding external market trends demands a blend of analytical rigor and interpretative intuition. Purely quantitative models, while essential, must be complemented by qualitative assessments that capture emerging shifts still invisible in hard data. Industry conferences, expert networks, and social media sentiment analyses provide textures of insight that enrich predictive accuracy. Layering these perspectives nourishes a panoramic workforce strategy, expansive enough to embrace complexity yet focused enough to generate actionable outcomes.

In closing, external market trends form the inescapable context within which workforce strategies unfold. They are the master rhythms guiding the symphony of talent demand, informing every note of hiring, development, and restructuring decisions. Organisations that cultivate a deep, ongoing understanding of industry currents and economic ebbs position themselves not merely as reactive actors but as visionary architects of their workforce futures. Embracing this external vantage point transforms workforce planning from a tactical exercise into an anticipatory art form—one where human potential is harmonized seamlessly with the unpredictable cadences of the marketplace. It is this mastery of external trend interpretation that equips leaders to compose workforce Plannings robust enough to navigate disruptions, agile enough to seize new horizons, and insightful enough to sustain lasting organisational success.

Internal Business Factors

In the intricate dance of workforce planning, understanding internal business factors is akin to tuning each instrument before the orchestra begins to play—without this atonement, even the most brilliant composition is bound to fall flat. These factors form the foundational rhythmic pulse that guides every decision regarding talent acquisition, development, and deployment within an organisation. At first glance, companies may be tempted to gaze outward, focusing heavily on external market trends and broader economic indicators to forecast talent needs. Yet, it is the internal environment—the unique constellation of organisational characteristics, strategies, culture, resources, and operational realities—that often serves as the true compass for workforce planning efficacy. Diving into these internal factors yields a rich appreciation of how personalized and fluid workforce strategies must be, for no two companies compose their future in quite the same key.

Central to this internal assessment is the company's strategic vision and its translation into tangible business objectives. A workforce plan devoid of alignment with long-term goals quickly loses its relevance and potency. Whether the organisation strives for rapid innovation, market expansion, cost leadership, or customer intimacy dramatically influences the shape of its human capital requirements. For instance, a company pursuing aggressive digital transformation will demand a markedly different cadre of skills—data scientists, software engineers, and agile project managers—compared to one focusing on manufacturing scale or traditional client services. These strategic priorities also interplay with the company's lifecycle stage. Start-ups and high-growth companies experience frenetic acquisition and development cycles, often requiring flexible talent models and a robust pipeline of versatile talent. In contrast, mature organisations may prioritize workforce stability, succession planning, and skills revitalization to maintain their competitive edge while navigating market saturation or disruption.

Beyond the statement of intent lies the organisational structure, which acts as the architectural Planning shaping workforce dynamics. Centralized versus decentralized models, the degree of matrix management, the level of cross-functional collaboration—all these structural nuances condition how talent flows, how roles evolve, and where critical skill gaps emerge. In organisations where decision-making processes are heavily layered, workforce planning must anticipate bottlenecks and plan for leadership development programs that cultivate middle management effectiveness to mitigate paralysis. Conversely, flatter organisations with distributed authority necessitate workforce plans that emphasize autonomous capabilities and soft skills such as communication, conflict resolution, and innovation. The structural DNA informs not only job design but also talent mobility, internal transfers, and career path fluidity, which are essential levers for building agility.

The cultural fabric of a company—its unwritten norms, values, and behavioural expectations—permeates every aspect of workforce planning. A culture that champions continuous learning and embraces change fosters an environment where upskilling, reskilling, and role reinvention are not only possible but expected. Such cultures create fertile ground for workforce strategies that hinge on internal talent development and dynamic role allocation. Conversely, risk-averse or siloed cultures may present formidable barriers to change, requiring deliberate interventions to embed capabilities that support a nimble workforce. Understanding the pulse of the culture enables planners to tailor engagement strategies, communicate change effectively, and design development programs that resonate authentically with employees. It also highlights potential resistance points and opportunities to celebrate talent initiatives that align with intrinsic motivations and shared purpose.

Financial resources and budgetary constraints constitute a pragmatic backbone upon which all talent strategies must be built. Workforce planning is not an abstract exercise but a continuous negotiation with available capital. Economic forecasts and revenue projections directly influence hiring capacity, training investments, and technological adoption. During periods of growth, companies might prioritize expanding headcount and attracting top-tier talent with competitive compensation and benefits, while in leaner times, emphasis may shift towards internal redeployment, performance optimization, and cost rationalization. The sensitivity of workforce costs, including wages, benefits, training, and turnover expenses, calls for meticulous financial modelling within planning processes to avoid strategic missteps that could jeopardize organisational stability. This financial lens also guides investment in human capital analytics and planning software, tools that increasingly enhance decision-making precision.

Operational considerations also weave into the fabric of internal business factors. The specific demands of production cycles, service delivery models, customer demand variability, and supply chain dependencies all ripple through talent requirements. For example, organisations operating in industries with cyclical workforce demands—such as retail with seasonal peaks or agriculture with harvest periods—must design plans that incorporate temporary talent, flexible scheduling, and rapid onboarding processes. Others facing tight regulatory environments or stringent quality standards need highly specialized skills and compliance-focused training that shape recruitment and development priorities. Additionally, technological infrastructure within the organisation can either enable sophisticated workforce analytics or constrain planners to more traditional, intuition-based methods. The state of digital maturity thus directly impacts the precision and agility of workforce forecasting and planning.

Human capital inventory—the current skills, knowledge, experience, and potential residing within the existing workforce—is arguably the most critical internal factor to grasp with granularity. Labor market shortages, while important, pale in comparison to the treasure trove of internal talent when effectively mapped and leveraged. Conducting comprehensive skills inventories, assessing employee motivations, identifying high-potential individuals, and evaluating performance trends provide invaluable insights that can recalibrate hiring needs and inform targeted development initiatives. This internal talent mapping also promotes strategic succession planning, ensuring leadership continuity and mitigating risk associated with unexpected attrition. The more nuanced and dynamic this inventory, the better an organisation can pivot its workforce composition in response to both strategic shifts and unexpected contingencies.

Employee engagement and retention statistics offer another key dimension within the internal landscape. High turnover rates, absenteeism, or disengagement can signal disconnects that jeopardize workforce stability and continuity, influencing planning decisions about employee experience enhancements and retention strategies. Conversely, an engaged workforce often translates to improved productivity, innovation, and discretionary effort, thereby extending the effective capacity of existing talent. These metrics also unearth which parts of the workforce, whether by department, geography, or job role, may require urgent attention—informing redeployment strategies and guiding more precise workforce condition monitoring. Leadership's commitment to fostering an inclusive and supportive work environment thus becomes an indispensable internal pillar, shaping not only attraction but also the sustained involvement of talent.

Parallel to these human factors are the internal communication channels and information flows that underpin data collection and decision-making for workforce planning. Organisations with transparent, integrated communication tend to benefit from rapid feedback loops—timely insights from managers and frontline supervisors that keep workforce assessments current and relevant. When information silos prevail or reporting mechanisms are antiquated, even the most sophisticated workforce plans risk being crafted on outdated or incomplete data, leading to misplaced investments or missed opportunities. Embedding efficient communication processes ensures that workforce planners remain attuned to evolving conditions within teams, departments, and the enterprise at large, thus enhancing responsiveness.

Moreover, the organisation's appetite for innovation and change management capacity forms a subtle yet powerful internal cohort of factors. Workforce planning is seldom a one-off exercise; it requires iterative cycles of review, adaptation, and recalibration. Companies with established change frameworks, agile governance, and a propensity to experiment with new workforce models are better poised to absorb disruptions and recalibrate talent strategies accordingly. This disposition shapes not only how workforce plans are constructed but how effectively they are executed, embraced by stakeholders, and embedded in organisational practice. Recognizing and nurturing this change readiness is therefore integral to designing workforce strategies that endure beyond initial formulation.

One cannot overlook the role of leadership within internal business factors either. Executives and managers act as both architects of strategy and champions of its communication. Their perspectives, priorities, and behaviours influence everything from resource allocation to cultural tone and operational discipline. Leadership's involvement in workforce planning can drive alignment across silos, galvanize collective commitment, and accelerate implementation. Conversely, misaligned or absent leadership endorsement often consigns workforce planning efforts to peripheral status, undermining their impact. Active leadership participation also fosters accountability, ensuring that workforce plans do not stagnate as mere documents but evolve into living roadmaps that guide decisions and measure progress.

Lastly, internal audit functions and governance mechanisms contribute to workforce planning by providing oversight and risk management. These frameworks ensure compliance with labour laws, ethical standards, and internal policies, which can constrain or direct workforce strategies. For example, union agreements, diversity mandates, or geopolitical considerations might impose boundaries that planners must navigate. Simultaneously, these oversight systems present opportunities to embed workforce planning within broader enterprise risk management, allowing organisations to anticipate and mitigate human capital risks proactively. Such integration elevates workforce planning from tactical necessity to strategic imperative, weaving it into the very DNA of corporate governance.

Synthesizing these internal business factors, it becomes clear that workforce planning is not a mechanical process of matching numbers to roles but a deeply intertwined orchestration of multiple, often nuanced elements that shape the workforce's capacity and character. It demands a continuous exploration of the company's internal ecosystem—its ambitions, structure, culture, financial reality, operational rhythm, human capital assets, and leadership essence—all harmonized to anticipate and prepare for an uncertain future. Mastery of this internal alignment allows organisations to transform workforce planning from a reactive chore into a strategic instrument that not only supports but propels business success. In this light, workforce planners emerge not merely as administrators of talent but as visionary conductors of an evolving human capital symphony, finely attuned to the internal melodies that will define tomorrow's organisational triumphs.

Competitive Intelligence

In the ever-shifting arena of business, where every organisation moves to the rhythm of its own unique score yet competes on the same stage, the role of competitive intelligence in workforce planning unfolds as both an art and a science—an orchestration of insight gleaned from the external environment, tuned finely to inform internal decisions. To grasp the full palette of competitive intelligence is to step beyond the familiar walls of one's own enterprise and immerse oneself in the swirling currents of market trends, economic shifts, and the subtle yet powerful dynamics that ripple through industries and labour pools alike. It is a canvas that demands not only keen observation but also strategic synthesis, whereby the cacophony of raw data—a symphony of figures, reports, and market movements—is transmuted into a comprehensible and actionable narrative, guiding the architect of workforce strategy toward building a future-ready team.

At its core, competitive intelligence within workforce planning is about positioning one's organisation not merely to respond but to anticipate; to decode the tacit signals buried within employment patterns, talent mobility, and the competitive behaviours of peer companies. It begins with the understanding that talent is no longer confined within organisational borders but is fluid, moving across industries, geographies, and even employment models with increasing velocity. This fluidity is shaped by macroeconomic indicators such as unemployment rates, wage inflation, and sector-specific growth cycles, which paint a broad yet intricate picture of the labour market's vitality and constraints. Leaders skilled in competitive intelligence learn to read these indicators as a skilled conductor reads a musical score—interpreting tempo changes, pauses, and crescendos—that alert them to opportunities and threats looming just beyond immediate perception.

Economic indicators are the backbone of competitive intelligence efforts, serving as a compass in the vast expanse of workforce ecosystems. Analysts track shifts in gross domestic product, productivity rates, and consumer confidence, weaving these strands into forecasts that suggest where industries might expand or contract, which skill sets could become scarce, and where strategic investments in talent development are paramount. Yet, it is the contextualization of these metrics against organisational realities and competitor moves that breathe life into otherwise static numbers. For instance, when a competitor announces automation initiatives aimed at reshaping their manufacturing process, it signals a probable realignment in their workforce requirements—an insight that becomes a lever for proactive talent acquisition or reskilling within one's own company. Similarly, observing wage trends across similar firms can inform compensation strategies, preventing costly talent attrition while optimizing labour costs.

Market trends encompass a broader narrative, encapsulating technological innovation, customer behaviour shifts, regulatory changes, and evolving societal expectations, all of which ripple through workforce needs. The rise of artificial intelligence, for example, not only disrupts traditional job roles but also catalyses demand for new competencies in data science, machine learning engineering, and human-machine collaboration. Competitive intelligence involves tracking these shifts rigorously, identifying talent pools that may emerge or dwindle, and anticipating the speed with which these changes will permeate various functions. Within this dynamic, organisations that master such intelligence can establish themselves as magnets for sought-after specialties, adjusting their recruitment and development frameworks to capture talent ahead of their rivals. Furthermore, the ability to interpret regulatory signals—such as new labour laws, immigration policies, or industry-specific compliance requirements—adds another layer of sophistication, ensuring that workforce plans remain not only competitive but also legally sound and socially responsible.

Beyond the economic and market lenses, organisational factors within competitive intelligence extend to cultural and strategic dimensions observable among industry peers. Understanding how competitors cultivate their employer brands, deploy flexible working arrangements, or design career pathways unveils subtleties that data alone may obscure. These insights often come from a blend of sources—public disclosures, social media, employee reviews, and industry forums—forming a mosaic of the human experience within rival workplaces. Translating such qualitative intelligence into workforce planning means acknowledging that talent decisions are deeply human and cultural, influenced by perceptions of opportunity, purpose, and work-life integration. A company that learns its peers are attracting top talent with compelling narratives of innovation and impact recognizes the imperative to craft a similarly resonant employer value proposition.

The process of gathering competitive intelligence demands rigorous discipline and ethical rigor. It is not merely about amassing information but about discerning which signals warrant attention amid the noise. Effective intelligence practitioners deploy an array of tools—from analytics platforms aggregating labour market data to specialized consulting services offering industry benchmarks. More importantly, they cultivate a mindset of continuous curiosity and agility, recognizing that intelligence is a living stream that must be refreshed regularly to remain relevant. The cadence of data collection is thus calibrated to the pace of industry evolution—more frequent in volatile environments such as technology sectors where disruption is rapid, perhaps quarterly or even monthly, and less often in more stable sectors, where annual or biannual reviews suffice.

Why does this matter so profoundly for workforce planning? The answer lies in the inherent uncertainties of the future. Strategic workforce planning without competitive intelligence risks becoming an echo chamber, guided solely by internal assumptions and historical data that may no longer hold true. To build a resilient and agile talent architecture, organisations must incorporate backward-looking analytics with forward-looking foresight, informed by a vivid understanding of competitive moves and market posture. For example, if market trends hint at an impending surge in demand for cybersecurity professionals driven by heightened regulatory scrutiny, workforce planners armed with this intelligence can initiate focused talent pipeline strategies, investing in specialized training, partnerships with educational institutions, and targeted recruitment campaigns. In contrast, a lack of this intelligence risks reactive hiring that lags behind demand, resulting in talent shortages and lost business opportunities.

Successful cases abound where competitive intelligence has translated directly into workforce advantage. Consider a global financial firm that recognized early on the increasing prominence of fintech startups and their aggressive hiring of software engineers and data analysts. By closely monitoring competitor hiring patterns, industry shifts, and regulatory changes favouring digital finance, the firm restructured its workforce planning to double investment in in-house skills development and flexible hiring models, including gig and remote talent. The result was not only reduced dependency on volatile external markets but also a revitalized, future-ready workforce attuned to emerging business models.

Another instructive example emerges from the manufacturing sector, where an automotive company leveraged competitive intelligence to navigate the accelerating transition to electric vehicles. By systematically examining competitors' talent acquisition strategies, partnerships with technology firms, and shifts in research and development staffing, the company anticipated the need for new engineering competencies and retrained legacy employees. This proactive approach enabled it to maintain market share and innovate without the bottlenecks that beset several rivals caught unprepared by the pace of transformation.

Moreover, the integration of technology amplifies the scope and precision of competitive intelligence in workforce planning. Artificial intelligence and big data analytics provide unprecedented capabilities to process vast datasets encompassing labour statistics, social media sentiment, competitor job postings, and economic forecasts. These tools create dynamic dashboards that reveal emerging trends or talent signals that may otherwise escape human notice. For leaders, the visualization of such data transforms competitive intelligence into strategic insight, a clear lens through which to view the future workforce landscape. This intersection of human judgment and machine-powered analytics forms the cutting edge of workforce strategy, enabling decisions rooted in evidence yet flexible enough to adapt as new data emerges.

Yet, the value of competitive intelligence is not confined to large multinational corporations with ample resources. Organisations of all sizes can harness well-structured approaches to data gathering and analysis, tailored to their context. In fact, the discipline of competitive intelligence fosters an organisational culture attuned to the external environment, enhancing overall strategic acumen. By involving cross-functional teams—including HR, finance, marketing, and operations—in intelligence gathering and interpretation, companies build collective ownership of workforce planning outcomes. Such inclusiveness ensures that intelligence is not siloed but embedded throughout the organisation, nurturing agility and an anticipatory mindset.

There is also a critical temporal dimension to competitive intelligence that shapes its effectiveness. Intelligence is most potent when it is forward-looking rather than reactive, enabling pre-emptive moves that confer competitive advantage. This requires leaders to embrace uncertainty not as a risk to avoid but as a dimension to navigate proactively. Workforce plans informed by real-time intelligence become living documents, updated regularly to reflect trend shifts, competitor actions, and internal progress. This dynamic quality transforms workforce planning from a static annual ritual into a continuous strategic dialogue, responsive to the nuances of market cadence.

Despite its manifold advantages, competitive intelligence must be handled with a keen appreciation of legal and ethical boundaries. Organisations must safeguard proprietary information and respect non-disclosure agreements, ensuring that all intelligence activities adhere to regulations and ethical guidelines. The trust and reputation of a company depend on maintaining these standards, even as it pursues aggressive strategic insight. Ethical competitive intelligence fosters sustainable relationships within industries and supports a healthy, transparent labour market that benefits all stakeholders.

In sum, the mastery of competitive intelligence within workforce planning is akin to tuning an orchestra to the subtle harmonies that ripple across the market landscape. It allows leaders to see beyond immediate internal constraints and perceive opportunities in the external tempo—emerging talent pools, shifts in competitor strategy, economic tremors, and evolving cultural currents. It converts the abstract into the actionable, enabling workforce strategies that are not only responsive but anticipatory, not only stable but agile, attuned to both the melody of immediate business demands and the symphony of long-term vision. The integration of competitive intelligence paramountly transforms workforce planning from a reactive exercise to a strategic core, positioning organisations to thrive amid both certainty and flux, harmonizing human potential with the cadence of an ever-evolving market.

Regulatory and Social Changes

The fabric of workforce planning is perpetually embroidered with the intricate threads of regulatory and social change, each stitch shaping the ultimate tapestry of an organisation's talent strategy. To navigate this evolving landscape with finesse demands more than a cursory nod to compliance or a reactive posture to new laws; it requires an anticipatory mindset, one that perceives legal and societal shifts not as external disruptions, but as integral signals guiding the orchestration of human capital. As organisations endeavour to master the complexity of workforce alignment, they must attune their strategic planning to the rhythm of fluctuating market trends, emerging economic indicators, and the dynamic pulse of societal values, all of which coalesce to inform the subtle art of forecasting and adaptation.

Legal frameworks act as the structural underpinning of workforce governance, delineating the permissible boundaries within which organisations may operate. These frameworks are neither static nor monolithic; rather, they are living instruments subject to continual refinement, influenced by political tides, public policy debates, and judicial interpretation. This fluidity means that workforce planners must cultivate a vigilant awareness of the current regulatory environment and, more importantly, develop the institutional agility to anticipate and respond proactively to impending legal reforms. Consider the surge in data protection regulations worldwide—a domino effect beginning with the European Union's General Data Protection Regulation (GDPR) rippled swiftly through other jurisdictions, compelling organisations to overhaul their data handling practices and talent management policies alike. Workforce strategies that embraced these shifts early were able to secure competitive advantages not only by compliance but by cultivating trust with employees and customers, thus enhancing employer brand and retention.

Likewise, labour laws continuously evolve to address pressing societal issues such as wage equity, workplace safety, and non-discrimination mandates. The growing emphasis on pay transparency laws, for example, has precipitated a significant transformation in compensation strategies. Forward-thinking organisations interpret these legal changes as opportunities to enhance fairness and reinforce cultural values, embedding equity as a cornerstone of their workforce Planning. They engage in comprehensive audits of pay practices, reconfigure job classifications, and enhance internal mobility pathways, ensuring that the workforce architecture is resilient to legal scrutiny and aligned with social expectations. This approach transcends mere compliance; it is the sculpting of a culture that resonates with authenticity and ethical leadership, fuelling engagement and attracting diverse talents who seek employers with a commitment to social justice.

Parallel to these legal shifts, societal changes continue to reshape the contours of the workforce in profound and often unforeseen ways. The social fabric that frames workforce planning is woven with threads of generational change, evolving demographic profiles, shifting cultural norms, and the ceaseless demands for inclusion and belonging. Each element exerts a subtle yet potent influence on how organisations conceive of work, talent acquisition, development, and retention. The rise of the millennial and Gen Z workforce segments, each characterized by distinctive values and expectations around work-life integration, purpose-driven employment, and continuous professional growth, has compelled a reassessment of traditional workforce models. Organisations that fail to internalize these social cues risk not only falling behind in competition for talent but also eroding the foundational trust necessary for long-term success.

The increasing diversity of the global workforce stands as both a challenge and a beacon for sophisticated workforce strategies. Social imperatives around equity, diversity, and inclusion are no longer peripheral corporate social responsibility ideals but strategic imperatives integral to innovation and market relevance. Organisations embracing this reality embark on nuanced workforce segmentation, crafting talent pathways that acknowledge diverse cultural contexts, varied career aspirations, and the myriad barriers historically faced by underrepresented groups. They employ sophisticated analytics to track not only diversity metrics but also the qualitative nuances of inclusion, such as employee engagement and psychological safety. Through these measures, workforce plans become living documents that reflect and respect the diversity of human experience, crafting an environment where all employees can thrive and contribute meaningfully.

Economic indicators, often seeming far removed from the immediate concerns of human resources, weave a vital thread into this tapestry of regulatory and social change. Macro-economic trends such as unemployment rates, inflation indices, and labour market fluidity influence the supply-demand equilibrium for talent, compelling organisations to recalibrate their workforce acquisition and development strategies. During economic downturns, for instance, workforce planning pivots towards optimization— redeploying existing talent, emphasizing cross-skilling, and judicious hiring freezes—while in periods of economic expansion, the focus shifts toward aggressive talent acquisition and onboarding. The interdependency of economic cycles and workforce dynamics underscores the necessity for planners to integrate robust environmental scanning mechanisms, continuously interpreting economic data within the context of their organisational mission and strategic goals.

Moreover, societal attitudes toward work and employment are increasingly governed by the broader economic realities facing communities and individuals. The gig economy, for instance, reflects a profound socio-economic shift fuelled by technological advancement and changing lifestyle preferences, resulting in a more fluid, contingent workforce composition. Organisations grappling with these trends find themselves reimagining traditional employment models, balancing the benefits of flexible arrangements against the challenges of maintaining organisational cohesion and knowledge continuity. Regulatory responses to the gig economy, such as debates over employment classification and benefits entitlement, further amplify the complexity of workforce strategy, highlighting the necessity for a keen legal acumen intertwined with empathetic social awareness.

Within this entwined web of regulatory mandates and social evolution lies the pivotal role of organisational culture, a living embodiment of values and behaviours that mediate the relationship between external changes and internal workforce responses. Workforce strategies grounded in a resilient and adaptive culture are better positioned to absorb shocks from legal shifts and societal expectations without friction. Leadership emerges here as the conductor who aligns values, communications, and organisational structures with the ongoing transformation in regulatory and social landscapes. Through transparent dialogue and participative change management, leaders foster an environment where new policies and social imperatives are not mere edicts but shared commitments. This cultural synergy accelerates the translation of external forces into strategic advantages, enabling organisations to move beyond compliance as an obligation and toward a proactive stance that embraces change as a driver of innovation and sustainability.

The interconnectedness of these factors—regulatory frameworks, social dynamics, economic realities, and organisational culture—creates a complex ecosystem within which workforce planning must operate. Successful strategies recognize that these are not separate silos but interdependent forces that demand simultaneous consideration and nuanced interpretation. For example, anticipating the impact of a shift in employment law requires understanding its social impetus, economic consequences, and cultural feasibility, integrating these insights into a cohesive plan that balances risk mitigation with opportunity maximization. The cultivation of such holistic insight calls for multidisciplinary collaboration within organisations, bringing together legal experts, human resource strategists, financial planners, and cultural architects to co-create workforce planning that is both compliant and compelling.

Navigating regulatory and social changes also involves embracing the power of scenario planning and predictive analytics to model the implications of emerging trends and legal reforms. By simulating various "what-if" scenarios—ranging from radical labour law overhaul to shifts in societal attitudes toward remote work—organisations can stress-test their workforce strategies against uncertainties. Advanced analytics enable planners to detect early signals and extrapolate potential workforce impacts, providing a data-driven foundation for agility. This methodology transforms workforce planning from a reactive checklist into a dynamic, foresighted process that aligns talent ecosystems with the contours of tomorrow's social and legal landscapes.

Furthermore, organisations dedicated to embedding social responsibility within their workforce plans excel in cultivating external partnerships and networks that provide real-time insights into regulatory developments and societal movements. Engagement with industry consortia, labour unions, governmental agencies, and community groups enriches the strategic perspective, ensuring that workforce planning is not only internally coherent but externally informed and validated. This outward-looking stance fosters credibility and legitimacy, key ingredients in building a workforce strategy that resonates authentically with employees, regulators, and the broader society alike.

In sum, understanding and integrating regulatory and social changes into workforce planning is an exercise in strategic symphony, where every legal update, societal shift, economic trend, and cultural signal plays a note essential to the composition's harmony. Those organisations that listen attentively, interpret insightfully, and respond creatively will not only safeguard compliance and mitigate risk but also unlock the latent potential within their workforce. This dynamic alignment facilitates sustainable growth, a vibrant culture, and an adaptive talent ecosystem ready to thrive amid the uncharted territories of the future world of work. The journey from awareness to mastery in this realm is continuous, demanding perpetual vigilance and inspired leadership, yet it is rewarded with the profound capacity to shape tomorrow's workforce with intention, integrity, and imagination.

Forecasting the Future: Talent Demand and Supply

Quantitative Forecasting Methods

In the intricate dance of workforce strategy, forecasting talent needs is akin to gazing into a shimmering crystal orb—an endeavour that requires both artful interpretation and scientific precision. Quantitative forecasting methods ground this vision in concrete data and statistical rigor, transforming intuitive guesses into measurable predictions. These approaches enable organisations to peer beyond mere present-day fluctuations, offering a numerical plan of the talent landscape that lies ahead. Harnessing historical data, labour market trends, and internal workforce patterns, quantitative techniques transform an ocean of numbers into a navigable map that guides leaders through uncertain terrain. At their core, these methods revolve around understanding the past and present dynamics within an organisation and extrapolating them to forecast future demand or supply of talent with mathematical confidence.

One of the foundational quantitative tools in workforce planning is trend analysis, which, at first glance, appears deceptively simple but reveals surprising depth upon closer inspection. Through examining historical hiring volumes, attrition rates, and productivity metrics over time, organisations construct a temporal narrative that exposes the ebbs and flows of workforce needs. For example, a manufacturing firm may map out its workforce size over the last decade, identifying steady increments tied to production expansions as well as abrupt declines following automation upgrades. By plotting these data points on a timeline, the firm can discern underlying growth rates and seasonal fluctuations, then project these into the future to anticipate staffing requirements. However, what elevates trend analysis from a mere numerical extrapolation to a strategic asset is the nuanced interpretation of external factors such as economic shifts or regulatory changes, which can act as accelerants or brakes to workforce changes. This dual lens—historical data tempered by environmental awareness—imbues trend forecasting with predictive power.

Another prevalent method of weaving numbers into talent foresight is regression analysis, which delves deeper than temporal trends by examining relationships between multiple workplace variables. This statistical technique quantifies how independent factors—like sales volume, customer demand, or technological implementation pace—influence dependent variables such as headcount or labour hours required. Imagine a retail chain grappling with fluctuating customer footfall that appears inconsistent across stores. By employing regression models, the chain can identify how sales promotions, store location demographics, or seasonality impact staffing needs in each outlet. The regression outcomes deliver coefficients that resonate like musical motifs, revealing which factors most strongly dictate workforce demand and the magnitude of their influence. Leaders armed with such insights can fine-tune their talent acquisition strategies by investing resources in areas predicted to experience increased demand rather than spreading efforts evenly and inefficiently. Crucially, regression models can be iteratively refined as new data streams come in, enhancing their accuracy and responsiveness to internal and external dynamics.

A particularly potent quantitative technique for forecasting talent demand, especially under conditions of uncertainty, is scenario modelling. This approach crafts multiple plausible future states based on different assumptions about business growth, market disruption, or technological adoption. Each scenario is explored through simulations, generating a range of potential workforce requirements rather than a single forecast. For example, a tech startup anticipating rapid product deployment might model scenarios that encompass high growth, moderate growth, and market contraction. Each scenario outlines corresponding talent demand curves, highlighting the necessary scale and skill mix of the workforce. The beauty of scenario modelling lies in its dynamic flexibility—rather than placing all bets on one predicted outcome, organisations prepare for multiple realities, including worst-case and best-case talent environments. This method fosters resilience, allowing leaders to allocate resources wisely, develop contingency plans, and adjust hiring pipelines fluidly based on how reality unfolds.

Time series analysis is another quantitative pillar, especially useful for data exhibiting cyclical patterns or seasonality. This method decomposes workforce data into components such as trend, seasonality, and irregular elements to unravel complex temporal patterns. For instance, a hospitality company might analyse employee count fluctuations across months, noting surges during holiday seasons and dips in off-peak periods. Through smoothing techniques and algorithms like ARIMA (Auto Regressive Integrated Moving Average), the company can generate forecasts that incorporate these regular cycles alongside longer-term trends. Time series analysis thereby equips organisations with the ability to synchronize hiring and training initiatives ahead of anticipated demand spikes, minimizing costly understaffing or overcapacity. While the mathematics involved can be intricate, the practical outcome is an intuitively aligned workforce calendar that resonates with operational rhythms.

Linear programming and optimization models also feature prominently in quantitative forecasting, often enriching strategic decision-making with cost-benefit analysis and resource constraints.

These methods do not merely predict demand; they suggest optimal allocations of talent resources to match future needs under various restrictions such as budget limits or skill shortages. Consider a healthcare system juggling nurse staffing across multiple hospital units, each with fluctuating patient intake and regulatory nurse-to-patient ratios. By framing the staffing challenge as an optimization problem, the system draws on quantitative forecasts and constraints to identify the most efficient distribution of personnel. The model's solution balances patient care quality, employee workload, and budget compliance, resulting in a workforce planning that maximizes impact while minimizing waste. These techniques underscore how quantitative forecasting transcends prediction to become a prescriptive instrument in workforce design.

The integration of predictive analytics and machine learning has ushered in a new era for quantitative workforce forecasting, amplifying traditional statistical methods with vast data processing and pattern recognition capabilities. Unlike conventional models reliant on pre-selected variables and assumptions, machine learning algorithms ingest diverse datasets—including unstructured data like employee sentiment surveys, social media trends, and even economic indicators—to detect hidden correlations and emerging talent demand signals. For example, a financial services firm might deploy machine learning to analyse hiring success metrics, employee engagement scores, and external labour market data simultaneously, uncovering nuanced predictors of turnover and skills gaps. These algorithms dynamically learn and adapt, producing forecasts that grow more precise over time. The fusion of human insight with algorithmic intelligence enables organisations to anticipate talent needs at a granular level and with real-time responsiveness, bridging the gap between static models and fluid business landscapes.

Despite their formidable promise, quantitative forecasting methods are not without challenges. Data quality issues such as missing records, inaccuracies, or outdated information can erode model reliability, akin to a symphony performed with discordant notes. Moreover, the inherent assumption that past patterns will mirror future realities may falter amid sudden industry disruptions, technological breakthroughs, or geopolitical upheavals. An overreliance on numbers risks neglecting qualitative signals—organisational culture shifts, leadership changes, or emergent employee aspirations—that elude quantitative capture yet dramatically impact talent dynamics. Thus, the most effective workforce forecasting marries statistical rigor with judicious interpretation, contextual awareness, and continuous validation.

Case studies vividly illustrate the transformative potential of quantitative forecasting when wielded with expertise and strategic insight. Take, for instance, a leading global logistics company that faced escalating demand volatility intensified by e-commerce surges and pandemic-fuelled supply chain shocks. By deploying a hybrid quantitative approach—combining time series analysis with scenario modelling and machine learning for real-time labour market analytics—the company developed a multifaceted forecast of driver and warehouse worker needs across regions. This forecast empowered them to synchronize recruitment campaigns with predicted market fluctuations, reducing hiring lag and minimizing costly overtime. Furthermore, they integrated optimization models into their workforce planning software, ensuring resource allocation adhered to budget constraints while meeting peak demand. The result was a harmonized workforce that played in concert with operational imperatives, enhancing customer satisfaction and profitability in an otherwise turbulent environment.

Similarly, a multinational pharmaceutical corporation navigating rapid digital transformation harnessed regression analysis and predictive analytics to anticipate the need for specialized data scientists and regulatory experts. By analysing internal project pipelines, external technology trends, and historical hiring success rates through sophisticated quantitative lenses, the company identified a looming talent shortfall. Proactively, they launched targeted upskilling programs and strategic partnerships, informed entirely by data-derived forecasts. The foresight embedded in their quantitative models allowed them to avoid costly recruitment delays and project bottlenecks, positioning their workforce as a competitive advantage in a knowledge-intensive industry.

Yet, the narrative around quantitative forecasting is incomplete without acknowledging its symbiotic relationship with qualitative methods. Quantitative data frames the "what" and "how many," while qualitative insights uncover the "why" behind workforce movements. For example, a retail chain's statistically modelled seasonal hiring needs align closely with qualitative feedback from store managers about customer experience strategies or employee morale issues. Integrating employee pulse surveys, leadership interviews, and expert panels alongside numerical models refines forecasts to be both accurate and actionable. This multidisciplinary approach transforms workforce planning into a living art form—where algorithms provide structure, but human experience infuses meaning and flexibility.

More than a toolkit of methods, quantitative forecasting represents a mindset that embraces complexity, continuous learning, and data-driven experimentation. Organisations mature in their forecasting capabilities by fostering cross-functional collaboration between HR analytics teams, business unit leaders, and external labour market experts. They invest in data infrastructure and predictive software while cultivating analytical literacy among decision-makers. Regular calibration of models occurs as data accumulates and market conditions evolve, ensuring forecasts remain relevant and credible. In this evolving landscape, workforce planners become akin to master conductors, orchestrating statistical symphonies that anticipate talent notes long before they sound aloud.

In essence, quantitative forecasting methods bring precision and depth to the strategic endeavour of workforce planning. They transform vague intuitions into calibrated expectations, guiding organisations through the haze of uncertainty with statistical beacons. While no model can promise flawless prediction, quantitative approaches illuminate pathways, expose risks, and reveal opportunities that would otherwise remain hidden. When woven seamlessly with qualitative insights and embedded within adaptive organisational cultures, these methods empower leaders to compose workforce strategies that are resilient, responsive, and ultimately harmonious with the ambitions of their enterprises. Through this confluence of data science and strategic vision, the future of talent management unfolds not as an unpredictable tempest but as a masterfully conducted opus, rich with promise and purpose.

Qualitative Insights

In the symphony of workforce planning, quantitative data often takes the spotlight, casting sharp rhythms and precise melodies that seem to define the contours of future talent landscapes. However, beneath this measurable surface lies an essential, rich undercurrent that breathes depth and nuance into the forecasting process: the qualitative dimension. This realm—anchored in expert judgment and scenario-based forecasting—adds vibrancy and texture to predictions, transforming cold statistics into living narratives with meaning and foresight.

Expert judgment, the cornerstone of qualitative insight, draws upon the wisdom, experience, and nuanced understanding of individuals who navigate the complexities of their fields daily. These experts often perceive subtle tremors of change and innovation long before they manifest fully in data sets. Imagine a seasoned R&D director in the pharmaceutical industry who senses emerging shifts in regulatory landscapes or a longstanding HR leader in manufacturing who discerns evolving skill demands rooted in technological adoption trends. Their perspectives, honed over years and tempered by countless scenarios, act like the keen ears of a concertmaster detecting slight discord or emerging harmony within an orchestra before the audience perceives anything. These insights are indispensable as they capture intangible elements— cultural shifts, emerging technologies, geopolitical nuances—that outstrip mere numbers.

Scenario-based forecasting elevates this qualitative approach by systematically exploring multiple plausible futures through narrative construction. Instead of relying on a single, deterministic projection, scenario planning creates vivid, diverse tapestries of what might lie ahead, allowing organisations to prepare for a spectrum of possibilities. Picture a multinational corporation anticipating talent needs for a decade ahead; rather than confining itself to linear growth models, its workforce planners envision scenarios ranging from rapid digital transformation accelerated by artificial intelligence to geopolitical regressions inducing stricter labour mobility restrictions or even environmental upheavals reshaping industry priorities. Each scenario is not a prediction but a "what if" story, a speculative performance that uncovers vulnerabilities, highlights opportunities, and ultimately enriches strategic readiness.

One compelling case illuminates the power of combining expert judgment with scenario-based forecasting in practice. A leading technology company found itself at a crossroads when the ever-accelerating pace of machine learning innovation began to undermine existing talent models. Data alone—from past hiring trends and turnover rates—failed to predict sudden shifts in emerging skill requirements. The company assembled a panel of internal and external experts, including AI researchers, project managers, and competitive analysts, who engaged in a structured dialogue reflecting on industry trajectories. They envisioned multiple futures in workshops, crafting scenarios ranging from widespread AI democratization that would amplify demand for data literacy across roles to a concentrated AI monopoly necessitating specialized expertise accessible only through elite networks. These scenarios, enriched by their shared experiential knowledge, guided the firm in prioritizing training investments, reimagining recruitment pipelines, and building strategic partnerships. What seemed abstract gained clarity—strategic initiatives that were both bold and adaptive.

Integral to the robustness of expert judgment is the deliberate process by which it is elicited, refined, and updated. Unstructured opinions can be misleading if swayed by individual biases or anchored assumptions. Techniques like the Delphi method—a structured approach where experts contribute insights anonymously in iterative rounds, gradually converging toward a consensus—mitigate these pitfalls. The anonymity shields contributors from social pressures, while the iterative feedback allows reflection and recalibration. In workforce planning contexts, this means assembling diverse groups of experts from different departments and even industries to illuminate blind spots and challenge prevailing wisdom. For instance, a financial institution anticipating disruptions from fintech innovation leveraged a Delphi panel that included traditional bankers, fintech entrepreneurs, regulatory experts, and data scientists. The iterative process helped reveal underlying uncertainties about talent needs related to cross-disciplinary skills such as compliance understanding intertwined with coding proficiency—a combination neither group fully anticipated on its own.

Similarly, scenario planning leverages storytelling and creativity as much as analytical rigor. Facilitators encourage participants to step beyond comfort zones, imagining futures that may initially feel improbable or even disconcerting. This frees organisations from the trap of "business as usual" mindsets, inviting fresh perspectives conducive to innovation. Methods vary widely: some use narrative scripts, others employ visual storyboards or role-playing exercises to immerse stakeholders in hypothetical worlds. The aim is not to assert accuracy but to provoke meaningful questions and strategic conversations grounded in plausible contexts. This iterative brainstorming often surfaces latent trends and interdependencies invisible in pure data models. For example, a global retail chain used scenario workshops to explore futures shaped by radical shifts in consumer behaviour catalysed by climate change anxieties. Through these narratives, they uncovered the potential for decentralized, hyper-local talent pools aligned with community values—a concept that reshaped how they approached workforce localization strategies.

The strength of qualitative insights lies not only in their anticipatory power but also in their capacity to reconcile ambiguity and complexity with strategic clarity. While quantitative models yield projections anchored on historical data and predictable patterns, they often falter amid disruptive breakthroughs or black swan events. By contrast, expert judgment and scenarios embrace uncertainty as a feature, not a flaw—an invitation to explore rather than deny complexity. This balanced approach empowers leaders to devise robust talent strategies that are flexible rather than brittle, tuned to multiple potential futures. Consider the example of a healthcare provider grappling with the implications of telemedicine's rapid adoption during a public health crisis. While metrics showed a surge in digital consultations, experts foresaw challenges in integrating virtual care into traditional workflows, anticipating the need for new hybrid skillsets combining clinical acumen with digital fluency. Scenario exercises depicted alternate timelines: from rapid technological harmonization to protracted resistance across demographics. These insights translated into tailored training programs and dynamic staffing models that ensured continuity of care amidst uncertainty.

Another dimension where qualitative methods demonstrate unique value is in understanding cultural and behavioural elements that influence workforce dynamics. Data quantifies turnover rates or skills gaps but rarely explains the underlying "why." Qualitative inquiry—through expert narratives, focus groups, and scenario workshops—uncovers attitudes, values, and implicit norms shaping talent attraction, retention, and development. This richness is particularly vital when organisations undergo transformational change, where culture is both a lever and a potential barrier. For example, a manufacturing company transitioning toward automation engaged frontline supervisors and engineers in scenario conversations that illuminated fears and aspirations about evolving roles. This qualitative exploration revealed deeply ingrained resistance tied to identity and job security fears that, if unaddressed, could derail retraining initiatives. Armed with this insight, leadership designed communication campaigns and supportive structures that resonated empathetically, aligning workforce strategy with organisational culture.

In practical terms, incorporating qualitative insights into workforce planning requires deliberate structures that balance rigor with creativity. Organisations can embed expert judgment into forecasting cycles by forming cross-functional advisory councils that routinely assess emerging trends and validate assumptions. These councils should represent diverse vantage points—technology, operations, HR, finance, strategy—to capture the multifaceted nature of workforce ecosystems. Complementing this, scenario workshops scheduled at regular intervals provide a dynamic playground where assumptions are challenged, strategies stress-tested, and new narratives forged. Importantly, both processes thrive on active leadership sponsorship and a culture that values curiosity and reflective practice over complacency.

Technology also plays a synergistic role in enhancing qualitative approaches. Digital collaboration platforms, virtual reality simulations, and sentiment analysis tools facilitate richer scenario exercises and expert interactions, especially in geographically dispersed organisations. Machine learning algorithms can analyse qualitative inputs—such as expert comments or scenario narratives—by identifying thematic patterns and hidden connections, thus augmenting human judgment rather than replacing it. For example, a global energy firm utilized natural language processing to synthesize vast amounts of expert commentary during scenario development, revealing emergent concern clusters around regulatory shifts and talent mobility. This enabled focused strategic discussions and informed targeted talent interventions.

Yet, while qualitative methods enrich forecasting, they also demand discernment and reflexivity. The richness of narratives and expert opinions carries the risk of anecdotalism, groupthink, or selective bias if not carefully managed. Transparency about assumptions, continuous validation against emerging data, and openness to revise scenarios are crucial safeguards. Workforce planners must cultivate facilitation skills that foster open dialogue, respect diverse voices, and encourage constructive scepticism. The aim is to weave qualitative and quantitative strands into a coherent strategic fabric, leveraging the strengths of each to compensate for respective limitations.

Ultimately, qualitative insights transform workforce planning from a mechanistic exercise into an imaginative, anticipatory art. They invite organisations to see beyond linear projections and prepare thoughtfully for complex, shifting talent landscapes. Just as an orchestra's conductor listens not only to the score but also to the subtle breaths and intentions of musicians—adapting tempo and dynamics in real time—organisational leaders who harness qualitative forecasting can orchestrate workforce strategies that resonate with authenticity, agility, and foresight. This blend of expert judgment and scenario thinking creates a strategic compass, guiding organisations through the fog of uncertainty toward a horizon where human potential and business ambition coalesce harmoniously.

By embracing this qualitative dimension, workforce planners cultivate not only predictive accuracy but also strategic wisdom. They recognize that the future is not predetermined but co-created through thoughtful anticipation and deliberate design. The stories told by experts, the futures imagined through scenarios, and the reflective processes that generate them become vital instruments in the hands of visionary leaders. These instruments help craft talent strategies that are not only resilient and responsive but inspiring—capable of rallying teams around shared purpose and collective growth in a relentlessly evolving world.

In this light, qualitative forecasting is no mere supplement to quantitative analysis; it is a transformative foundation that infuses workforce planning with humanity and strategic depth. It frames the unknown as a canvas for creativity rather than a barrier to action and equips organisations to not just survive but thrive amidst complexity. Through continuous dialogue between data and narrative, between numbers and nuance, workforce planning becomes a living art, a dynamic interplay that tunes human capital to the rhythms of tomorrow's promises and challenges.

Balancing Demand and Supply

In the intricate dance of workforce planning, the act of balancing demand and supply emerges as both the heartbeat and the compass, guiding organisations through the labyrinthine corridors of future talent needs and labour market realities. Imagine for a moment a grand clockmaker, meticulously assembling gears to ensure that each tick resonates harmoniously with the rhythms of time. Similarly, workforce strategists must calibrate their approach to align precisely with anticipated business demands while corresponding fluidly with the external labour environment. This balancing act is neither static nor straightforward; it is a dynamic interplay of forces, continuously influenced by shifting business strategies, evolving technologies, demographic trends, and economic fluctuations. To navigate this complexity, organisations employ a panoply of forecasting techniques, blending quantitative precision with qualitative insight, ensuring that their talent pipeline neither overflows with surplus nor dries up into scarcity.

Quantitative forecasting serves as the analytical backbone of demand and supply balancing, drawing upon historical data, statistical models, and algorithmic projections to chart plausible talent scenarios. Consider a multinational technology firm preparing to launch a new line of artificial intelligence products. Their human resource analysts begin by mining years of recruitment data, turnover rates, productivity metrics, and training durations. Using regression analysis, time-series forecasting, and scenario simulations, they estimate the number of software engineers, data scientists, and product managers required over the next five years. These numerical forecasts act as a beacon, illuminating probable talent deficits or surpluses. Yet, the audacity of numbers, while seemingly definitive, carries intrinsic limitations; it cannot fully capture the nuances behind workforce behaviours, future skill shifts, or sudden industry disruptions. Therefore, quantitative methods achieve their full potential when interwoven with qualitative wisdom.

Qualitative forecasting techniques infuse a human element into the numerical tapestry, drawing on expert opinions, market intelligence, and nuanced assessments of industry trends. This approach is akin to a seasoned navigator interpreting not only the stars but also the feel of the wind and waves to steer a vessel safely. For example, a global pharmaceutical company, anticipating the impact of emerging regulatory policies and technological innovations on talent needs, convenes panels of internal leaders, industry analysts, and academic experts. Through Delphi methods and scenario workshops, these diverse voices brainstorm plausible futures, identifying nascent skill requirements such as expertise in gene editing or regulatory affairs specialists adept at navigating new compliance landscapes. Such qualitative insights enrich the quantitative forecasts, adding flexibility and contextual depth, allowing organisations to accommodate ambiguities and uncertainties inherent in long-term planning.

Real-world cases vividly illustrate the potency of combining quantitative and qualitative forecasting in balancing labour demand and supply. Take the retailer that faced a sudden surge in e-commerce growth during an unforeseen market shift. Their initial quantitative forecast, based on pre-pandemic sales trends, underestimated the need for supply chain analysts and digital marketing experts. However, by incorporating qualitative inputs from frontline managers and customer service teams, the company identified emerging skills and roles vital to navigating the new normal. Consequently, they rapidly adjusted recruitment strategies, developed training programs, and forged partnerships with digital academies, effectively bridging the gap between their workforce capacity and evolving demand. This synergy of data and insight enabled swift adaptation, preventing the organisation from being overwhelmed or caught unprepared—a testament to the critical importance of balancing demand and supply with a multifaceted lens.

Delving deeper, the methodologies to predict supply— meaning the available external and internal talent pools—are equally complex and consequential. Internal supply forecasting usually involves talent inventories, succession planning, and assessments of workforce mobility, skill pathways, and potential retirements. It requires not only granular data on current employee competencies and career aspirations but also an understanding of organisational culture and engagement levels. For instance, a financial institution, grappling with the retirement of its experienced risk managers, found that despite an internal bench of capable mid-level candidates, cultural shifts and aspirations towards digital roles limited upward mobility. By conducting qualitative interviews alongside quantitative skills mapping, they crafted a comprehensive internal supply forecast that highlighted the need for targeted development programs and cultural initiatives to prepare successors adequately, balancing the supply side with the upcoming demand.

Externally, forecasting labour market supply demands an acute reading of macroeconomic indicators, educational outputs, demographic shifts, immigration policies, and competitor behaviours. One cannot overlook the subtle, often slow-moving changes in the talent ecosystem, such as the aging workforce in manufacturing or the increasing number of STEM graduates in emerging economies. For example, a global manufacturing firm projected a shortage of skilled machinists and engineers over the next decade due to an aging population and declining vocational enrolments. Their labour market analysis blended quantitative data from government statistics and labour market information systems with qualitative conversations with educational institutions and industry associations. They then proactively partnered with technical schools to sponsor apprenticeships and integrated technologies like augmented reality to attract younger talent, effectively balancing supply risks with demand imperatives.

Beyond forecasting techniques, strategic interventions play a pivotal role in balancing talent demand and supply. Organisations often adopt workforce segmentation to tailor approaches for critical, core, and support roles—devoting resources and development initiatives proportionally to the strategic value and scarcity of roles. For instance, in the creative sector, where talent is inherently scarce and fiercely contested, companies not only forecast demand meticulously but also invest in employer branding, talent communities, and innovative sourcing strategies to secure a stable supply. Conversely, for roles with abundant supply, such as entry-level administrative positions, organisations focus more on efficiency and scalability. This segmentation, informed by rigorous demand-supply analysis, ensures that limited resources are allocated strategically, avoiding blanket approaches that dilute effectiveness.

Technology integration accelerates and deepens the precision of balancing strategies. Artificial intelligence and machine learning algorithms sift through mountains of workforce data to uncover hidden patterns, predict turnover risks, and simulate various demand-supply scenarios under different economic or organisational conditions. One illustration is a large healthcare provider using AI-powered analytics to predict nurse staffing needs, factoring in patient load forecasts, seasonal illnesses, and employee burnout indicators. This forward-looking capability grants leadership unprecedented agility, enabling timely interventions such as targeted recruitment drives, flexible scheduling, or cross-training initiatives. Meanwhile, digital labour marketplaces offer new avenues to supplement supply via gig and freelance talent, thus injecting flexibility that traditional workforce planning models struggle to accommodate.

A profound challenge embedded in balancing demand and supply lies in navigating uncertainty and volatility. No forecast can claim absolute accuracy over extended horizons, especially amid disruptive forces like technological breakthroughs, geopolitical shifts, or pandemics. Therefore, organisations must embrace adaptive workforce strategies, embedding continuous monitoring, feedback loops, and scenario planning into their core processes.

Through regular recalibration, scenario comparisons, and sensitivity analyses, organisations transform static forecasts into living documents, capable of evolving in tandem with reality. This agility not only mitigates talent mismatches but also fosters resilience, enabling organisations to pivot swiftly without compromising strategic momentum.

Narratives of organisations exposed to unforeseen disruptions underscore this imperative vividly. During the COVID-19 pandemic, many companies discovered that their workforce demand and supply forecasts were rendered obsolete overnight. Yet, those with robust strategic planning frameworks that integrated real-time labour market intelligence, flexible staffing models, and rapid upskilling capabilities managed to rebalance their talent resources on the fly. One logistics firm, facing fluctuating delivery volumes, leveraged predictive analytics and a pool of trained gig workers to dynamically scale its workforce, preserving continuity while avoiding costly overstaffing. Such examples illuminate that balancing demand and supply extends beyond forecasts; it necessitates a culture of preparedness, learning agility, and leadership committed to continuous evolution.

Leadership, indeed, functions as the conductor orchestrating this delicate balance. By fostering cross-functional collaboration between business units, HR, and analytics teams, leaders ensure that talent strategies resonate with executive priorities and operational realities. Transparent communication channels facilitate the flow of qualitative insights from frontline managers and employees back into forecasting models, enriching accuracy and buy-in. Furthermore, embedding workforce planning into strategic dialogues accentuates its role as a vital driver of competitive advantage rather than a mere administrative exercise. Leaders who champion such integration empower their organisations to synchronize talent rhythms with corporate ambitions deftly and responsively.

Finally, balancing talent demand and supply is not an endpoint but a continuous journey, a cyclical process demanding vigilance, creativity, and courage. It calls for embracing complexity rather than seeking simplistic answers, leveraging the confluence of data and human judgment, technology and empathy, foresight and adaptability. When executed with artistry and precision, it transforms workforce planning into a strategic symphony— ensuring that the right people with the right skills appear on the stage precisely when the organisational crescendo demands, harmonizing human potential with business aspirations in an ever-changing opera of success.

Navigating Risks: Identifying and Mitigating Workforce Challenges

Types of Workforce Risks

In the intricate dance of strategic workforce planning, risks are the silent undertows beneath the surface, constantly shaping and reshaping the stability and effectiveness of an organisation's human capital. Understanding these risks is akin to a conductor discerning the subtle dissonances within the orchestra before they swell into disruptive cacophonies. Workforce risks are multifaceted, spanning a vast spectrum from the tangible shortages of essential skills to the often-unpredictable currents of economic volatility, each threatening to unsettle the harmony of meticulously laid plans. To truly master the art of workforce planning, one must deeply explore these risk categories, not merely as abstract threats but as dynamic forces that require both anticipation and deft mitigation.

One of the most palpable forms of workforce risk is skill shortages, a perennial challenge that acts like a recurring motif in the grand symphony of talent management. In industries accelerating towards innovation, the gap between available skills and those demanded by evolving organisational needs can widen rapidly. This scarcity does not arise in a vacuum; it is the product of technological disruption, demographic shifts, educational lag, and changes in career aspirations. When an organisation faces such shortages, it is akin to an orchestra missing a section of violas right before a pivotal performance—the sound is incomplete, the balance disrupted. The consequences can cascade, affecting productivity, quality, and ultimately, customer satisfaction. Addressing skill shortages requires more than recruitment; it demands a strategic foresight that anticipates future competencies and proactively shapes workforce development. This includes investing in custom training programs, forging partnerships with educational institutions, and embracing continuous learning cultures that encourage employees to evolve alongside technological and market changes.

Closely related yet distinct is the risk of high employee turnover, a phenomenon that can strike unpredictably and with profound effect. Turnover, especially when concentrated in critical roles or departments, fractures the cohesion of teams and drains the institutional knowledge that forms the backbone of sustained success. The departure of seasoned professionals is like losing lead instruments in a performance—no matter how skilled the replacements, the nuances and depth of experience take years to replicate. Turnover risks are often symptoms of deeper organisational challenges: misaligned culture, lack of career progression, inadequate recognition, or poor leadership. However, they can also arise from external forces such as competitive poaching or life-stage changes of employees. Mitigating turnover risk involves weaving retention strategies into the very fabric of the workforce plan. Cultivating a strong employer brand, fostering inclusive and engaging work environments, providing meaningful growth opportunities, and ensuring fair compensation are essential threads in this tapestry. Moreover, using predictive analytics to identify flight risks can enable pre-emptive interventions, transforming potential crises into opportunities for renewed commitment.

Beyond the immediate sphere of individual workforce dynamics lies the broader, often volatile landscape of economic risks that ripple through labour markets and organisational capacities. Economic volatility—whether triggered by global financial crises, trade disruptions, technological shifts, or pandemics—casts long shadows on workforce stability. These macroeconomic tremors shape hiring capacities, morale, and the very feasibility of long-term talent investments. Organisations caught unprepared may find themselves forced into reactionary downsizing, furloughs, or hiring freezes, disrupting not just operational continuity but also their reputation as an employer of choice. Conversely, economic upswings present their own challenges, ushering in competitive talent markets where poaching and wage inflation threaten to erode cost structures. Navigating these economic risks demands a blend of agility and prudence—a balanced approach that preserves financial health without sacrificing strategic workforce initiatives. Scenario planning emerges as a critical tool, enabling leaders to visualize diverse economic conditions and craft flexible workforce responses accordingly. Building reserves of talent through talent pools, contingent workforce strategies, and robust cross-training programs can provide the elasticity needed to absorb economic shocks.

Emerging alongside these traditional risk categories are newer, yet equally consequential, challenges that stem from the evolving nature of work itself. One such risk is technological displacement, where automation and artificial intelligence sweep through job functions, rendering certain roles obsolete or fundamentally transformed. This phenomenon introduces uncertainty and potential resistance within the workforce, as employees grapple with fears of redundancy or skill irrelevance. Failure to manage this transition can lead to disengagement, productivity dips, and reputational harm. Successful mitigation of technological risk hinges on transparent communication, proactive upskilling, and reimagining roles to complement human strengths rather than replace them. By framing technology as an enabler rather than an adversary, organisations can foster a culture of innovation and resilience.

Parallel to this is the increasing complexity of workforce demographics and expectations, which introduce risks related to diversity, equity, and inclusion, as well as work-life balance demands. Ignoring these dimensions can result in disengagement, reputational damage, and legal challenges, undermining the cohesiveness of the workforce. The modern workforce seeks meaningful work, flexibility, and authenticity; when these are absent or insufficiently addressed, turnover risk escalates, and employer branding suffers. Integrating these cultural and social considerations into workforce planning requires a nuanced understanding of employee aspirations, supported by inclusive policies, diverse leadership, and adaptable work arrangements.

Health and well-being risks have surged to the forefront in recent years, particularly amplified by global health crises and rising awareness of mental health. Unaddressed, these risks precipitate increased absenteeism, reduced productivity, and can ripple into broader cultural malaise. The workforce is no longer merely a collection of skills and tasks but a community whose holistic health underpins performance. Organisations that embed well-being into their strategic planning through comprehensive health programs, flexible scheduling, and supportive leadership build a resilient human capital foundation capable of weathering internal and external storms.

Risk stemming from regulatory changes and compliance mandates adds another layer of complexity. Shifts in labour laws, immigration policies, data protection regulations, and occupational safety standards can abruptly alter workforce parameters, imposing constraints or necessitating costly operational adjustments. Staying ahead of these changes requires vigilant environmental scanning and agile policy adaptation. Moreover, engaging with policymakers and industry groups can offer a proactive voice in shaping favourable conditions.

Globalization extends the risk horizon further, as organisations increasingly source talent across borders, navigating geopolitical tensions, cultural differences, and varied legal frameworks. The promise of a global talent pool is counterbalanced by risks of workforce fragmentation, communication barriers, and challenges in embedding a unified organisational culture. Successful navigation demands sophisticated workforce segmentation, leveraging technology for seamless connectivity, and cultivating intercultural competence among leaders and employees alike.

Underlying many of these risk categories is the critical influence of leadership and organisational culture. Weak or misaligned leadership can amplify workforce risks by eroding trust, clarity, and motivation. Conversely, strong leadership acts as a stabilizing force, guiding the workforce through uncertainty with vision and empathy. Cultivating a culture that embraces change, values transparency, and empowers employees mitigates risks by transforming potential disruptions into shared challenges that galvanize collective action.

Mitigating workforce risks is not a passive insurance policy but a dynamic, ongoing process that demands strategic integration and operational rigor. It begins with comprehensive risk identification and prioritization, employing tools such as risk registers and heat maps to visualize exposures. These must be coupled with robust data collection and analytics capabilities to detect early warning signs and inform predictive models. Importantly, risk mitigation strategies must be embedded across organisational functions—from HR and finance to operations and strategy—ensuring that workforce considerations are front and centre in decision-making.

Contingency planning is vital, creating flexible pathways that allow rapid response to unforeseen workforce disruptions. This might include cross-training employees to create multi-skilled teams, establishing strategic partnerships for talent sharing, or developing alternative labour models such as gig or freelance arrangements. Communication plans are equally crucial; transparent dialogue before, during, and after risk events fosters trust and minimizes uncertainty.

Finally, cultivating a learning organisation where risk experiences are systematically captured, analysed, and translated into continuous improvement closes the risk management loop. Organisations that review and refine their workforce risk frameworks adapt more readily to shifting landscapes, maintaining competitiveness and resilience.

In sum, the tapestry of workforce risks is rich and varied, intersecting in complex ways that can either unravel organisational ambitions or fortify them against the unknown. Leaders who master the subtle art and rigorous science of identifying, understanding, and mitigating these risks compose a workforce planning that not only survives but thrives amid uncertainty. This mastery transforms workforce risks from looming shadows into guiding beacons, illuminating pathways to sustainable success and innovation.

Risk Assessment Techniques

In the complex symphony of workforce planning, risk assessment emerges as the conductor's baton—it directs attention to those dissonant notes before they become a cacophony that can derail an entire performance. At its core, risk assessment in workforce planning is about envisioning the invisible fissures that might crack the organisational foundation when least expected. It requires a finely tuned sense for identifying, evaluating, and prioritizing the myriad risks that could impact talent pipelines, employee engagement, or operational continuity. These risks, spanning skill shortages, turnover spikes, and the unpredictable waves of economic volatility, are not mere abstract threats; they are shadows lurking in the interstices of strategy and execution, demanding a lens sharpened with clarity, foresight, and methodical judgment.

Beginning with skill shortages, one must appreciate that the gap between the workforce's current capabilities and future organisational needs is not a static void but a shifting landscape that morphs with technological advances, market demands, and industry disruptions. The tools for assessing this risk demand a panoramic gaze across multiple dimensions: an audit of existing competencies, an analysis of strategic business directions, and an ongoing scan of labour market dynamics. Competency mapping frameworks serve as a vital instrument here, allowing organisations to chart skill inventories across roles, departments, and geographies, juxtaposing them against projected requirements informed by strategic initiatives and emerging trends. This mapping transcends simple checklists; it becomes a living document, enriched with qualitative insights from managers and frontline employees who understand the nuances of indispensable skills and those becoming obsolete. In parallel, predictive analytics drawn from labour market data and industry foresight inject quantifiable rigor into these assessments, spotlighting occupations at risk of supply-demand imbalances before they crystallize into tangible shortages.

However, identifying a skill gap is merely the prologue to risk evaluation—it is imperative to contextualize the severity and likelihood of such shortages. Risk matrices become invaluable here, enabling planners to assign scores based on the criticality of the role impacted, the difficulty of sourcing niche skills, and the speed at which the shortage could affect operations. A specialized data scientist for AI initiatives, for example, carries a different risk profile than a general administrative support position; the former's scarcity and strategic importance demand heightened vigilance, proactive talent scouting, and robust succession pipelines. This prioritization guides how limited resources are funnelled—whether into aggressive upskilling programs, strategic hiring partnerships, or investments in automation as a hedge—all of which comprise the mitigation tactics essential to transform risk awareness into actionable resilience.

Turnover risk, a perennial concern embroidered into the workforce fabric, demands equal sophistication in assessment. Unlike skill shortages, turnover encompasses a multitude of causes—ranging from voluntary departures driven by disengagement or external opportunities, to involuntary separations due to restructuring or performance issues. An effective risk assessment in this domain rests on understanding both quantitative indicators and qualitative undercurrents. Analysing historical turnover rates segmented by demographics, tenure, and job functions provides a foundational baseline, but the richer insights emerge from employee engagement surveys, exit interviews, and pulse check initiatives that illuminate why individuals consider leaving. This degree of introspection blends art and science, requiring a culture receptive to honest feedback and an analytical framework equipped to transform sentiments into predictive risk profiles.

To elevate turnover risk assessment beyond reactive analysis, many organisations now integrate attrition risk models leveraging machine learning algorithms. These models synthesize HR data—performance ratings, promotion history, compensation trends, commute times, and even social network analysis within the company—to flag high-risk employees potentially poised to exit. Importantly, these models underscore the necessity of ethical application; transparency and respect for employee privacy must be carefully balanced against the strategic imperative to mitigate turnover. Once the high-risk segments are identified, leaders can initiate targeted retention strategies, personalized career development plans, or enhanced recognition programs, thereby transforming insights into preventative action.

Economic volatility, a grand macro-level force, introduces a different tenor to the risk assessment concerto. Unlike the circumscribed variability inherent in skill shortages or turnover, economic turbulence—whether triggered by recessions, geopolitical upheavals, or pandemics—can precipitate workforce risks with widespread reach and uncertain consequences. Assessing these risks demands a robust environmental scanning process that synthesizes economic indicators, industry forecasts, and policy changes. Scenario planning emerges as a powerful technique here, allowing organisations to craft multiple future narratives that consider varying degrees of economic disruption and their probable impact on workforce needs. This approach refuses the fatalism of prediction and instead embraces agility through preparedness, fostering strategic conversations around flexible staffing models, cross-training, and contingency reserves.

Within these economic scanning efforts, specialized financial risk tools such as sensitivity analyses, stress testing, and Monte Carlo simulations can be harnessed to quantify the workforce cost implications of economic swings. By modelling salary inflation, hiring freeze impacts, and severance expenses under different scenarios, organisations gain clarity on where their vulnerabilities most lie. This analytical rigor informs decision-making about the volatility tolerance of the workforce strategy and identifies the "shock absorbers" needed—be it variable work arrangements, contractual labour blends, or investment in automation—to dampen the blow.

Beyond these core categories, workforce risk assessment must consider emerging dimensions such as regulatory compliance risks, reputational risks tied to workforce grievances, and technology adoption risks that could destabilize morale or productivity if mishandled. The multifaceted nature of these threats demands an integrative approach, weaving together diverse data streams into coherent risk dashboards that bring to life the interplay and cumulative effects of various risks. Advanced risk management platforms now offer real-time data fusion, visual heat maps, and predictive analytics, enabling leaders to not only monitor but also simulate responses to complex risk constellations. By converting abstract risks into vivid, manageable challenges, these tools empower organisations to act decisively rather than react frantically.

Mitigation tactics emerge as indispensable companions to risk identification, transforming passive awareness into proactive resilience. The arsenal for addressing workforce risks is rich and varied, from talent pipeline diversification strategies that shield against supply chain shocks in human capital to sophisticated succession planning that cultivates bench strength for critical roles. Cross-training programs spin a safety net beneath operational key points, ensuring work continuity despite personnel fluctuations.

Moreover, responsive learning ecosystems, fostering continuous skill development, buffer against obsolescence and anchor talent retention by nurturing a growth mindset. In some forward-looking organisations, risk pooling—sharing talent resources across business units or even with partner organisations—further diffuses individual exposure and builds collective resilience.

Crucially, the leadership's role in weaving risk assessment and mitigation into the organisational fabric cannot be overstated. Risk conversations must permeate all levels, nurtured by a culture that values transparency, agility, and continuous learning. Leaders act as both sense-makers and orchestrators, ensuring that risk insights translate into investment decisions, process redesigns, and communication strategies that align stakeholders toward a shared commitment to precaution and preparedness.

In essence, workforce risk assessment is a sophisticated process that illuminates the shadowy uncertainties surrounding human capital strategy. It combines the vivid clarity of data-driven tools with the nuanced understanding of human behaviours and market realities. By rigorously evaluating risks of skill shortages, turnover, economic volatility, and beyond, organisations gain the power not simply to survive but to thrive amidst uncertainty— mastering their workforce strategy like a virtuoso navigating a complex musical score, anticipating every crescendo and rest with confidence and grace.

Mitigation Strategies

In the intricate tapestry of workforce planning, mitigation strategies emerge as the vital threads that strengthen the fabric against the unrelenting pressures of change and uncertainty. When viewed through the lens of an orchestra, these strategies are the subtle yet deliberate rehearsals and sound checks—carefully orchestrated efforts that prepare the ensemble not just to perform beautifully under ideal conditions, but to adapt seamlessly when a musician falters, or a sudden shift in tempo is required. The landscape of workforce vulnerability is a terrain marked by diverse and complex risk categories, each demanding a tailored approach to buffering potential disruption. Among the most persistent and impactful are skill shortages, employee turnover, and economic volatility, all of which can unsettle the delicate harmony of organisational talent alignment. Addressing these challenges proactively hinges on the recognition that such vulnerabilities are not isolated incidents but interconnected dynamics that ripple through every layer of the organisational structure, from frontline production teams to executive leadership.

Skill shortages stand as a formidable challenge in the modern workforce ecosystem, where the velocity of technological change continuously redefines the core competencies needed for success. The stark reality of a skills gap is akin to an orchestra lacking a critical section of instruments; no matter how talented the musicians present, the absence of specific, critical skills diminishes the richness and completeness of the performance. Organisations confront this risk not only through reactive hiring but more importantly, via comprehensive forecasting and cultivation efforts designed to pre-empt skill shortages before they reach crisis levels. Central to this endeavour is the strategic investment in continuous learning and development programs that evolve in lockstep with industry advances. This entails more than generic training; it involves a deep diagnostics process—employing data analytics to identify emerging skill requirements at granular levels, followed by crafting personalized development pathways that inspire and empower employees to grow in meaningful, future-proof ways. Partnerships with educational institutions and industry consortia serve as another critical pillar, forming pipelines of fresh talent while ensuring curricula reflect real-world, applied knowledge that organisations will need downstream. Furthermore, rotational programs and cross-functional assignments can be leveraged as internal incubators of talent versatility, enabling employees to acquire complementary skills that both enrich their careers and furnish the organisation with agile resources ready to pivot in times of change.

Turning to employee turnover, the metaphor of the orchestra translates into the costly and demoralizing act of losing a principal player mid-performance—a disruption that reverberates not only through the immediate team but also threatens the overall tempo and cohesion. Mitigating turnover risk involves a sophisticated understanding of the underlying causes, which range from misaligned expectations and inadequate engagement to insufficient career pathways and external market poaching. At its core, effective mitigation converts the organisation into a magnet for talent rather than merely a place of employment. This magnetism is generated through a culture of trust, transparency, and recognition—a culture that communicates value beyond pay checks, encompassing meaningful work, development opportunities, and a supportive environment. Early warning systems powered by well-crafted employee engagement surveys, exit interviews, and predictive analytics allow leaders to detect attrition risks with a level of sensitivity akin to a maestro sensing a musician's bias or fatigue before a note is missed. Interventions may include tailored retention incentives, mentorship programs, and proactive career coaching that reinforce employees' sense of belonging and growth. Additionally, succession planning is a critical component, ensuring that key roles have ready and capable successors, thereby alleviating the operational shock of unexpected departures.

Economic volatility adds a formidable layer of complexity, introducing external forces that no organisation can fully control but can strategically anticipate and buffer against. The unpredictability of market downturns, sudden regulatory shifts, or global crises acts like abrupt changes in a musical score's dynamics, demanding swift recalibration and resilience from all performers. Organisations poised to navigate economic turbulence do so through the cultivation of an agile workforce that balances flexibility with stability—a structure that embraces contingent workforces, remote capabilities, and adaptable scheduling. This agility allows rapid scaling up or down, redeployment of talent to emerging priorities, and cost efficiencies that do not compromise core competencies. Financial resiliency in workforce investments is enhanced by scenario planning, where multiple future states are envisioned, and strategic options are pre-positioned, enabling a response that is both decisive and nuanced. For instance, by establishing talent pools with varied contract terms or maintaining a reserve of internal freelancers who can be mobilized on demand, companies can dampen the shocks of sudden workforce reductions or expansions and maintain continuity in critical knowledge areas. Moreover, transparent communication channels and change management initiatives are vital to maintain trust and morale during economically challenging times, preventing the erosion of engagement that can amplify turnover when uncertainty strikes.

Beyond these individual risk categories, effective mitigation strategies are characterized by their integrative and anticipatory nature. A workforce plan that incorporates risk assessment as a dynamic, ongoing process—not a static point in time—is better equipped to detect subtle shift signals that precede larger disruptions. This requires a departure from traditional, linear planning models toward an ecosystem perspective that continuously monitors internal capabilities alongside external market conditions, technological trends, and socio-economic factors. Advanced digital tools and predictive analytics play an indispensable role here, enabling organisations to simulate the impact of different risk scenarios and test the resilience of various workforce configurations in virtual environments. This virtual rehearsal process refines mitigation tactics, allowing decision-makers to fine-tune responses before real-world crises demand action. Furthermore, cultivating a culture that embraces learning from near-misses and small-scale disruptions enhances organisational resilience by embedding adaptive muscles into the workforce's DNA.

At the tactical level, diversification strategies further strengthen mitigation capabilities. Just as an orchestra benefits from a wide variety of instruments capable of producing layered harmonies, organisations benefit from talent heterogeneity in experience, skill sets, and work modalities. Hybrid models that blend full-time employees with gig workers, contractors, and remote collaborators broaden the talent base and increase strategic options. This diversity fosters organisational innovation and resilience by reducing overreliance on any one source of expertise or labour segment. However, such diversification demands deliberate integration strategies to ensure that all contributors, regardless of engagement status, are aligned with the company's mission, values, and performance expectations. Technology platforms that facilitate seamless collaboration and knowledge sharing underpin this integration, preserving the cohesion vital for collective success.

Leadership emerges as a critical lever in the successful deployment of mitigation strategies. Leaders act as conductors who must not only anticipate potential discordant notes but also cultivate an environment where every musician feels accountable and empowered to adjust their performance in real time. This leadership involves a delicate balance of transparency, decisiveness, and empathy—a communication style that confronts risks openly without breeding fear and mobilizes teams toward shared solutions with clarity and purpose. Executive sponsorship of workforce mitigation efforts visibly signals their strategic importance and aligns resource allocation accordingly. Additionally, leaders must champion a culture of agility that rewards experimentation and rapid learning rather than penalizing mistakes, thereby fostering an atmosphere where mitigation strategies are continuously refined through collective insight.

Ultimately, the art of mitigating workforce vulnerabilities lies not in eliminating risks entirely—a near-impossible task in a world of constant flux—but in building a robust and responsive system that minimizes exposure while maximizing adaptive capacity. This system is akin to a finely tuned symphony where each section anticipates the cues of others, maintaining balance and harmony through both rehearsed composure and spontaneous creativity. Organisations that master this art gain a decisive advantage, able to sustain performance levels, seize emerging opportunities, and traverse uncertainty with confidence. Through an integrated approach combining predictive foresight, targeted development, strategic diversification, and empathetic leadership, workforce mitigation strategies become a powerful shield and guiding compass, ensuring that the organisation's human capital not only survives but thrives amid the evolving score of tomorrow's business landscape.

Building Workforce Resilience

In the symphony of organisational life, workforce resilience serves as the crucial undercurrent that steadies the composition when unforeseen disruptions threaten to throw it into discord. To build resilience within the workforce is to cultivate a form of collective adaptability, an elasticity that allows individuals and teams not only to endure shocks but to emerge from them renewed, stronger, and more aligned with a shifting business landscape. This resilience is not an accidental byproduct; it demands deliberate, strategic acts of foresight, careful orchestration of talent resources, and a nuanced understanding of the multifaceted risks that loom ever-present in contemporary organisational ecosystems. Skill shortages, employee turnover, and economic volatility are among the most pervasive risk categories that threaten to unravel even the most finely tuned workforce plans, and in facing these challenges, organisations must develop layered, multifaceted mitigation tactics that transform potential fragilities into sources of strength.

The initial and perhaps most vivid risk to workforce resilience is the spectre of skill shortages. In a world propelled by rapid technological advancement and shifting industry standards, the obsolescence of skills can be alarmingly swift. Leaders often describe this phenomenon as a daunting game of catch-up—where the pace of innovation outstrips the speed with which the workforce can adapt. This results in gaps that ripple across operational effectiveness, innovation capacity, and customer satisfaction. The consequences are not merely strategic; they percolate to the core of employee morale and engagement, as talented individuals find themselves burdened with the frustration of inadequate preparation or resources. In confronting skill shortages, resilience begins with a proactive commitment to continuous learning and development. Organisations that embed a culture of growth, where upskilling and reskilling are viewed as perpetual imperatives rather than episodic fixes, transform their workforce into a dynamic reservoir of capability. This reframing shifts the workforce from a static inventory of current skills to a rapidly evolving asset that anticipates future needs.

A cornerstone of these efforts includes leveraging precise talent analytics and environmental scanning to identify emergent skills before shortages become critical. By harnessing sophisticated data models, organisations can peer over the horizon, spotting trends and projecting talent demands with greater accuracy. When combined with agile learning pathways—such as modular training programs, micro-credentials, and mentoring initiatives—this creates a continuous feedback loop wherein individual capabilities are expanded in harmony with strategic goals. Moreover, smart workforce design entails not only filling immediate skill gaps but also cultivating T-shaped talent – professionals who possess a deep skill in one area but have a breadth of knowledge across multiple domains, enabling versatile deployments in times of uncertainty. Such adaptability diminishes the vulnerability that arises when niche expertise becomes stranded within siloed teams.

Complementing this investment in skills is the reinforcement of strong internal mobility programs. Encouraging and facilitating lateral moves within an organisation fortifies resilience by making skills portable across functions and geographies. When employees experience career growth through varied assignments, they develop richer perspectives and networks, amplifying their ability to navigate complexity and pivot when conditions shift. This also mitigates the risk of attrition that arises when career pathways stagnate. As employees sense the ecosystem as supportive of their evolving ambitions, their emotional and professional investment deepens, tethering them more closely to the organisation's shared mission and forestalling losses to competitors. Therefore, the act of pre-emptively managing skill shortages is inseparable from fostering an environment that prizes learning agility, cross-pollination of expertise, and robust career frameworks.

Turnover, the second formidable risk to workforce resilience, acts as a disruptor not only of operational continuity but also of organisational memory and cultural coherence. The departure of seasoned employees can create voids in institutional knowledge, undo complex team dynamics, and impose significant costs related to recruitment, onboarding, and lost productivity. While some turnover is natural and even necessary to infuse fresh perspectives, excessive or untimely exits signal deeper underlying challenges that can cascade into destabilizing patterns. Resilient organisations view turnover through a dual lens: as a metric to be managed and as a symptom to be understood. Recognizing the emotional and psychological underpinnings of employee retention becomes paramount in this endeavour.

Building resilience against turnover requires a sophisticated understanding of workforce sentiment, engagement drivers, and evolving expectations. It is here that leadership sensitivity and organisational culture intertwine to shape outcomes. Cultivating a workplace environment characterized by trust, recognition, inclusion, and meaningful work fortifies individuals' commitment and willingness to weather inevitable hardships. Open communication channels where employees can voice concerns and participate in shaping their work experience elicit a sense of ownership that anchors them even amid external uncertainties. Moreover, leaders who model empathy and provide clear, transparent pathways for career development signal to employees that their growth is intrinsically valued, reinforcing the connective tissue that binds them to the collective enterprise.

In addition, resilience to turnover demands bespoke retention strategies that transcend generic incentives. Tailoring rewards and development opportunities to diverse employee segments—recognizing that motivations and aspirations vary widely across generational cohorts, skill levels, and life stages—enables targeted interventions that resonate deeply and authentically. For example, younger talent may prioritize purposeful work and rapid skill acquisition, whereas established professionals might seek stability and influence within the organisation. Embedding flexibility through remote work options or personalized benefits also enhances the organisation's ability to accommodate life's uncertainties, further reducing attrition risks. In this way, workforce resilience is intimately connected to the organisation's capacity to humanize the work experience, aligning institutional needs with individual well-being.

Economic volatility surfaces as another profound disruptor threatening the equilibrium and foresight of workforce strategy. Shocks from fluctuating markets, geopolitical events, or global recessions can instantaneously scramble projections, erode financial buffers, and squeeze operational budgets, leaving organisations scrambling to recalibrate workforce needs in compressed timeframes. When economic tides shift, the frequency and magnitude of workforce adjustments increase dramatically, from hiring freezes to layoffs and strategic redeployments. The crude bluntness of these reactions often exacerbates vulnerability, sabotaging morale and undermining the organisational cohesion essential for rebound.

True resilience in the face of economic volatility necessitates a strategic paradigm that marries financial prudence with workforce agility. Companies fortified with robust scenario planning processes—engaging cross-functional teams in rigorous "what-if" explorations—build mental and operational muscle to anticipate various contingencies. These exercises, far from abstract, translate the unpredictability of economic fluctuations into tangible strategic responses, preparing leaders and workforce partners to implement calibrated workforce adjustments without resorting to knee-jerk decisions. When coupled with dynamic workforce segmentation— where roles and talent pools are evaluated for their core strategic importance, scalability, and risk exposure—organisations can tailor resource allocation in ways that preserve critical capabilities while enabling flexible scaling.

Furthermore, a resilient workforce includes an adaptable talent architecture that blends permanent employees with contingent workers, freelancers, and gig economy participants. This diversified model functions as a shock absorber, allowing organisations to deepen capacity or contract swiftly in accordance with market signals, all while mitigating the social and financial costs associated with more rigid employment structures. Technology facilitates this agility, as integrated talent management platforms provide real-time visibility into workforce composition and utilization, enabling precise alignment with fluctuating demand. Still, this shift towards hybrid talent models requires a renewed emphasis on cultural coherence and communication strategies that transcend traditional organisational boundaries to maintain engagement and shared purpose across diverse employment statuses.

Another critical facet in confronting economic volatility lies in nurturing a financial mindset within workforce planning that regards human capital as a strategic asset rather than a mere cost centre. Organisations that systematically integrate workforce analytics with financial performance metrics gain a holistic lens into the value generated by different talent segments, enabling smarter decisions that optimize both economic and human outcomes. Transparent dialogue around the business realities encourages shared responsibility, fostering resilience not just in structures and processes, but in collective attitudes oriented toward adaptability and mutual support.

Beyond these categorical risks, building workforce resilience demands a holistic architecture encompassing mental and emotional well-being, leadership agility, and cultural vitality. The relentless pace of change imposes psychological tolls, exposing employees to stress, burnout, and uncertainty that can erode individual and collective effectiveness. A resilient workforce is therefore one in which psychological safety is cultivated, and stigma around seeking support is dismantled. Progressive organisations embed wellness programs, mindfulness practices, and mental health resources into their operational fabric, signalling a genuine commitment to sustaining human potential in its full complexity.

Leadership emerges as the central conductor of workforce resilience, charged with setting tone, vision, and response cadence. Resilient leaders embody agility, decisiveness, and empathy, orchestrating their teams through turbulence with clarity and compassion. They cultivate inclusive environments where diverse perspectives fuel innovative problem-solving and foster a collective capacity to absorb shocks. Importantly, these leaders practice reflective learning, openly acknowledging setbacks as learning moments to be integrated into ongoing adaptation rather than sources of blame or inertia.

The vitality of organisational culture in shaping resilience cannot be overstated. Cultures characterized by trust, transparency, experimentation, and shared purpose serve as fertile ground, where resilience flourishes organically. When psychological safety is embedded, employees are empowered to voice concerns early, collaborate in pivoting strategies, and co-create solutions — dynamics critical to withstanding disruptions. Conversely, cultures that quash dissent or prioritize rigid hierarchies breed fragility, where vulnerabilities go unseen until they metastasize into crises.

To operationalize these insights, many organisations turn to resilience-building frameworks that integrate strategic planning, risk management, and workforce development into cohesive cycles of continuous improvement. These frameworks are augmented by technology platforms that enable real-time data collection, scenario mapping, and workforce modelling, rendering resilience a living, actionable attribute rather than an aspirational ideal. Regular resilience assessments, akin to stress tests in finance, allow organisations to identify emerging weaknesses, refine their contingency plans, and sharpen their response agility.

This ongoing commitment cultivates a workforce ecosystem structured not around static hierarchies but dynamic networks capable of fluid collaboration, rapid learning, and adaptive redeployment. In this ecosystem, resilience is woven into the DNA of everyday operations and strategic planning alike, infusing the organisation's rhythm with a spirit of readiness and renewal. Rather than viewing disruptions as catastrophic interruptions, resilient organisations embrace them as inflection points—a dissonant motif within a larger composition that, when skilfully managed, enriches the overall harmony.

Ultimately, building workforce resilience is less about predictive certainty and more about nurturing a mindset and operational capacity to thrive amidst uncertainty. It is the art of fostering talent ecosystems where change is not merely survived but leveraged, where the workforce itself becomes both a compass and a ballast for the organisation's journey through volatile seas. This resilience transforms workforce strategy from a static plan into a living symphony—flexible, vibrant, and poised to orchestrate success no matter what the future unfolds.

Segmenting Talent: Understanding Workforce Diversity and Needs

Demographic Analysis

In the symphony of workforce planning, demographic analysis serves as a foundational instrument, tuning the initial notes that guide organisational talent strategies with precision and nuance. When we speak of demographics in this context, we move beyond mere headcounts and age brackets to a rich tapestry of characteristics that reveal the intricate human patterns shaping the workforce landscape. Demographics, in their most potent application, offer a lens through which organisations can discern not only who makes up their workforce but also how these individuals' intrinsic qualities—ranging from generational identities to cultural backgrounds—intersect with skill sets and behavioural tendencies. This layered understanding is vital; it transforms workforce planning from a static exercise of filling roles into a dynamic orchestration of aligning people's unique capacities and motivations with the evolving demands of the business.

At its core, demographic analysis within workforce strategies begins with segmented insights into age, tenure, gender, education, and ethnicity, but it quickly transcends these basics to explore how these factors relate to broader talent management questions. For instance, understanding generational clusters within the workforce—the Baby Boomers, Generation X, Millennials, and Generation Z—enables leaders to anticipate differing career aspirations, learning preferences, motivations, and even adaptability to technology. This awareness is crucial when designing engagement initiatives or succession plans. The contrast between a Boomer planning retirement within the next five years and a Millennial seeking rapid skill development offers direction for differentiated interventions. Such targeted focus prevents the traditional pitfall of one-size-fits-all human resources policies that tend toward mediocrity rather than excellence.

Expanding demographic analysis to skill-based segmentation sharpens the lens further. While demographics paint the picture of who employees are, their skills articulate what they bring to the table, and this combination unlocks strategic clarity. Much like departments within an orchestra—the strings, woodwinds, brass, and percussion—each skill cluster has a unique voice and role, yet must harmonize with the others for a masterpiece to emerge. Profiling workforce skills through competency frameworks, certifications, and experiential milestones allows organisations to map talent at macro and micro levels. They can identify critical skill shortages or surpluses, anticipate retiring expertise, and foresee emerging skill demands driven by market shifts or technological advancement. Embedding this intelligence into planning cycles results in a workforce planning responsive to present and future operational rhythms.

However, the true artistry of demographic analysis unfolds when behavioural segmentation enters the stage. People's work behaviours, attitudes, values, and personality traits heavily influence not only individual performance but also team dynamics and organisational culture. Behavioural insights gleaned through surveys, performance reviews, and sophisticated psychometric tools provide colour and texture to the demographic canvas. For example, behavioural profiles might reveal clusters characterized by high adaptability and innovation, which are invaluable in disruptive environments. Conversely, segments exhibiting risk aversion or a preference for stability may excel in roles requiring consistency and attention to detail. Aligning these behavioural tendencies with organisational needs ensures deliberate placement and development, minimizing friction and maximizing engagement.

The integration of demographic, skill-based, and behavioural segmentation works synergistically to optimize talent management strategies. Consider a global technology firm experiencing rapid market evolution; demographic data may highlight an aging workforce concentrated in legacy system maintenance roles. Skill-based analysis could reveal a dearth of expertise in emerging cloud platforms, while behavioural data may uncover resistance to change within traditional teams. These intersecting insights allow leadership to pivot decisively, crafting targeted hiring, training, and culture transformation strategies that attract younger digital natives and reskill existing employees with adaptive learning structures. Without such multidimensional segmentation, organisations risk misallocating resources, perpetuating talent gaps, and facing declines in productivity or innovation.

Moreover, demographic analysis has macroeconomic and societal implications that ripple into strategic workforce planning. Trends such as declining birth rates in developed nations, increasing diversity, or evolving educational pathways meld the available talent pool outside the organisational boundary. Forward-thinking organisations extend demographic scrutiny beyond internal compositions to include community and labour-market dynamics. For example, firms located in regions with growing immigrant populations may capitalize on expanded talent diversity, blending cultures and perspectives that fuel creativity and customer empathy. Conversely, understanding demographic shifts like urban migration patterns or aging populations may inform decisions about where to locate operations or how to invest in remote work infrastructure. This external demographic awareness enriches strategic foresight and adaptability.

Yet, demographic analysis, while powerful, demands a cautious and ethical approach. The temptation to rely on categories raises the risk of stereotyping or unconscious bias, which can undermine inclusion and fairness. It is essential that organisations adopt demographic segmentation not as boxes limiting individual potential but as guideposts helping to tailor strategies thoughtfully. Integrating diversity, equity, and inclusion (DEI) principles throughout the analytic process can foster a culture where demographic differences are celebrated rather than pigeonholed, driving both social responsibility and business performance. Transparency in data use and respect for privacy must underpin demographic initiatives, especially in an era of intensified scrutiny on data ethics.

Technological advances have revolutionized how demographic analysis is conducted and applied. Big data analytics, machine learning algorithms, and AI platforms empower organisations to sift through vast volumes of workforce data with unprecedented granularity and predictive power. For example, predictive demographic modelling can forecast retirement waves years in advance, enabling timely succession planning or recruitment campaigns. Similarly, real-time analytics can detect shifts in employee engagement among demographic cohorts, offering early warnings for retention risks. Visualization tools translate complex demographic insights into accessible dashboards for leaders, making strategic decision-making more intuitive and evidence-based. This technological integration elevates demographic analysis from retrospective reporting to proactive talent orchestration.

Nonetheless, the art lies in balancing quantitative data with qualitative context. Numbers alone do not capture the lived experiences behind demographics. Storytelling, ethnographic research, and empathetic leadership dialogues enrich demographic insights with texture and empathy. Listening to employee voices across demographic segments uncovers deeper motivations and barriers that statistics obscure. For instance, a demographic group underrepresented in leadership may reveal systemic challenges such as limited mentorship opportunities or biased promotion criteria. Addressing these revelations holistically ensures that strategic workforce planning is not only statistically sound but also human-centered.

Crucially, demographic analysis informs the delicate equilibrium between workforce stability and agility. An organisation heavily weighted toward a specific demographic—say, a predominant age group or skill cluster—may face vulnerabilities when market conditions shift abruptly. Alternatively, overly heterogeneous demographics without integration can provoke fragmentation and disengagement. Strategic planners use demographic data to craft balanced workforces that combine seasoned expertise with fresh perspectives, stable performers with change agents, and diverse backgrounds with common purpose. This equilibrium underpins resilience, enabling organisations to pivot fluidly while maintaining core identity and operational continuity.

Practical implementation of demographic analysis for workforce strategies often unfolds through cross-functional collaboration. HR leaders, data scientists, business strategists, and operational managers converge to define relevant demographic parameters aligned with business objectives. Regular updates and scenario modelling ensure demographic insights keep pace with organisational and external dynamics. Workforce development programs are designed with an eye toward demographic trends, such as tailored leadership training for emerging female talent or flexible work arrangements accommodating multi-generational preferences. Incentive systems also reflect demographic realities, recognizing the motivational nuances among varied age, cultural, and skill groups.

Case studies vividly demonstrate the transformative power of demographic analysis. A multinational financial services firm, grappling with rapid digitization, leveraged demographic segmentation to map an aging workforce against emerging digital talent pools. This insight prompted a multi-pronged approach that combined phased retirement programs, digital upskilling boot camps, and recruitment drives targeting younger demographics, resulting in a revitalized talent pipeline and enhanced innovation capacity. Meanwhile, a healthcare system employed behavioural and demographic analyses to personalize retention programs, thereby lowering turnover rates among critical care nurses across diverse age groups by addressing both work-life balance needs and culturally sensitive engagement.

In summation, demographic analysis in workforce planning is less about demographics as static descriptors and more about decoding the dynamic human kaleidoscope that underlies every organisational heartbeat. It weds empirical rigor with empathetic insight, enabling leaders to compose workforce strategies that are simultaneously analytical, adaptive, and inclusive. By weaving together demographic, skill-based, and behavioural threads, organisations gain a robust framework to anticipate talent challenges, leverage human diversity as a strategic asset, and cultivate an energized workforce attuned to the rhythms of tomorrow's market demands. This nuanced composition ultimately empowers businesses to not only survive but flourish in the face of uncertainty, conducting their workforce like a finely tuned symphony where each member's unique contribution resonates in harmony with shared success.

Skill and Competency Mapping

In the orchestral masterpiece of workforce planning, skill and competency mapping emerges as the essential score, a complex and intricate plan detailing every note and rest that each musician must perform to harmonize the collective output. This mapping transcends mere inventories of capabilities and enters the nuanced realm where the textures of talent, behavioural propensities, and demographic attributes intertwine to form a rich tapestry, facilitating strategic alignment that transcends simplistic categorization. When organisations embark on this critical task, they are not merely creating lists but constructing multidimensional portraits that capture not just what employees can do, but how they do it, and who they are within the evolving ecosystem of the enterprise. This depth of understanding allows leaders to move beyond traditional human resource paradigms, enabling the crafting of tailored interventions designed to optimize performance, foster development, and accelerate innovation within their unique cultural milieu.

At its core, skill and competency mapping initiates with the comprehensive identification of essential skills, which can range from technical proficiencies to soft competencies that often evade straightforward quantification. The process requires penetrating insight into the organisation's current and future strategic objectives, anticipating shifts in market dynamics, technological advances, and competitive landscapes. It demands looking beyond static job descriptions toward a dynamic interpretation of how a role serves the organisation's mission and vision, and what skills will drive success amid uncertainty. This approach inherently incorporates an understanding that roles evolve, and so must their requisite skill sets, heralding the importance of agility in workforce design. Skill mapping is thus both a forward-looking and reflective exercise, evaluating not only current expertise but also latent potential, adaptability, and learning agility.

An indispensable dimension in this effort is the recognition that skills seldom exist in isolation but rather cluster into competencies — integrated patterns of behaviour, knowledge, and abilities that are observable and measurable. Competency frameworks provide a structured language for communicating performance expectations and potential across diverse organisational units, bridging gaps between departments and fostering a unified understanding of talent. They offer a prism through which leadership can evaluate individual and collective capacity, forging alignment between human capital and strategic imperatives. However, the richness of competency mapping is fully realized only when it embraces the often-overlooked behavioural and attitudinal elements, acknowledging that workforce effectiveness hinges on the interplay of what employees do, how they approach their work, and the environments in which they thrive.

Integral to this construct is the segmentation of talent through demographic, skill-based, and behavioural lenses, an analytical approach that adds granularity and precision to talent management strategies. Demographic segmentation considers variables such as age, tenure, education, and cultural background, bringing forth insights about the diversity and generational dynamics within the workforce. These factors influence how employees learn, engage, and contribute, affecting retention and development initiatives. For example, younger cohorts may prioritize career progression and technological fluency, while seasoned employees often hold critical institutional knowledge and leadership potential. This layered understanding enables the design of differentiated engagement and support mechanisms that respect individual circumstances while advancing collective objectives.

Skill-based segmentation builds upon this foundation by categorizing employees according to their specific capabilities and experience levels, whether in technical disciplines, leadership, or specialized functional areas. This categorization is not limited to the identification of current competencies but extends to the recognition of emergent skills driven by transformational trends such as digitalization, artificial intelligence, and cross-functional collaboration. Organisations armed with this insight can strategically allocate resources, prioritize learning journeys, and foster communities of practice tailored to distinct talent pools, thus maximizing both individual growth and organisational capacity. The dynamic nature of skill sets, often shaped by rapid technological advancements, demands continuous revaluation and adaptability in segmentation frameworks.

Behavioural segmentation adds a further critical dimension, delving into personality traits, work styles, motivational drivers, and interpersonal skills that influence how individuals perform and interact within teams and broader organisational networks. These characteristics provide a predictive window into employee engagement, resilience, and potential for leadership or collaboration. For example, mapping behavioural tendencies such as openness to change, conscientiousness, or proactivity can reveal latent capabilities essential during periods of transformation and uncertainty. Recognizing and aligning these behavioural attributes with appropriate roles and development programs fosters a more cohesive and effective workforce, enhancing both individual satisfaction and collective outcomes.

The synthesis of these three segmentation dimensions culminates in a multidimensional workforce profile — a living atlas that guides talent decisions ranging from recruitment and deployment to development and succession planning. It enables the agility to anticipate talent gaps, tailor learning pathways, and sculpt teams with complementary skills and dispositions, optimizing performance and innovation. This nuanced perspective transcends traditional HR reporting, connecting data-driven insights with a human-centered narrative that appreciates the complexity and variability of the workforce as an interconnected organism, rather than a collection of interchangeable parts.

Practical application of skill and competency mapping requires an orchestration of methodologies and tools that span qualitative assessments and quantitative analytics. Techniques such as competency-based interviews, psychometric testing, 360-degree feedback, and skill inventories converge to paint detailed pictures of individual and group capabilities. Advances in technology and data analytics now empower organisations to collect, integrate, and interpret vast pools of talent information, enabling predictive modelling and scenario analysis that elevate workforce planning from reactive to proactive disciplines. These tools help surface hidden strengths and potential risks, supporting targeted interventions and optimizing resource allocation.

Yet, the efficacy of these mapping initiatives depends equally on leadership and cultural factors. Effective leaders foster environments where transparency, trust, and continuous dialogue about skills and aspirations encourage employee participation and authenticity in assessments. They champion a learning culture that sees competency development not as a chore but as an ongoing journey aligned with individual and organisational growth. By embedding skill and competency mapping into the fabric of organisational routines and decision-making, leaders convert abstract data into actionable intelligence, empowering managers and employees alike to navigate complexity with clarity and confidence.

Moreover, the narrative and metaphor of the orchestra extend naturally into the strategic application of skill and competency mapping. Just as a conductor understands the unique voice of each instrument and guides them in concert to produce a coherent composition, strategic workforce planning guided by skill mapping harmonizes the diverse talents and potentials of employees to achieve resonance with business objectives. It acknowledges individual brilliance without losing sight of collective performance, balancing specialization with orchestration. This metaphor reminds practitioners that talent is living and dynamic, requiring attentive tuning and opportunities for improvisation amid changing tempos and thematic shifts in the business environment.

Crucially, this process also lays the foundation for workforce agility and resilience by identifying not only current competencies but also developmental potential and learning flexibility, thereby building a talent pipeline that can pivot as conditions evolve. Skill and competency mapping foregrounds the importance of continuous re-skilling and up-skilling, vital in an era where technological disruption and shifting customer expectations redefine job roles at an unprecedented pace. It enables organisations to anticipate forthcoming talent deficits and proactively develop capabilities through targeted learning initiatives, rather than merely reacting to crises or external shocks.

In practice, organisations that excel in skill and competency mapping often discover unexpected reservoirs of talent and capacity within their ranks. They unveil cross-functional synergies and emergent leaders previously obscured by conventional appraisal methods. This deep understanding fosters more equitable talent management practices, supporting diversity and inclusion efforts by illuminating non-traditional career pathways and recognizing varied expressions of competence. It enables the dismantling of silos and the promotion of collaboration by connecting talents and passions that might otherwise remain latent.

Ultimately, skill and competency mapping embodies a forward-leaning mindset, a commitment to viewing talent through a multi-faceted prism that respects complexity and interdependence. It transforms workforce planning from a static, transactional activity into a strategically rich conversation about potential, aspiration, and alignment, woven into the very DNA of organisational strategy. By embracing demographic diversity, skill dynamism, and behavioural nuance, it equips leaders with the foresight and precision required to cultivate a workforce not just capable of fulfilling the demands of today but also of evolving and flourishing amid the inevitable uncertainties of tomorrow.

In sum, skill and competency mapping stands as one of the most profound instruments in the strategic planner's toolkit — a form of talent cartography that charts pathways through uncharted landscapes, illuminating the intersections of capability, motivation, and identity. It reveals the hidden architectures underpinning workforce performance and potential, guiding decisions that weave individual threads into a resilient, high-performing organisational fabric. As with any artful composition, the beauty and power arise not just from isolated skills or traits but from their harmonious integration, yielding a workforce symphony attuned to the rhythms of change and poised to deliver enduring success.

Behavioural and Cultural Segmentation

Within the intricate mosaic of workforce planning, understanding the behavioural and cultural contours of talent is not simply a supplemental task—it is an essential art form that breathes life into strategic engagement. Segmenting employees and potential hires by demographics or skill sets offers a foundational layer, much like the framework of a building, but diving deeper into the subtleties of behaviour and organisational culture enables leaders to cultivate a vibrant, dynamic, and cohesive workforce ecosystem. This process transcends traditional categorizations and ventures into the realm of attitudes, values, and social dynamics, which ultimately drive motivation, collaboration, and adaptability. Behavioural and cultural segmentation invites us to peer beneath surface-level qualifications and roles, to unearth the underlying human narratives that shape how individuals relate to their work and to one another—an understanding that proves indispensable for optimizing talent management in an era where engagement and alignment carry unprecedented weight.

Imagine the workforce as a vast forest, not merely a collection of trees, but an intertwined system where the health of each tree depends on the soil, the climate, and the symbiotic relationships among species. Just as an ecologist would study patterns of growth, interactions, and resilience within a forest, strategic workforce architects must explore behavioural and cultural patterns to nurture an environment where human potential can flourish sustainably. Demographic segmentation—by age, gender, or tenure—provides a useful outline, while skill-based segmentation clarifies functional expertise, but without behavioural insights, these frameworks risk becoming rigid and mechanical. In contrast, behavioural segmentation captures the dynamic aspects of individuals' work styles, communication preferences, risk tolerance, and capacity for innovation. It acknowledges that two employees with identical qualifications can respond in profoundly different ways to change, pressure, and opportunity. Similarly, cultural segmentation focuses on shared norms, beliefs, and values within a group or organisation, recognizing that culture is the invisible current that channels everyday decisions and shapes collective identities.

To truly grasp the significance of behavioural and cultural segmentation, one must start by appreciating how attitudes toward work vary across individuals and groups. Some employees thrive in highly structured environments with clear guidelines and hierarchical decision-making, bringing exceptional reliability and focus. Others flourish in flexible, open atmospheres that invite creativity and risk-taking, often pushing innovation frontiers. These contrasting behaviours create a spectrum that demands nuanced understanding. For example, a tech startup that values agile responsiveness and creative experimentation may struggle if a majority of its workforce prefers entrenched routines and cautious approaches. Conversely, a financial institution, where stability and compliance reign supreme, may find a highly experimental culture disruptive. Therefore, leaders must diagnose these behavioural patterns not as static traits but as adaptive preferences that interact with the broader organisational culture and strategic imperatives.

Overlaying this is cultural segmentation, which delves into the shared ethos that binds employees beyond their individual behaviours. Organisational culture is the symphony conductor guiding the rhythm of collaboration, trust, and conflict resolution.

Within a single multinational corporation, cultural segments may manifest as distinct microcultures defined by geography, departmental priorities, or even hierarchical levels. An engineering team in Berlin might emphasize precision, process optimization, and direct communication, while a marketing unit in New York might prioritize creativity, speed, and relational dynamics. These cultural markers influence not only how team members engage with their work but also how they interpret leadership intent, respond to incentives, and cope with disruptions. The delicate interplay of cultural segments requires leaders to act with cultural intelligence, tailoring communication, recognition, and development approaches to resonate authentically with each segment's values and expectations.

Behavioural and cultural segmentation also has profound implications on employee engagement strategies—a vital component in optimizing workforce effectiveness. When organisations recognize and respond to different segments' unique motivators, they move beyond one-size-fits-all approaches and tap into deeper wells of commitment and productivity. For instance, younger employees often value opportunities for continuous learning, mentorship, and purposeful work that align with societal impact. Their behavioural profile may be characterized by a preference for collaborative technologies, social recognition, and an openness to challenging the status quo. Older segments might prioritize job security, clear career trajectories, and respectful acknowledgment of experience, reflecting a more risk-averse or tradition-oriented behavioural style. Cultural segmentation sharpens this focus further by highlighting how various groups within the same age or skill demographic might approach these motivators differently based on their cultural orientation, such as collectivist versus individualist mindsets. Leaders who attune themselves to these nuances can craft tailored engagement interventions that resonate powerfully with each segment, driving higher retention and performance.

Delving into workforce agility, behavioural and cultural segmentation provides a crucial lens for resilience-building in turbulent environments. Agility demands not just structural flexibility but a workforce mindset capable of embracing ambiguity, learning rapidly, and pivoting with purpose. Behavioural profiles that favour curiosity, adaptability, and proactive problem-solving become invaluable assets in such contexts. Segmentation tools can reveal pockets of latent agility scattered across departments or teams, enabling targeted development and deployment of these human capital elements. Meanwhile, cultural segmentation sheds light on collective readiness to embrace change—some subcultures within the organisation may be more open to experimentation and failure as a learning process, while others might demonstrate risk aversion rooted in deeply ingrained norms. Recognizing these cultural fault lines equips leaders to design change management initiatives that respect these distinctions and build bridges between segments, preventing fragmentation or disengagement during transitions.

In practical terms, behavioural segmentation can be constructed through a variety of methodologies, combining quantitative data with qualitative insights. Psychometric assessments, 360-degree feedback mechanisms, and employee surveys uncover patterns related to personality traits, decision-making styles, and motivational drivers. Advanced analytics platforms leverage machine learning algorithms to detect clusters of behaviours predictive of performance outcomes or turnover risk. By integrating these behavioural data points with demographic and skills information housed in human capital management systems, organisations create sophisticated profiles that inform workforce strategies at multiple levels—from recruitment and onboarding to training and succession planning. Cultural segmentation, while more elusive, emerges through ethnographic research, cultural audits, and employee dialogue forums. Leaders who engage directly with diverse employee segments gain empathy and insight, capturing the subtleties that statistical measures alone cannot reveal. Together, behavioural and cultural segmentation foster a multidimensional portrait of the workforce rich in texture and context, empowering decisions that deliver both precision and humanity.

The symbiosis of behavioural and cultural dimensions also guides leadership development and performance management practices. Effective leaders are not monolithic figures imposing uniform templates but sensitive architects of environments where diverse behavioural styles and cultural backgrounds harmonize. Segment-tailored leadership approaches—whether emphasizing coaching for intrinsically motivated innovators or providing structure for diligent executors—enhance alignment and fulfillment. Performance management systems that respect these segments avoid the pitfalls of unfair evaluations and homogenized incentives, instead fostering clarity around expectations and recognition tailored to motivational drivers. For example, a highly collaborative cultural segment may respond best to collective rewards and team-based outcomes, while an autonomy-valuing segment might prioritize individual goal achievement and personalized recognition. By weaving behavioural and cultural segmentation into leadership frameworks, organisations amplify trust, clarity, and sustained high performance.

At a strategic level, embedding behavioural and cultural segmentation into talent acquisition enables organisations to build not only capability but also congruence with desired cultural attributes and behavioural norms. This alignment acts as a talent filter, increasing the likelihood that new hires will integrate smoothly and contribute fully from day one. Sourcing strategies that combine traditional qualifications with behavioural assessments and cultural fit evaluations produce richer candidate profiles and enhance workforce diversity in perspectives and approaches. However, this process must be nuanced to avoid homogenization or exclusion; it is not about seeking cultural clones but about identifying complementary behavioural and cultural elements that enrich the existing fabric. For example, introducing behavioural diversity—such as balancing risk takers with risk mitigators—creates a robust system of checks and balances within project teams. Incorporating cultural sensitivity ensures that diverse backgrounds and worldviews synthesize rather than clash, fuelling innovation and engagement.

The emergence of hybrid and remote work models introduces new dimensions to behavioural and cultural segmentation, challenging leaders to rethink engagement and collaboration paradigms. Remote work dissolves traditional geographic and social boundaries, exposing behavioural differences in communication styles, self-management capacities, and social connectivity needs. Some employees may excel in autonomous, digitally mediated environments, demonstrating high self-discipline and a preference for asynchronous workflows. Others might experience feelings of isolation or disengagement without face-to-face interactions, reflecting deep-seated behavioural needs for social validation and immediate feedback. Culturally, remote work environments demand heightened awareness of inclusion practices and culturally calibrated digital communication norms. The absence of shared physical space intensifies the importance of articulating and embodying organisational values within virtual rituals, language, and symbols that resonate across cultural segments. Behavioural and cultural segmentation, therefore, becomes an essential compass in designing virtual collaboration strategies, technology adoption, and well-being programs that preserve connection and cohesion.

Behavioural and cultural segmentation also plays a pivotal role in the delicate art of managing conflict and fostering psychological safety within teams. Behavioural differences often surface as sources of misunderstanding or friction, especially when amplified by cultural divides. For instance, direct communicators may unintentionally overwhelm those preferring indirect expressions, or a results-driven subgroup may clash with process-focused individuals over priorities. Without deliberate segmentation-informed insights, conflict resolution efforts can default to superficial treatments, leaving underlying tensions to simmer. Conversely, by recognizing the behavioural language and cultural context of each segment, leaders and HR professionals can craft customized mediation practices and dialogue frameworks that validate different viewpoints while promoting mutual respect. Psychological safety—the cornerstone of innovation and engagement—thrives in environments where diverse behaviours are not just tolerated but embraced as integral to collective strength. Segmentation thus transforms conflict from a disruptive force into a creative catalyst.

Training and development initiatives further gain precision and impact through behavioural and cultural segmentation. Recognizing that employees learn differently and bring varied cultural lenses to education allows mentors and trainers to tailor content, delivery methods, and pacing. Some behavioural segments might excel in experiential learning environments that harness peer-to-peer interaction and real-time feedback, while others may prefer structured, self-directed modules with clear objectives. Cultural variations influence preferences for individual versus group learning, forms of recognition during achievement, and receptivity to hierarchical versus collaborative facilitation styles. Designing segmented learning journeys elevates engagement and retention of knowledge, accelerating workforce upskilling and transformation efforts. In the increasingly complex terrain of digital skills and continuous learning imperatives, segment-aligned development becomes a strategic lever for maintaining competitiveness and innovation.

Beyond the internal organisational landscape, behavioural and cultural segmentation offers strategic insights for managing talent in a globally interconnected marketplace. Multinational enterprises must navigate an intricate web of national cultures, linguistic diversity, and regulatory environments. Uniform talent management policies risk misalignment and disengagement when deployed without cultural calibration. Behavioural segmentation enables the identification of work styles and motivational factors prevalent in different regions, allowing HR functions to customize programs that align with local realities while reinforcing global objectives. For example, performance metrics successful in one cultural context might prove demotivating or confusing in another, necessitating localized interpretation. Cultivating a global talent architecture grounded in nuanced segmentation fosters inclusivity and leverages diversity as a strategic advantage.

The growing integration of technological tools amplifies the capacity for behavioural and cultural segmentation while simultaneously introducing ethical considerations. Artificial intelligence and advanced analytics platforms now process vast datasets to reveal intricate patterns of behaviour and cultural markers with precision unimaginable in previous eras. Predictive models anticipate turnover risks, engagement dips, and skill gaps segmented by behavioural and cultural characteristics, empowering proactive interventions. Yet, the deployment of such technologies must be anchored in transparent ethical frameworks to avoid biases, privacy infringements, or mechanistic reductions of human complexity. Workforce planners must balance the power of data-driven segmentation with unwavering commitment to dignity, fairness, and the preservation of individual autonomy. By doing so, technology becomes a trusted ally in crafting personalized, respectful talent management rather than a cold instrument of control.

In sum, behavioural and cultural segmentation is not a mere technical exercise, but a rich narrative woven into the fabric of strategic workforce planning. It illuminates the human dimensions behind organisational charts and skill matrices, revealing the vibrant psychological and social textures that animate sustainable engagement and performance. Leaders who master this form of segmentation unlock the ability to orchestrate their workforce with empathy and precision, sculpting environments where diverse talents resonate harmoniously with shared purpose. By embracing the complexities of behaviour and culture—attuned to the subtle shifts and enduring patterns—organisations position themselves not merely to survive but to thrive amid the ascending demands of tomorrow's talent landscape. The symphony of human potential plays strongest when every voice is understood, every rhythm recognized, and every cultural nuance honoured—a masterpiece crafted through the deliberate art of behavioural and cultural segmentation.

Tailoring Strategies for Segments

In the intricate dance of workforce planning, the power to tailor strategies based on finely tuned segment insights emerges as a vital conductor's skill — an essential art form that moves beyond generic approaches toward a landscape where the unique characteristics of each group guide deliberate, nuanced action. Imagine the workforce not as a homogenous mass but as a richly layered mosaic, each tile distinct yet indispensable to the integrity of the whole picture. To navigate this complex composition, one must dive deeply into the realm of segmentation, a process that illuminates the diverse threads woven through an organisation's human capital. It is here that demographic, skill-based, and behavioural segmentation converge, each offering a prism through which to understand and ultimately optimize talent management. This strategic focusing lens transforms the abstract concept of workforce planning into a vibrant, living plan, enabling leaders to craft bespoke tactics that resonate with the authentic needs, aspirations, and potential of each segment, thereby unleashing a more dynamic, responsive, and aligned human ecosystem.

Demographic segmentation, often the most immediate and tangible approach, sets the stage by categorizing employees according to observable and quantifiable characteristics such as age, gender, tenure, educational background, and geographic location. While these dimensions might seem merely administrative on the surface, their implications ripple through every facet of workforce strategy. For example, the generational contours shaped by demographic data—think Boomers, Gen X, Millennials, and Gen Z—are not just numbers but vibrant narratives filled with distinct values, work preferences, and motivational triggers. Recognizing that younger cohorts may prioritize flexibility, purpose-driven work, and rapid learning opportunities while older generations might value stability, recognition, and a legacy of contribution allows organisations to calibrate engagement initiatives and retention programs with precision. Furthermore, demographic insights alert workforce planners to inevitable transitions such as impending retirements that could trigger knowledge drain or leadership vacuums if left unplanned. Yet demographic segmentation's true power unfolds when combined thoughtfully with other segmentation factors, eschewing simplistic stereotyping in favour of richer, multi-dimensional profiles that reveal both challenges and opportunities.

As critical as demographics are, the depth of understanding sharpens substantially when overlaid with skill-based segmentation. This layer shifts the focus from who employees are to what they bring to the table in capabilities, competencies, and potential. Skills, both current and evolving, constitute the lifeblood of any organisation's competitive advantage, and taking stock of them with surgical detail enables workforce planners to map out precisely where gaps, surpluses, and bottlenecks lie. By clustering employees around expertise domains, proficiency levels, certifications, and even learning agility, organisations can engineer targeted development pathways and succession plans that not only fill immediate vacancies but also cultivate a pipeline aligned with future business trajectories. Skill-based segmentation also empowers leaders to adopt a more agile stance, redeploying talent swiftly in response to shifting market demands or internal pivots, thus transforming workforce planning from a rigid forecast into a dynamic, living strategy. Here, the metaphor of an orchestra gains renewed vigour: knowing the unique sound and skill of each musician ensures the conductor can assign solos and harmonies that showcase strengths and shroud weaknesses, crafting a resonant performance attuned to every note's nuances.

The third—and perhaps most nuanced—dimension of segmentation arises in behavioural analysis. This approach ventures into the psychological and cultural terrain, parsing employee attitudes, work ethics, risk tolerance, collaboration styles, and engagement levels. Behavioural segmentation unlocks the secret rhythms that fuel motivation, loyalty, innovation, and resilience within the workforce. Understanding who thrives as a solo virtuoso and who flourishes in ensemble settings enables workforce designers to build teams that not only complement skills but also blend personalities and behavioural tendencies for peak performance. Beyond team composition, these insights extend to leadership development, suggesting tailored coaching and mentoring approaches that align with individual behavioural patterns, increasing the likelihood of sustainable growth. Moreover, behavioural data can unveil early signals of disengagement or burnout, often invisible in conventional metrics, allowing proactive interventions that reduce turnover and preserve institutional knowledge. When behavioural insights are integrated with demographic and skill data, the result is a multi-dimensional portrait of talent that moves beyond static profiles, capturing the vibrant humanity that propels an organisation forward.

Customizing strategies based on such segmentation is not a mere academic exercise but a transformative practice that bridges the gap between abstract workforce planning and tangible organisational outcomes. For instance, consider an innovative technology company grappling with rapid growth and skill shortages in specialized fields like artificial intelligence and cybersecurity. Through skill-based segmentation, the company might identify critical talent gaps and develop customized upskilling programs targeted at mid-career professionals already within the firm, providing them with training pathways that blend formal education with immersive projects. Simultaneously, demographic data may reveal a surplus of early-career talent in regions not aligned with headquarters' evolving needs, prompting initiatives around relocation incentives or remote work models. Complementing this, behavioural segmentation might uncover that certain high-potential employees exhibit risk-taking and learning agility traits, earmarking them for leadership acceleration tracks. The synergy of these tailored approaches creates a finely tuned talent orchestra capable of executing complex strategies with agility and grace.

An additional dimension that demands deep appreciation is how segment-tailored strategies weave seamlessly into broader organisational culture and leadership dynamics. Leaders who grasp the diverse tapestries of their workforce exhibit the acumen to craft communication, recognition, and reward systems that resonate authentically across segments. Instead of a "one-size-fits-all" approach, nuanced messaging celebrates the unique contributions of diverse groups, fostering inclusivity while preserving a unified sense of purpose. Leadership development programs, too, can be calibrated to mirror the behavioural and skill profiles of rising leaders, optimizing impact and engagement. For example, a leadership cohort composed predominantly of early-career employees may require a heavier focus on foundational management skills integrated with coaching around emotional intelligence and resilience, whereas seasoned leaders may benefit from programs that cultivate transformational leadership styles and strategic foresight. This segmentation-driven personalization elevates workforce engagement and cultivates a culture where talent not only aligns with strategy but feels intrinsically valued and motivated to contribute.

Yet, segmenting and tailoring must not fall prey to static rigidity; they are dynamic, iterative practices intimately tied to continuous learning and adaptation. Market conditions, technological innovation, and societal changes constantly reshape the contours of workforce segments, demanding that organisations maintain fluidity in their approach. An effective tailored strategy incorporates feedback loops, performance reviews, and pulse surveys disaggregated by segments, ensuring that insights remain fresh and actionable. For example, a retail giant might discover through ongoing behavioural analytics that Millennial staff prioritize career progression over compensation more than previously thought, prompting adjustments in incentive structures. Similarly, skill-based segmentation may reveal emergent technical proficiencies or obsolete skills requiring swift recalibration of learning investments. Technical tools, including AI-driven analytics platforms, further amplify segmentation precision and responsiveness, enabling leaders to visualize trends and recalibrate strategies in near real-time. The question shifts from "what is our workforce makeup?" to "how is this evolving, and how must we respond?"—underscoring the ongoing vitality of tailored approaches.

One must also acknowledge the ethical dimension woven into segmentation strategies. While richly instructive, segmentation must be wielded with conscious care to respect employee privacy, avoid stereotyping, and promote equity. Overreliance on demographic labels without context can unintentionally entrench biases or marginalize groups. The careful integration of anonymized data, transparent communication about how segmentation informs strategy, and inclusive decision-making processes help to build trust. An ethical, segment-informed workforce approach not only safeguards employee dignity but also enhances organisational reputation, critical in an era where socially conscious business practices influence talent attraction and retention. By framing segmentation as a tool for empowerment rather than classification, organisations transform potential pitfalls into foundations of equity and inclusion.

The practical mechanics of crafting segment-specific strategies draw upon an arsenal of techniques. Workforce planners might deploy targeted talent acquisition tactics refined by demographic and skill analytics, such as sourcing candidates through specialized channels that align with cohorts or expertise areas. Learning and development investments can be stratified, balancing broad-based programs fostering foundational competencies with micro-learning interventions tailored to behavioural learning styles and professional aspirations. Engagement campaigns benefit from segment-specific messaging and incentives, designed to optimize motivation drivers ranging from recognition and career mobility to work-life balance initiatives. Retention efforts may involve bespoke career pathing, flexible work arrangements, or mentoring relationships attuned to segment-specific needs and challenges. In essence, segment-tailored strategies transform what might otherwise be generic organisational efforts into precision instruments measured to hit the sweet spot of individual and collective workforce aspirations.

Reflecting on numerous case studies, the fruits of segmentation-driven, tailored strategies emerge in vibrant relief. For example, a global professional services firm used skill-based segmentation to identify a shortage of data analytics experts and implemented an accelerated reskilling initiative that cut time-to-competency for mid-career consultants by half. Concurrently, behavioural segmentation revealed a subset of highly collaborative employees who thrived in fast-paced project teams; this insight led to the intentional design of cross-disciplinary squads, resulting in higher client satisfaction scores and reduced project turnover. In another instance, a multinational consumer goods company deployed demographic segmentation data to craft flexible retirement options and phased exit programs for their aging workforce, preserving institutional memory while offering dignity and choice. These stories underscore an essential truth: segmentation is not about dividing people into silos but about illuminating pathways for holistic workforce vitality and strategic alignment.

As organisations further mature in their segmentation capabilities, the horizon expands toward dynamic workforce ecosystems where segmentation is integrated with continuous scenario planning and predictive analytics. Here, segments are not fixed categories but fluid groupings reflecting evolving roles, emerging skills, and shifting engagement profiles. AI-powered platforms synthesize multiple data layers, identifying emergent segments and enabling leaders to simulate varied strategic responses to hypothetical scenarios — from economic downturns to technological disruption. Tailoring, therefore, becomes a living dialogue between data insights and human judgment, fostering not only preparedness but true anticipatory intelligence. Companies that embrace this future mindset find themselves less vulnerable to surprise and more capable of harmonizing talent deployment with nuanced, evolving business strategies.

Ultimately, the art of tailoring strategies based on segment insights crystallizes into an organisational imperative, one that elevates workforce planning from a static function to a dynamic, strategic capability. It is a process as much about empathy and human understanding as about data and analytics, requiring leaders to listen deeply, analyse rigorously, and act decisively. The payoff is a workforce symphony that plays in harmonious alignment with business objectives, where every segment's unique melody enriches the collective performance. In a world of unprecedented change and complexity, this nuanced approach is not optional but foundational to sustained success—transforming workforce planning into a vibrant, adaptive, and deeply human endeavour.

Data and Technology: Tools for Strategic Planning

Workforce Analytics Fundamentals

In the intricate dance of workforce planning, data has evolved from mere numbers on spreadsheets to become the lifeblood that fuels informed, strategic decision-making. Understanding the fundamentals of workforce analytics, therefore, is akin to learning the language that transforms ambiguous intuitions into clear, actionable insights, empowering organisations to anticipate needs and pivot swiftly in the face of change. At its core, workforce analytics is about harnessing data — both historical and real-time — to paint a detailed portrait of the current workforce landscape and forecast the path ahead with increasing precision. This transformation owes much to advances in technology, which have unlocked access to vast reservoirs of information and introduced powerful tools to process, analyse, and visualize complex datasets as never before.

The journey into workforce analytics begins by recognizing that the human capital within any organisation is not static; it is a dynamic, ever-evolving entity shaped by myriad internal and external factors. By systematically collecting data on employee performance, skills, turnover rates, recruitment, and engagement, among other dimensions, leaders can map patterns that reveal strengths, weaknesses, and potential gaps. But data alone is insufficient without the context and analytical frameworks that ascribe meaning and predictive power. Here, the fundamentals encompass the principles of data quality, integration, and interpretation—ensuring that the numbers reflect reality and that stakeholders can trust the insights derived from them.

Emerging technologies such as artificial intelligence, machine learning, and sophisticated data visualization platforms have revolutionized this arena. AI algorithms sift through mountains of data, identifying correlations and trends that human analysts might miss or take years to uncover. Predictive analytics shifts workforce planning from a reactive exercise, responding to past or current events, to a proactive approach that anticipates future demands based on a range of variables, including market trends, economic indicators, and internal organisational dynamics. This leap from hindsight to foresight transforms strategic planning into a living, breathing discipline that synchronizes with the volatile rhythm of the modern business environment.

At the heart of effective workforce analytics is the seamless integration of diverse data sources. An organisation might possess information ranging from payroll records and employee surveys to customer feedback and external labour market intelligence. The challenge—and the opportunity—lies in weaving these disparate threads into a coherent tapestry that reveals actionable insights. Basic analytics might involve descriptive statistics to understand current workforce composition and performance levels. Beyond this, diagnostic analytics delve into root cause analysis, helping identify why certain trends or issues arise. Predictive analytics then leverages historical data and sophisticated algorithms to forecast future states, such as predicting which departments are at risk of turnover or spotting emerging skill shortages that could hinder competitiveness.

However, the true power of workforce analytics manifests only when it moves beyond number crunching and model building to influence decision-making. It transforms intuition and anecdote into evidence-based strategies that balance short-term operational demands with long-term talent development goals. For instance, a company using workforce analytics may detect that a critical segment of its technical talent is nearing retirement age without a robust pipeline of successors. This early warning allows targeted upskilling programs and recruitment efforts, preventing costly talent gaps. Moreover, analytics can guide the design of incentive systems aligned with strategic priorities, ensuring that motivation and performance are channelled effectively. It supports myriad decisions, from hiring and promotions to succession planning, diversity initiatives, and even organisational restructuring.

Another essential component of workforce analytics fundamentals is the ethical and responsible handling of data. As organisations increasingly rely on personal and sensitive employee information, they must uphold the highest standards of privacy and transparency. Building and maintaining trust is paramount when employees understand how their data is used and can see that analytics serve their interests—supporting career growth, wellbeing, and fair treatment—rather than surveillance or unjust bias. A culture that embraces data-driven decisions while respecting individual rights becomes fertile ground for innovation and collective resilience.

Perhaps most transformative is how workforce analytics democratizes planning by breaking down silos and involving diverse stakeholders in the conversation. Digital dashboards and collaborative platforms make insights accessible beyond HR specialists, allowing managers and even employees to engage with relevant data. This transparency fosters a shared understanding of workforce dynamics across the organisation, empowering teams to contribute to and own solutions. It aligns with the metaphor of an orchestra, where each section tunes its instruments not in isolation but in harmony with the whole, guided by a conductor whose baton is the insight bestowed by workforce analytics.

As organisations navigate rapid technological change, globalization, and shifting workforce expectations, the fundamentals of workforce analytics offer a compass pointing toward agility and resilience. They enable an anticipatory stance, where talent strategies are continuously refined through data-enabled experimentation, scenario modelling, and real-time feedback loops. This adaptive mindset turns workforce planning from a periodic, static exercise into a continuous, evolutionary practice attuned to both opportunity and risk.

In sum, the foundation of workforce analytics lies in its ability to translate raw data into meaningful stories about people and their roles within an organisation, stories that empower leaders to compose the future workforce with foresight and precision. It is a blend of art and science—requiring technical acumen to extract insights, strategic vision to interpret their significance, and human empathy to apply them in ways that nurture engagement and growth. As the curtain rises on this new era of data-driven workforce planning, mastering these fundamentals becomes not a luxury but an imperative for any leader seeking to orchestrate talent into a harmonious and thriving symphony.

AI and Predictive Modelling

In an era where data streams flow ceaselessly from countless sources, the challenge is no longer the scarcity of information but the ability to harness it with precision, intuition, and foresight. Artificial intelligence (AI) emerges not merely as a tool but as the masterful conductor within the orchestra of workforce planning, seamlessly integrating voluminous data and dynamic variables to compose a symphony of predictive insight. The heart of predictive modelling beats to the rhythm of AI's unparalleled capacity to analyse complex patterns, sift through noise, and distil clarity from the enigmatic swirl of uncertainty that once clouded strategic workforce decisions. When organisations tap into the potency of AI-driven predictive analytics, they move beyond reactive measures, stepping confidently into a future where anticipating talent needs becomes an art guided by science.

Envisioning AI's role in workforce forecasting requires embracing a landscape where human intuition and machine intelligence coalesce. Traditional workforce planning often relied on historical trends and linear projections—methodologies invaluable yet inherently limited by their backward gaze. They painted a portrait of the past well, but faltered when the canvas stretched into the unpredictable contours of tomorrow's market flux. AI disrupts this static narrative by deploying advanced algorithms capable of interpreting multifaceted data layers, including employee performance metrics, cultural sentiment gleaned from natural language processing, economic indicators, shifts in consumer behaviour, and even emergent skill demands surfacing from the submerged currents of innovation. This expansive data tapestry provides a foundation to model not just what is probable, but what is possible, opening the gateway to scenario analyses that were once too cumbersome or speculative to consider.

At the core of AI's transformative influence lies machine learning (ML), a subset of AI that empowers systems to improve autonomously through exposure to data and experience. Unlike traditional programming constrained to pre-defined rules, ML algorithms evolve, recognizing hidden relationships and subtle cues within datasets that defy manual examination. For instance, an organisation employing ML-driven predictive models for workforce needs might uncover nuanced early indicators of voluntary turnover long before any overt signs appear. By analysing communication patterns, engagement scores, and workload fluctuations, these models can flag potential retention risks with remarkable accuracy, enabling proactive interventions that preserve talent and continuity. Furthermore, talent acquisition becomes a more strategic endeavour as predictive models, enriched with data on candidate success predictors and attrition patterns, refine sourcing strategies and reduce costly hiring mismatches.

The domain of AI-based workforce planning extends beyond personnel metrics, integrating external environmental factors that influence talent dynamics. Advanced predictive models assimilate macroeconomic trends, labour market shifts, geopolitical developments, and even social movements, creating a multidimensional forecasting matrix. For example, the implementation of natural language processing enables the scouring of news feeds, social media, and industry reports to detect emerging skills gaining traction or identify rising competitive threats to talent pools. This real-time environmental scanning, powered by AI, ensures that workforce strategies remain agile and anticipatory, not caught flat-footed by sudden disruptions or shifts in talent availability. Here, AI serves not just as an analyst but as a vigilant sentinel, perpetually monitoring and signalling changes relevant to human capital planning.

Another profound contribution of AI to predictive workforce modelling is the capacity for hyper-personalization at scale. In a conventional environment, workforce planning tends to aggregate roles and skills into broad categories, losing sight of individual potential and nuanced differences. However, AI can dissect workforce data down to single employees, forecasting career trajectories, developmental needs, and readiness for critical roles with granular insight. By analysing performance evaluations, learning histories, collaboration networks, and motivational indicators, AI-powered models craft dynamic profiles that empower leaders to tailor retention efforts, succession planning, and internal mobility strategies more effectively. This bespoke understanding catalyses a culture of opportunity and growth within organisations, fostering greater engagement and reducing the often-devastating voids caused by unexpected departures.

A particularly captivating facet of AI's application lies in its ability to simulate future workforce scenarios through sophisticated 'what-if' analyses. These simulations enable decision-makers to explore the outcomes of various strategic options before committing resources or executing change. For example, an organisation contemplating automation's impact on its workforce might model scenarios ranging from minimal disruption to wholesale role transformation, revealing the timing, scale, and skill recalibrations necessary for a smooth transition. AI enhances these simulations by incorporating probabilistic modelling and reinforcement learning techniques, which learn from each scenario iteration to optimize recommendations continuously. Such dynamic experimentation cultivates visionary planning, allowing companies to prepare contingency plans, optimize resource allocation, and build robust yet flexible workforce architectures aligned with anticipated business pivots.

Despite its promise, the integration of AI in predictive workforce models demands mindfulness of the pitfalls that could undercut its effectiveness. Models are only as reliable as the data and assumptions underpinning them, and biases embedded within historical datasets risk perpetuating inequities or flawed forecasts if not carefully monitored. Moreover, AI's opaque decision-making processes—often referred to as the "black box" phenomenon—can stymie trust among human stakeholders who seek a transparent rationale behind critical workforce decisions. The solution resides in adopting ethical AI frameworks and interpretability techniques that elucidate how predictions emerge, enabling human leaders to scrutinize, challenge, and complement AI insights rather than surrender judgment entirely. Workshops, cross-functional committees, and continuous validation of model performance nurture a governance environment that balances algorithmic power with human wisdom.

Another frontier where AI infuses vigour into workforce strategic planning is through the fusion of predictive analytics with real-time operational data, enabling what some call 'always-on workforce intelligence.' This continuous feedback mechanism transforms static planning cycles into dynamic, adaptive systems that respond fluidly to emerging conditions. Consider global supply chain disruptions that cascade through an organisation's production teams; AI sensors and analytics instantly relay impact signals, prompting workforce redistributions, urgent upskilling programs, or remote deployment of niche expertise. The immediacy and precision offered by such integrated predictive capabilities shift the workforce strategy from a theoretical Planning to a living organism, capable of evolving seamlessly as the market evolves.

Real-world examples illuminate AI's vivid impact on workforce forecasting. One multinational technology firm employed AI-powered predictive models to refine its talent pipeline, embedding algorithms that tracked not only skills gaps but also cultural fit and leadership potential. This holistic approach reduced hiring cycles and significantly improved retention rates within two years. In the healthcare sector, a large hospital network leveraged AI to project nurse staffing needs amidst fluctuating patient volumes caused by seasonal illness spikes and pandemics. The predictive insights enabled timely recruitment and redeployment, mitigating burnout and enhancing patient care continuity. Similarly, a global retailer integrated AI forecasting with customer purchasing trends and regional economic indicators, allowing it to anticipate labour demands at store levels with remarkable foresight, optimizing both operational efficiency and employee satisfaction.

Furthermore, the evolution of natural language generation technologies linked with AI-driven analytics facilitates the translation of complex predictive outputs into vivid, narrative forecasts accessible to a broad leadership audience. Instead of inundating decision-makers with raw data streams or impenetrable model outputs, these tools craft tailored reports that tell a story rich with actionable insights and strategic implications. This narrative augmentation bridges the technical divide, democratizing workforce intelligence and embedding it more deeply into organisational dialogues, planning forums, and executive decision-making processes.

The Guide to Workforce Planning

The marriage of AI and predictive modelling reshapes the ethos of workforce planning from a function rooted in static spreadsheets to a dynamic, continuously learning discipline. It empowers leaders to look beyond static headcount targets and instead cultivate a living panorama of human potential—one that reflects evolving skills, emerging markets, and the growing importance of diversity and inclusion as integral drivers of innovation and resilience. In this new paradigm, workforce planning is no longer a sterile calculation but a vibrant, anticipatory endeavour, pulsing with the energy of predictive intelligence and human creativity entwined.

Yet, to fully realize the advantages AI offers, organisations must also invest in upskilling their strategic planners to collaborate effectively with these digital tools. This demands a cultural shift where data literacy and technological fluency are embraced by HR professionals and leadership alike, cultivating a symbiosis between human insight and machine precision. As AI surfaces new patterns and offers predictions, human strategists must interpret these insights within the context of nuanced organisational values, external realities, and ethical considerations—ensuring not only that the predictions are accurate but that the actions they inspire align with the company's long-term vision and purpose.

AI's role is expansive but not infallible; its greatest value lies as an enhancer of strategic thinking rather than its replacement. It handles vast complexity, recognizes signals obscured to unaided analysis, and continuously refines forecasts as fresh data emerges. Yet, the human element remains indispensable in guiding AI, interpreting its nuances, and infusing workforce planning with empathy, creativity, and contextual judgment. This interplay embodies the future of strategic workforce management—a collaboration where the symphony of human potential performs in harmony with the cadence of artificial intelligence, creating not just a workforce prepared for tomorrow but a workforce inspired for the extraordinary.

As we continue to navigate an ever-accelerating digital and economic landscape, the AI-powered predictive modelling framework stands as a beacon for organisations seeking clarity amidst chaos. By transforming intangible data into vivid foresight, AI enables strategic planners to peer beyond the immediate horizon, crafting workforce strategies that are resilient, responsive, and remarkably attuned to the evolving needs of business and humanity alike. In this alchemy of innovation and insight, workforce planning transcends prediction, becoming a fertile ground where possibility unfolds, risks are mastered, and opportunity is orchestrated with the confidence of a maestro commanding an ensemble primed for a masterpiece of sustained success.

HR Technology Platforms

The Guide to Workforce Planning

In the intricate symphony of workforce planning, HR technology platforms serve as the masterful instruments amplifying the orchestra's harmony and precision. These platforms, often underestimated as mere administrative aids, have evolved into sophisticated, dynamic ecosystems that empower organisations to orchestrate their human capital with the nuance of a seasoned conductor. The evolution of these tools is not merely incremental but transformative, weaving together data, analytics, and artificial intelligence to provide predictive insights that were once in the realm of intuition and guesswork. At their core, HR technology platforms unify disparate elements of workforce management into a coherent, intelligent framework that breathes life into strategic planning.

At the foundation, these platforms streamline the traditionally fragmented HR processes, from recruitment and onboarding to performance management and succession planning, embedding capabilities that allow companies to see beyond the present and anticipate talent needs. The evolution from basic HR information systems that merely stored employee data to sophisticated suites offering predictive analytics has been nothing short of revolutionary. Modern systems harness the power of machine learning algorithms to analyse patterns in employee performance, turnover likelihood, engagement levels, and even external labour market trends. Such analyses enable leaders to make decisions grounded in data-driven foresight rather than reactive measures, reducing uncertainty in workforce planning and sharpening strategic alignment.

Consider, for example, a global technology firm grappling with rapid industry shifts and an impending wave of retirements among skilled developers. Utilizing an integrated HR platform with advanced analytics, leadership can uncover hidden trends—such as a subtle decline in engagement among mid-career employees or signals that certain skill sets are becoming scarce in the external market. The platform's AI modules sift through mountain ranges of internal and external data, blending historical performance, training completion rates, market demand forecasts, and compensation benchmarks to forecast impending talent gaps with remarkable accuracy. This predictive capability shifts the company from firefighting talent shortages to proactively shaping recruitment, development, and retention strategies that ensure continuity and innovation.

Beyond forecasting, HR technology platforms provide immersive visualization tools that transform complex data into clear, compelling narratives accessible to stakeholders across the organisation. Decision-makers can interact with dynamic dashboards that illustrate workforce composition, skill distribution, and scenario-based projections. These visual metaphors serve not only as analytical tools but as catalysts for strategic conversations, enabling leadership teams to explore "what-if" scenarios and weigh the impact of various talent initiatives. For instance, by simulating the introduction of a new remote work policy, decision-makers can assess how talent attraction, engagement, and cost structures might evolve, adjusting plans accordingly. This level of insight turns workforce planning from an opaque process into an agile, communicative dialogue aligned closely with business imperatives.

The integration capabilities of modern HR platforms further underscore their transformative potential. Contemporary ecosystems no longer function as isolated silos but interconnect seamlessly with payroll systems, learning management systems, project management tools, and even financial planning software. This bi-directional flow of information enriches the predictive models and ensures that workforce data resonates holistically throughout the organisation. For example, linking learning management systems with performance data enables a clear line of sight into skill development journeys, making it possible to tailor reskilling programs precisely where and when they are needed. Simultaneously, these integrated insights empower finance leaders to model the cost implications of talent strategies with granular accuracy, fortifying the strategic business case for workforce investments.

Crucially, these platforms are evolving with a human-centered design philosophy that emphasizes usability, accessibility, and inclusivity. The goal is to democratize strategic insights by making complex data intelligible and actionable not only for HR specialists but also for line managers, team leaders, and even individual employees. Empowering managers with real-time visibility into team capabilities, workload balance, and developmental trajectories fosters a culture of continuous engagement and agile adjustment. Employees, too, benefit from personalized career growth roadmaps and real-time feedback mechanisms embedded within these platforms, enhancing motivation and retention while aligning individual aspirations with organizational goals. This alignment creates a virtuous loop in which technology facilitates a deeper human connection and mutual growth.

The incorporation of cutting-edge technologies such as natural language processing and chatbots further enriches workforce engagement and efficiency. Instead of sifting through cumbersome data reports or waiting days for HR responses, managers and employees can interact with AI-powered assistants that provide instant answers on benefits, policy changes, or learning opportunities. These conversational interfaces also gather valuable qualitative data by capturing employee sentiment and feedback through natural dialogue, offering nuanced insights that complement quantitative analytics. This fusion of human touch and machine intelligence amplifies the organisation's responsiveness to evolving workforce needs, nurturing resilience amidst change.

Security and ethical considerations have become paramount as these platforms handle ever-growing volumes of sensitive data. Leading vendors prioritize robust data governance frameworks that ensure compliance with global privacy regulations and uphold employee trust. Encryption protocols, anonymization techniques, and transparent data usage policies work together to balance the need for insightful analysis with respect for individual privacy. Such ethical stewardship is not only a legal imperative but a strategic differentiator that fosters a culture of trust, essential for the honest data exchange necessary to power accurate predictive models.

Despite their profound capabilities, the successful adoption of HR technology platforms requires more than just installing software—it demands a cultural shift and strategic vision. Organisations must cultivate digital literacy across their leadership and workforce to unlock the full potential of these tools. Training programs, change management initiatives, and ongoing support play vital roles in embedding these platforms into the fabric of daily decision-making. Moreover, the human expertise in interpreting data remains irreplaceable: technology provides the notes, but it is leaders and strategists who compose the melodies that move the organisation forward.

In practical terms, a strategic workforce planner's toolbox equipped with these platforms' functions much like the conductor's baton—subtle yet commanding. It guides attention to critical moments where intervention is needed, surfaces hidden tensions in workforce balance, and sets the tempo for talent development initiatives that synchronize with market demands. Organisations leveraging these platforms find themselves with an elevated vantage point, able to foresee talent storms ahead and chart a course that secures competitive agility and sustained innovation.

The promise of HR technology platforms to unlock workforce potential is immense, yet it is only beginning to be realized. As artificial intelligence grows more sophisticated and data ecosystems become richer and more interconnected, these platforms will continue to push the boundaries of what is possible in workforce planning. They are no longer just tools, but strategic partners that enable organisations to transcend reactive HR management and embrace a visionary, data-informed approach. By weaving technology deeply into the tapestry of workforce strategy, organisations can craft a symphony of talent that is not just responsive to the future but compellingly anticipatory— transforming uncertainty into opportunity and human capacity into enduring success.

Integrating Data Across Systems

In the ever-evolving landscape of workforce planning, the integration of data across disparate systems emerges as not merely a technical necessity but a strategic fulcrum upon which the entire edifice of talent management pivots. Imagine a grand symphony orchestra where each instrument, though exquisitely tuned, produces a cacophony if not delicately harmonized. Similarly, organisations today grapple with numerous data silos, each harbouring invaluable information resting in isolation—human resource management systems offering employee demographics, learning management platforms chronicling skill development, performance evaluation tools capturing qualitative and quantitative feedback, and external Labor market analytics providing vital economic and competitive intelligence. Without a cohesive data flow linking these fragments into a unified stream, leaders and strategists are left with fragmented melodies—partial narratives that obscure the orchestral vision of workforce strategy.

Cohesion in data integration is the key that unlocks transformational insights, turning static numbers into dynamic foresight. Emerging technologies, particularly artificial intelligence and advanced analytics, act as the masterful conductors, weaving together the individual data threads into rich tapestries of understanding. The journey toward seamless integration begins with acknowledging the complexity of existing organisational landscapes, where systems often operate on incompatible architectures and differing data standards. Overcoming these challenges demands intentional architecture design that embraces interoperability from the ground up, utilizing open APIs, standardized data formats, and middleware solutions that act as digital translators, bridging chasms between legacy software and modern platforms.

One cannot overstate the potency of predictive analytics empowered by integrated data ecosystems. When workforce data flows unhindered across functional boundaries, predictive models gain access to a panoramic vista of variables—employee engagement scores entwined with productivity metrics, turnover patterns intersecting with succession planning data, skills inventory aligned with project pipeline forecasts. This multidimensional perspective enables algorithms to not only identify current talent gaps but also anticipate emergent needs shaped by business pivots, market trends, and technological disruptions. In this sense, data integration transforms from a back-office chore to an ambitious endeavour that fuels strategic foresight, enabling organisations to move from reactive decision-making to proactive orchestration of their human capital.

Moreover, the tangible benefits ripple through operational efficiency and agility. Integrated data systems empower leadership to generate real-time dashboards that transcend departmental confines, delivering holistic views accessible at every organisational tier. This democratization of insights nurtures informed dialogue among executives, HR leaders, and line managers, catalyzing aligned actions that resonate with overarching business objectives. For instance, talent acquisition teams can pivot recruitment strategies armed with an immediate understanding of evolving skill demands, while learning and development units rapidly tailor upskilling initiatives grounded in current workforce analytics. The synchronization fostered by integrated data flow is akin to a well-conducted orchestra where every section's output complements the other, creating a resonance that pushes organisational performance toward new crescendos.

Yet, the path to seamless integration is laden with challenges that transcend mere technology. Data quality remains paramount; an integrated system is only as reliable as the inputs it ingests. Inconsistent or erroneous data can propagate errors across connected platforms, misleading predictive models, and skewing strategic projections. This compels organisations to institute rigorous data governance frameworks that encompass standardized data entry protocols, continuous cleansing processes, and clear ownership roles to ensure accountability across the data lifecycle. Equally vital is cultivating a culture that values data literacy and ethical stewardship, encouraging stakeholders to engage with data critically and responsibly, appreciating the profound impact it wields over workforce decision-making.

Security and privacy considerations further complicate this landscape. Integrating data across systems often involves consolidating sensitive employee information, potentially exposing it to heightened risk if not meticulously managed. Modern encryption techniques, role-based access controls, and compliance with regulations such as GDPR and CCPA form the protective scaffolding that underpins trust in integrated data environments. Organisations must strike an intricate balance—leveraging comprehensive data for strategic gains without compromising individual privacy or ethical obligations. Achieving this equilibrium necessitates transparent communication with employees about data usage and implementing safeguards that align with both legal mandates and organisational values.

Advancements in cloud computing have supercharged data integration capabilities, dissolving the barriers imposed by geographic dispersion and siloed infrastructure. Cloud-based platforms facilitate scalable, agile data architectures, enabling organisations to ingest, process, and analyse vast datasets with unprecedented speed and flexibility. This technological leap dovetails elegantly with increasing trends toward remote and hybrid workforces, where data flows must transcend physical boundaries to inform timely workforce strategies across global operations. Furthermore, integrating human and machine data—melding biometric insights, collaboration patterns, and even sentiment analysis derived from communication platforms—propels strategic workforce planning into a realm of nuanced, human-centered understanding enriched by technological precision.

Real-world examples illuminate how organisations have harnessed integrated data flows to achieve transformative outcomes. Consider a multinational technology firm that consolidated disparate regional HR databases into an integrated talent intelligence platform. By layering this data with external market analytics and internal project demand forecasts, leadership anticipated critical skills shortages months ahead, enabling targeted reskilling programs that reduced talent gaps by nearly thirty percent and avoided costly project delays. Similarly, a healthcare system integrated patient care schedules, staff certifications, and burnout indicators into a single analytic dashboard, empowering managers to optimize shift allocations, dynamically boosting staff satisfaction while maintaining superior patient outcomes.

The essence of integrating data across systems lies not only in technical execution but in the strategic mindset that embraces complexity and fosters collaboration across organisational silos. It calls for visionary leadership that champions investment in technological infrastructure while cultivating cross-functional partnerships anchored in shared goals. The process transforms workforce planning from a static function into an evolving art, where data serves as the palette blending diverse colours into cohesive, future-forward portraits of talent landscapes.

As the digital era accelerates, organisations that master the integration of data across systems will find themselves not merely reacting to change but anticipating and shaping it. The promise of cohesive data flow extends beyond improved decision-making—it offers a competitive symphony; an orchestration of human potential aligned intricately with the rhythms of business strategy. In this symphony, data integration is the invisible conductor's baton, guiding every note, every pause, every crescendo toward a harmonious future where workforce plans resonate with clarity, precision, and visionary insight.

Leadership's Baton: Driving Workforce Strategy

Leadership Roles in Workforce Planning

Leadership in workforce planning transcends the traditional confines of hierarchical authority and becomes a dynamic force orchestrating the alignment of human potential with evolving organisational ambitions. At the heart of a successful workforce strategy lies not only the careful articulation of talent requirements but the visionary guidance and influence wielded by leaders who shape the strategic narrative, galvanize commitment, and nurture a culture attuned to agility and innovation. This influence manifests in diverse facets—from the leadership style adopted, through the nuanced art of communication, to the deft navigation of change management—all converging to create the fertile ground upon which strategic workforce plans can flourish.

Effective leaders understand that workforce planning is not an isolated administrative task but a living, breathing strategic imperative that demands their proactive engagement. The leadership style they exhibit plays a pivotal role in setting the tone, priorities, and momentum of workforce initiatives. A transformational leadership approach, for instance, inspires and motivates individuals by cultivating a shared vision that transcends immediate operational concerns. Leaders adopting this style act less as commanders and more as architects of possibility, instilling a sense of purpose that aligns employees' personal aspirations with the broader business objectives. This alignment fosters intrinsic motivation, encouraging teams to embrace workforce changes not as mere compliance but as essential evolutions toward a collective future.

In contrast, transactional leadership, with its emphasis on structured rewards and clear expectations, can provide the necessary scaffolding to maintain accountability during the rigors of strategy implementation. While sometimes perceived as rigid, when balanced with vision-driven approaches, transactional leadership ensures that the day-to-day execution of workforce plans proceeds with discipline and measurable progress. However, the most impactful leaders tend to embody adaptive styles that fluidly blend inspiration and pragmatism, responding to shifting internal dynamics and external market forces with agility. This versatility is critical in workforce planning, where unpredictable disruptions require leadership not only to envision future talent landscapes but to recalibrate approaches with speed and clarity.

Integral to these leadership styles is the mastery of communication—a subtle yet powerful tool in shaping workforce strategy. Leaders must articulate the why, what, and how of workforce planning with clarity and empathy, transforming abstract strategic planning into tangible narratives that resonate across all organisational layers. Effective communication transcends mere information dissemination; it weaves a compelling story that engages stakeholders emotionally and intellectually, fostering a collective ownership of the workforce agenda. Leaders who communicate transparently build trust, a crucial currency in navigating the uncertainties inherent in workforce transformations. When employees understand the rationale behind talent shifts, anticipate the implications for their roles, and see their leaders' genuine commitment to their wellbeing, resistance diminishes and collaboration flourishes.

Moreover, communication in this context is invariably two-way. The most progressive leaders cultivate environments where open dialogue and feedback are not just encouraged but expected. This reciprocal communication enriches workforce planning by surfacing ground-level insights and anxieties that might otherwise remain hidden, allowing leadership to refine strategies in real time. Such inclusivity also signals respect and value for diverse perspectives, strengthening organisational cohesion. As workforce planning inherently involves change — often unsettling — empathetic communication softens transitions, converts sceptics into advocates, and maintains morale through periods of ambiguity.

Change management lies at the crossroads where leadership style and communication converge to produce tangible workforce planning outcomes. Leaders must become adept change agents, possessing a nuanced understanding of the human psyche, organisational culture, and systemic barriers that can impede strategic shifts. Implementing workforce plans frequently entails disruption—redefining roles, adopting new technologies, reconfiguring team structures—each with potential to unsettle established norms and provoke resistance. Leaders, therefore, must anticipate these challenges, crafting change initiatives that are not one-size-fits-all mandates but tailored journeys acknowledging the varied readiness and resilience of different parts of the organisation.

Successful change management in workforce planning begins with building a compelling vision that makes the future state desirable and attainable. Leaders serve as the visible champions of this vision, modelling behaviours and attitudes that align with strategic goals. Their visible commitment sets a precedent, signalling to employees that workforce planning is a priority woven into the organisational fabric. They deploy structured change frameworks—which may include phased rollouts, pilot programs, and continuous monitoring—ensuring that strategy implementation is both deliberate and adaptive. Such frameworks enable the identification and mitigation of risks early, turning potential roadblocks into learning opportunities.

Beyond process, leaders must also recognize the emotional journey their people undertake during workforce transformations.

They cultivate psychological safety by encouraging expression of concerns and actively addressing fears related to job security, competency shifts, and identity within the evolving organisation. Change is as much about managing emotions as it is about managing tasks; leaders who master this duality sustain engagement and foster resilience. By providing learning opportunities, coaching, and support systems, they empower employees to not only survive but thrive amid change, building a culture that embraces continuous adaptation as a source of strength.

Leadership influence in workforce planning also encompasses the strategic allocation of resources, including nurturing leadership at all levels. Recognizing that complex talent challenges cannot be addressed by a single individual, effective leaders build leadership pipelines that embed workforce planning capabilities across functions. This distributed leadership fosters ownership, accelerates decision-making, and reinforces alignment. Leaders cultivate these capabilities through mentorship, targeted development programs, and by setting clear expectations for managers to assume active roles in talent identification, development, and retention. This cascading influence ensures that the workforce strategy is lived daily, not relegated to strategy documents.

Importantly, leaders must balance short-term operational demands with long-term talent imperatives. Workforce planning often involves investing in capabilities that will only bear fruit years into the future, requiring leaders to champion patience and strategic foresight amidst a climate of immediate performance pressures. They must skilfully advocate for resources and attention to workforce initiatives, articulating their return on investment not only in potential profitability but also in organisational resilience and innovation capacity. By framing workforce planning as a continuous strategic dialogue, rather than a sporadic project, leaders embed adaptability into the organisational DNA, equipping the enterprise to weather uncertainties and capitalize on emergent opportunities.

The influence of leaders extends to shaping the organisational culture—a subtle yet decisive factor in workforce planning success. Culture acts as both the soil and the air through which talent strategies germinate and take root. Leaders who cultivate cultures of trust, learning, and collaboration create fertile conditions for workforce planning to unfold organically. In such cultures, workforce agility becomes a shared value, employees embrace development opportunities, and cross-functional collaboration thrives, enabling swift realignment of talent to shifting strategic priorities. Conversely, cultures marked by silos, fear, or rigidity create friction that can stall or distort workforce initiatives.

Leaders influence culture not solely through formal policies but through everyday behaviours, rituals, and storytelling. Their visible commitment to workforce planning—whether through transparent decision-making, recognition of talent contributions, or openness about challenges—signals authenticity and seriousness. This cultural signalling amplifies workforce strategy messages and ensures they resonate throughout the organisation. Furthermore, leaders must actively dismantle cultural barriers—such as unconscious biases or rigid hierarchies—that limit talent mobility and innovation. By championing inclusivity and psychological safety, they unlock the full spectrum of capabilities and perspectives necessary for crafting adaptive and forward-looking workforce plans.

In today's fast-evolving business landscape, leadership roles in workforce planning also demand an astute sensitivity to technological shifts reshaping talent ecosystems. Leaders must possess the acumen to integrate digital tools and data analytics into strategic decision-making while balancing the human touch that imbues workforce plans with empathy and ethics. This hybrid leadership proficiency enables the proactive anticipation of emerging skills needs informed by predictive insights rather than retrospective data. Leaders who cultivate data literacy and encourage experimentation with workforce technologies foster environments where innovation in talent strategy is continuous and evidence-based rather than ad hoc.

The orchestration of leadership across these dimensions—style, communication, change management, culture, and technology—resonates like a symphony, where each element interweaves to produce harmonized outcomes greater than the sum of its parts. When leaders harmonize their roles effectively, workforce planning ceases to be a fragmented or reactive exercise and transforms into a strategic masterpiece that empowers the organisation to navigate uncertainty with confidence and creativity. They do not merely direct talent deployment but inspire a collective movement toward a future where human capital and business aspirations converge seamlessly.

Ultimately, leadership influence in workforce planning is an ongoing journey of learning, adaptation, and courageous vision. Leaders must remain vigilant against complacency, continuously refining their approaches in response to emergent challenges and opportunities. This leadership vigilance ensures that workforce strategies remain vibrant, relevant, and robust, fuelling sustainable organisational success. Their stewardship is the compass guiding the enterprise through workforce complexities, turning what might appear as daunting challenges into symphonic possibilities ripe with innovation, resilience, and shared prosperity.

Communicating the Vision

In the grand symphony of workforce strategy, communication functions as the conductor's baton—guiding, shaping, and harmonizing disparate elements into a unified performance. Without an articulate, resonant message that conveys the vision with clarity and conviction, even the most meticulously designed workforce plans risk languishing in misunderstanding or dissonance among teams. The art of communicating the vision transcends simply disseminating information; it demands crafting a narrative that stirs the hearts and minds of every individual within the organisation, aligning their personal motivations with the collective ambition. Leadership, in this critical phase, plays an indispensable role—not only through the words spoken but through the tone, presence, and authenticity conveyed. How leaders communicate, and the styles they adopt, become the catalyst for successful workforce strategy implementation, allowing teams to internalize and embody the mission rather than merely obliging with it.

At its core, effective messaging is about connection. It slices through corporate jargon and complex analytics to deliver a narrative that feels tangible and meaningful. The vision, when communicated well, becomes a living story—a shared purpose that resonates across hierarchical layers and job functions. This is where leadership style converges with communication practices to ignite enthusiasm and commitment. Transformational leadership, for instance, is uniquely suited to this Endeavor because it energizes through inspiration and vision casting, inviting employees not just to comply but to co-create the future. Leaders adopting this style do not simply issue directives but engage in dialogues that challenge, uplift, and invite innovation, making the workforce strategy a collective quest rather than an imposed mandate. This style encourages vulnerability—leaders openly share both the promise and the uncertainty inherent in strategic change, fostering trust and psychological safety within their teams. In such an environment, communication becomes a two-way street where feedback flows freely, enriching the implementation process and enabling adaptive evolution of the strategy.

Additionally, the charismatic, empathetic leader taps into emotional intelligence to tailor messages that resonate with diverse audiences within the organisation. Understanding the unique concerns, motivations, and aspirations of different groups allows communication to be precise and compelling. For some, the framing may emphasize career development and new opportunities for personal growth, while for others, security and stability during transitional times take precedence. Leaders adept at reading these emotional and cultural cues shape their narratives, accordingly, using stories, analogies, and metaphors that speak directly to the varied lenses through which employees perceive change. This emotional atonement is a powerful lubricant for reducing resistance, as it acknowledges the human element often overshadowed by data and performance metrics. Through such sensitive, contextual communication, workforce planning ceases to be an abstract exercise and becomes a shared saga—personal and purposeful.

Yet even the most charismatic communication must be supported by strategic consistency and clarity. The vision cannot be a fleeting spark; it must be a steadfast beacon that withstands the complexities and frictions of execution. Leaders who communicate the vision effectively ensure that every message, meeting, and touchpoint reinforces the core themes of the workforce strategy. This repetition is not mere redundancy but a vital mechanism for embedding the vision into the organisational psyche. The language used is accessible yet aspirational, inviting not just understanding but belief. Terminology is chosen deliberately to avoid alienation or confusion, knitting together technical precision with inspired storytelling. Transparency and honesty become bedrocks during this process, as employees increasingly value Candor in times of transformation. When leadership openly acknowledges challenges, setbacks, and the need for collective problem-solving, they reinforce a culture of resilience and shared ownership.

Embedded within this process is an often-underestimated aspect of communication: timing. The cadence at which messages are delivered can crucially influence morale and momentum. Leaders orchestrate communication flows in waves—initially building anticipation and curiosity, followed by detailed clarifications as teams seek to understand their roles, and continuing with periodic reinforcements and celebrations of milestones. This dynamic approach prevents fatigue and keeps engagement levels high. Importantly, meaningful pauses are incorporated to allow reflection and dialogue, encouraging employees not just to absorb information but to interact with it, challenge it, and internalize it. In doing so, communication becomes a dynamic conversation rather than a static proclamation. Such dialogic engagement is the hallmark of high-functioning organisations where workforce strategy is not a distrustful edict but a shared venture.

Change management techniques further enhance the impact of communication. Recognizing that introducing a new workforce strategy inevitably disrupts established routines, leaders employ frameworks like Kotter's Eight Steps or ADKAR to structure messaging and interventions. These models emphasize the creation of urgency and coalition-building among influencers within the organisation, not only at the executive level but throughout operational tiers. Leaders identify natural leaders and early adopters who can champion the vision in practical, relatable ways, connecting top-down direction with bottom-up momentum. This networked approach to communication weaves the workforce strategy into daily conversations and decision-making, reducing the friction of change. Leaders also ensure adequate training and resources accompany messaging so that employees feel equipped, not overwhelmed, by new expectations. In this way, communication becomes a scaffold supporting behavioural shifts and skills development, rather than a mere announcement of strategic imperatives.

Technological advancements today provide leaders with powerful tools to amplify and customize their communication strategies. Digital platforms enable real-time updates, rich multimedia storytelling, and tailored messaging to diverse segments—bridging geographical distances and organisational boundaries. However, technology must be used thoughtfully to prevent messages from becoming fragmented or impersonal. Leaders who excel in this realm balance virtual and face-to-face interactions, recognizing that empathy and nuance thrive in human connection. Town halls, small group discussions, and informal check-ins complement emails and intranet posts to create multidimensional communication ecosystems. Furthermore, analytics derived from these platforms offer feedback on engagement levels, message reach, and sentiment, empowering leaders to refine and recalibrate their approaches continuously. This iterative process transforms communication from a one-off event into an evolving dialogue attuned to the organisation's pulse.

Moreover, leaders recognize that communication is inseparable from culture—both shaping and being shaped by it. An organisational culture characterized by openness, learning, and psychological safety naturally facilitates the transparent exchange necessary for strategy alignment. Leaders act as cultural architects, modelling behaviours that demonstrate commitment to shared values and encouraging candid conversations about the challenges and opportunities unfolding. Storytelling becomes a cultural practice, passing down not just rational explanations but the collective wisdom of the organisation, weaving the workforce strategy into its fabric. This cultural embedding ensures that communication transcends superficial compliance to become a lived experience, where vision alignment is reinforced daily in actions as much as words.

Resistance, a natural human reaction to change, often manifests as a communication challenge. Leaders tackling resistance do so not by overpowering or dismissing dissent but by listening intently and addressing concerns with empathy and evidence. They engage sceptics through open forums and personalized conversations, validating emotions while strategically guiding the dialogue toward shared goals. This responsive communication approach underscores a fundamental truth: a workforce strategy succeeds when people feel heard and respected, not coerced. By transforming resistance into participation, leaders unlock valuable insights that enrich the vision and enhance its feasibility.

In sum, communicating the vision in workforce strategy is a sophisticated, nuanced Endeavor that demands more than mere information sharing. It is a multifaceted orchestration involving inspiring storytelling, emotional intelligence, cultural cultivation, technology utilization, and change management savvy. Leaders who master this art create a resonant narrative that aligns hearts and minds, nurturing a workforce energized to navigate uncertainty and seize emerging opportunities. Such communication is the connective tissue binding strategy to execution, turning the promise of vision into the lived reality of organisational transformation. It transforms workforce planning from an intangible Planning into a vibrant, collective symphony—one that inspires every player to contribute harmoniously to the enduring success of the enterprise.

Change Management Essentials

Change is the ever-present undercurrent in the vast ocean of organisational life, a force that both frightens and invigorates, disrupts and renews. Navigating this sea requires not only a sturdy vessel but an astute captain—someone who understands that guiding a workforce through transformation is equal parts art and science. At its core, change management is the deliberate orchestration of human dynamics, woven through the intricate fabric of leadership, communication, and cultural adaptation. To master this Endeavor, organisations must embrace change not as a series of isolated events but as a continuous rhythm that flows through every layer of their strategic Planning. It's here, within the charged atmosphere of transitions, that leaders emerge as conductors of a symphony of minds and hearts, each movement demanding thoughtful direction to ensure the harmonious evolution of the workforce.

Leadership, often romanticized as the charismatic figure who rallies troops in a decisive charge, takes on a far richer and complex dimension in the realm of change management. It is less about the forceful imposition of will and more about cultivating a vision so compelling that it transforms uncertainty into opportunity. This vision must be deeply anchored in empathy—an understanding of the workforce's fears, aspirations, and resistance. Transformational leadership, the approach most suited for workforce transformations, thrives by inspiring and empowering individuals to embrace new paradigms, encouraging ownership rather than compliance. Leaders who invest in storytelling, crafting narratives that connect change to a broader purpose, invoke the imagination and motivation necessary for engagement. When employees see themselves not as passive recipients but active participants in the organisational evolution, the daunting spectre of change dims, replaced by a sense of shared agency.

The Guide to Workforce Planning

Equally vital is the leadership style's adaptability, for no single approach fits all contexts. While transformational leaders emphasize inspiration and vision, servant leadership shines through in nurturing and supporting teams through unsettling transitions, attending to emotional and psychological needs. Authenticity and transparency become pillars, building trust that often acts as a fragile bridge over turbulent waters. When leaders openly acknowledge challenges and uncertainties, they invite dialogue rather than silence, inviting collective problem-solving. The juxtaposition of authoritative yet approachable leadership sets a tone of resilience, where accountability and compassion coexist seamlessly, coaxing the workforce toward embrace rather than retreat.

Communication emerges as the sinew binding the entire change management framework. It is through words, symbols, and shared experiences that the abstract concept of workforce transformation crystallizes into a tangible reality. Yet, communication here is not merely transactional or informational; it is transformational and relational. The cadence of messaging—its timing, frequency, and channels—must be orchestrated with precision, ensuring that information flows outward and feedback streams inward. This dynamic interchange nurtures a two-way street where concerns are voiced, clarifications made, and adjustments applied, fostering a culture of openness and continuous learning.

Effective change communication transcends the conventional memo or corporate email; it must activate the senses and emotions. Stories of early adopters who have flourished under new frameworks, vivid metaphors that paint the journey from 'old' to 'new,' and candid discussions about setbacks collectively create psychological scaffolding for acceptance. Communication strategies must also be highly segmented, recognizing that different groups—executives, mid-level managers, frontline employees—interpret and react to change through unique lenses. Tailoring messages to address these varied perspectives prevents misinformation and rumours from taking root and bridges generational and cultural divides within the organisation. Transparency about the rationale behind changes, the expected benefits, and the anticipated challenges prevents a vacuum of uncertainty from permeating the workforce.

In tandem with leadership and communication, the mechanics of change management demand robust processes that move beyond rhetoric into actionable frameworks. The adoption of established models—such as Kotter's eight-step process, Lewin's three-phase approach, or the ADKAR model—provides organisations with a structured roadmap to guide transformation efforts systematically. These models emphasize stages from creating a sense of urgency, building guiding coalitions, to anchoring new approaches in the organisational culture, each step helping to mitigate resistance and build momentum. Yet, the true power of these methodologies lies in their flexible interpretation, tailored to align with unique organisational contexts rather than rigid prescriptions.

Resistance to change, often framed as an obstacle, is better viewed as a natural and invaluable signal. It reveals underlying concerns, gaps in communication, or misalignments between strategy and workforce realities. Successful change managers listen attentively to this resistance, engaging respectfully and empathetically with dissenting voices. By framing resistance as feedback rather than rebellion, organisations can co-create solutions that resonate more deeply and sustainably. Incorporating employees as active architects of change enhances buy-in and prevents the alienation that so often derails transformation efforts.

The cultural dimension within change management is frequently the most elusive yet pivotal element. Culture represents the collective mental models, values, beliefs, and behaviours that define 'how things get done'—a force that can either accelerate or choke change. Altering culture requires intentionality and patience, often necessitating subtle shifts over extended time horizons. Leaders must identify and cultivate cultural champions— individuals who exemplify desired traits and serve as role models— creating ripples of influence that gradually permeate through social networks. Embedding new values into everyday practices, rituals, and symbols reinforces the transformation, anchoring it in lived experience rather than transient directives.

In practical terms, organisations embarking on workforce transformations benefit from a layered approach to change management, integrating people-focused tactics with data-driven insights. Technology offers powerful tools to monitor the pulse of change initiatives, identifying bottlenecks or pockets of disengagement through sentiment analysis, pulse surveys, and predictive analytics. These insights enable leaders to intervene proactively, adapting strategies in real time rather than reacting to crises post-facto. Moreover, the rise of digital collaboration platforms allows for more transparent and inclusive communication, breaking down silos and fostering cross-functional engagement essential to complex workforce redesigns.

Training and development play a crucial supporting role, equipping employees not only with new skills but also with the mindset to thrive amid flux. Robust learning interventions— workshops, coaching, peer learning groups—embedded within the change journey empower individuals to build competence and confidence concurrently. When the workforce perceives transformation as an opportunity for personal and professional growth, resistance gives way to curiosity and commitment.

Crucially, the cadence and scale of change must align with organisational capacity. Overwhelming employees with rapid-fire transformations risks burnout and retreat; conversely, excessively incremental approaches may sap momentum and urgency. Leaders who cultivate an acute sense of timing—balancing the imperative for progress with the human need for assimilation—steer their organisations through change with grace and resilience. Celebrating milestones, recognizing contributions, and acknowledging challenges along the way create a rhythm of progress that sustains morale.

Finally, change management's success hinges on embedding adaptability into the organisational DNA. The post-transformation workplace is less a fixed state than a continuous evolution, requiring a mindset that embraces experimentation, feedback, and iteration. Leaders who foster psychological safety encourage risk-taking and innovation, key to sustaining agility amid persistent uncertainty. By institutionalizing mechanisms for ongoing workforce dialogue and feedback loops, organisations transform change from episodic upheaval into a continuous symphony of growth and responsiveness.

In this evolving landscape, the essential truth emerges that managing change effectively is not the achievement of a one-time victory but the cultivation of enduring capabilities that empower organisations and their people to navigate the unknown with confidence and coherence. The craft of change management, anchored in empathetic leadership, transparent and engaging communication, cultural atonement, and agile processes, becomes the lodestar guiding workforce strategy from the disruptive unknown toward the orchestrated possibility of a thriving future. It is through this meticulous, human-centered approach that organisations can transform workforce initiatives from daunting challenges into defining opportunities, harmonizing human potential with the evolving rhythm of business imperatives.

Cultivating Strategic Mindsets

In the ever-shifting landscape of workforce strategy, cultivating strategic mindsets within leadership stands as a pivotal force that can either propel an organisation toward its envisioned future or leave it mired in reactive stagnation. Encouraging forward-thinking within leadership transcends the mere adoption of new policies or frameworks; it requires a fundamental recalibration of how leaders perceive their roles, influence their teams, and communicate vision amidst uncertainty. It demands a dynamic interplay between the wisdom to navigate the complexity of today's challenges and the imagination to foresee the contours of tomorrow's opportunities, melding prudence with innovation in an ongoing dance of adaptation.

The concept of a strategic mindset is not confined to a rigid set of behaviours but rather manifests as an evolving cognitive and emotional orientation. Leaders who embody this mindset engage deeply with the organisational ecosystem, sensing shifts in market forces, technological advancements, and societal expectations as melodies that presage shifts in the orchestral arrangement of talent. They strike a delicate balance between the analytical rigor of planning and the intuitive agility necessary to pivot when the unexpected arises. This duality marks the essence of strategic leadership—anchored in clarity yet buoyed by creativity, confident in purpose yet open to continual learning.

Nurturing such a mindset begins fundamentally with the identification and refinement of leadership styles that inherently support strategic thinking. Transformational leadership, with its emphasis on inspiring and intellectually stimulating followers, closely aligns with the goals of workforce strategy. Unlike transactional approaches fixated on routine exchanges and incremental performance metrics, transformational leaders foster an environment where ideas percolate, perspectives broaden, and challenges are reframed as opportunities for growth. They serve as catalysts in the metamorphosis of organisational culture, encouraging teams to transcend habitual mindsets and participate actively in shaping the future narrative. Their communication is marked not by top-down directives but by dialogues that invite curiosity, critical thinking, and shared ownership of outcomes.

Simultaneously, strategic mindsets demand the discipline to ground visionary aspirations in pragmatic execution. Authentic leadership, characterized by transparency, consistency, and ethical grounding, complements the expansive vision by ensuring trust and credibility. When leaders model authenticity, they create psychological safety, a space where employees feel empowered to express ideas, confront uncertainties, and engage with change without fear of reprisal. This trust forms the substratum on which complex workforce strategies are built; it smooths the friction that arises from disruption and accelerates the collective journey toward new configurations of talent deployment.

Communication, within this framework, becomes an art form—a conduit through which strategic intent flows clearly and compellingly across the diverse strata of an organisation. The orchestration of workforce strategy necessitates more than memoranda and presentations; it requires storytelling that bridges the abstract and the tangible, weaving data-driven insights with narratives that resonate emotionally. Leaders must articulate the 'why' behind strategic initiatives with clarity, weaving a tapestry that connects individual roles with the broader mission and vision. Through such communication, they animate strategy, transforming it from a static document into a living, breathing guide, much like a conductor conveying nuances of tempo and emotion to an orchestra, ensuring all players move in harmonious accord.

Moreover, this communication is iterative and adaptive rather than prescriptive and fixed. Feedback loops become integral, allowing leaders to gauge pulse points across departments, interpreting subtle shifts in morale, resistance, or enthusiasm. Awareness of these signals guides adjustments that keep workforce strategy both responsive and resilient. In this way, leaders move beyond the paradigm of "telling" toward a richer, more inclusive model of "engaging," inviting colleagues at every level to contribute to strategic dialogue, thereby deepening commitment and cultivating collective intelligence.

Change management emerges as a core competence entwined with the strategic mindset. The full orchestra may have the score, but without the conductor's skill in navigating transitions, the performance risks falling into discord. Leaders must recognize that change is less a linear process and more a journey marked by cycles of awareness, resistance, exploration, and integration. They champion this journey by embodying patience tempered with persistence, demonstrating empathy to those unsettled by shifting expectations while articulating unwavering faith in the ultimate purpose. This delicate navigation requires a fusion of rational planning and emotional intelligence—a capacity to read both market analytics and human signals, aligning them to forge pathways that minimize disruption while maximizing engagement.

Effective change management within workforce strategy is not merely about mitigating risk but about embracing disruption as an engine of evolution. Leaders holding strategic mindsets see change less as a hurdle and more as a catalyst. They anticipate that emerging technologies, evolving workforce demographics, and new employment paradigms like gig and remote work will unsettle traditional models, but through adaptive resilience, these forces become sources of vitality rather than threats. They cultivate a culture where continuous learning and experimentation are prized, where failure is reframed as a stepping stone rather than a setback, and where agility enfolds every team member, enabling nimble responses to dynamic conditions.

At the intersection of leadership style, communication, and change management lies a critical leadership capability: the capacity to foster strategic foresight across the organisation. This involves not only a personal disposition toward long-term thinking but also the ability to embed foresight processes into daily operations. Leaders encourage scenario planning exercises, horizon scanning, and talent analytics as regular rituals, transforming these from abstract, sporadic efforts into ingrained habits. They leverage cross-functional collaboration to broaden perspectives, inviting voices from frontline employees to senior executives to knit together a multidimensional understanding of potential futures. This collective foresight acts as a navigational compass, informing hiring priorities, skills development, and workforce allocation decisions before the winds of change necessitate reactive measures.

Interestingly, fostering strategic mindsets sometimes requires unlearning deeply ingrained behaviours that favour short-term gain or operational comfort. Leaders must disentangle themselves from the seductive appeal of immediate metrics and outputs, cultivating patience and curiosity attuned to complexity and emergent phenomena. This recalibration often occurs through intentional developmental experiences—immersive simulations, leadership retreats focused on futurist thinking, and mentorship programs that challenge conventional assumptions. Organisations that invest in such developmental interventions equip their leaders to think expansively, to tolerate ambiguity, and to harness paradoxical tensions, such as stability and change, innovation and discipline.

The reward for this investment manifests not only in sharper strategic alignment but also in the creation of organisational ecosystems that are robustly adaptive. When leaders internalize strategic mindsets, they become stewards of an evolving workforce architecture capable of sculpting talent pools that mirror the contours of both present operational needs and foreseeable transformations. The dual gaze—simultaneously inward at organisational capabilities and outward at market dynamics—infuses decision-making with depth and agility. This perspective cultivates a workforce culture suffused with purpose and possibility, where employees are not merely cogs in a machine but engaged artisans contributing to a collective masterpiece.

Yet, the journey toward cultivating strategic mindsets is not a solitary venture confined to individual leaders; it spreads through networks of influence, creating cascading effects that permeate all levels of the organisation. Peer coaching, collaborative strategy sessions, and communities of practice become fertile grounds for nurturing shared mental models. Within these forums, leaders grapple collectively with complex dilemmas, challenge biases, and build adaptive capacities. This social dimension enhances the networked intelligence of the organisation, embedding strategic mindsets as a foundational norm rather than an occasional attribute.

Integral to this socialization of strategic thinking is the recognition that diversity of thought enriches the process. Leaders who actively seek diverse perspectives—across functional areas, demographic backgrounds, and cognitive styles—amplify their organisation's ability to anticipate and respond to complex challenges. This enrichment crosses cultural boundaries, fosters innovation, and combats groupthink, thereby sharpening workforce strategies that are both inclusive and incisive. In embracing this multiplicity, leaders extend the metaphor of orchestration to its fullest: every instrument's unique timbre contributes to a symphony's depth and resonance, just as every leader's distinct viewpoint enhances strategic clarity and creativity.

In practical terms, cultivating strategic mindsets involves intentional rituals and frameworks that reinforce forward-thinking. Regular strategic retreats, integrated dashboards combining qualitative and quantitative workforce indicators, and mechanisms for horizon scanning become part of organisational rhythm. Leaders champion these mechanisms not as check-box exercises but as dynamic, context-sensitive tools that evolve in tandem with the organisation's trajectory. They foster a culture where curiosity is rewarded and failure is interpreted as data for better strategy, thus perpetuating a virtuous cycle of learning and adaptation.

Underlying all these efforts is the recognition that leadership capacity to enable strategic workforce planning is grounded in a mindset infused with humility and courage. Humility to acknowledge the limitations of any single viewpoint and the fluidity of future conditions, courage to challenge entrenched norms, and to advocate for bold yet thoughtful changes despite uncertainty. This duality creates a fertile environment where strategic thinking flourishes, empowering organisations not just to respond to change but to shape it proactively.

Ultimately, encouraging forward-thinking within leadership is about creating a living laboratory of learning and innovation where strategic mindsets are nurtured, tested, and matured. It demands continuous commitment to personal and collective development, an openness to complexity, and an unwavering focus on aligning human potential with organisational purpose. When leaders embrace this challenge, they become instruments of transformation—conductors guiding their orchestras through symphonies of change, harmony, and sustained success. Here, the strategic mindset is not merely a cognitive stance but a pulse that infuses every decision, every conversation, and every action, orchestrating an ensemble of talent perfectly attuned to the demands of tomorrow's world.

Building Agility: Creating a Flexible Workforce

Cross-Training and Skill Development

In the symphony of an organisation's workforce, every musician's ability to play multiple instruments transforms the orchestration from routine harmony into a vibrant masterpiece of adaptability and resilience. Cross-training and skill development emerge as pivotal pillars in this dynamic, underpinning workforce versatility and unleashing an organisation's capacity to respond with agility to an ever-shifting business landscape. The essence of cross-training surpasses mere operational efficiency; it cultivates an environment where employees are empowered to navigate seamlessly across different roles, breaking down silos, fostering collaboration, and igniting innovation through broadened perspectives. This multifaceted approach to workforce development is not simply an HR initiative but a strategic imperative that reverberates through every corner of an enterprise, ensuring the collective can pivot fluidly in the face of disruptions, capitalize on emergent opportunities, and sustain competitive advantage.

Cross-training unfolds as more than a series of instructional sessions — it is a transformative journey where employees branch out beyond their foundational expertise to acquire the skills, knowledge, and confidence required to perform in diverse capacities. This process nurtures a mindset where flexibility becomes second nature, enriching the workforce's ability to reconfigure itself in response to fluctuating demands. Consider the manufacturing plant where a line worker who traditionally focuses on assembly is trained to understand basic maintenance tasks and quality control checks. This worker, once limited by a singular skill scope, evolves into a resourceful node capable of bridging gaps when equipment falters or quality issues arise, thus enabling the line to maintain momentum without costly downtime. Such carefully cultivated redundancy in capabilities not only enhances operational continuity but also fosters a culture of ownership and agility, where each team member functions as a versatile contributor rather than a fixed cog.

In addition to expanding technical competencies, cross-training cultivates empathy and cross-functional awareness within the workforce. When employees are exposed to the realities and challenges of roles beyond their own, they develop a richer appreciation for the interdependencies that sustain the organisational ecosystem. This holistic understanding inspires more effective collaboration and communication, dismantling the "us versus them" mentality that can erode morale and productivity. For instance, in a tech company, a software developer cross-trained in customer service gains frontline insights into client pain points, enabling them to design more consumer-centric solutions. In turn, this deepens engagement and accelerates innovation cycles. Thus, cross-training functions not only as a tool for versatility but also as a catalyst for empathy-driven leadership and cooperative problem-solving.

Flexible work models complement cross-training by embedding adaptability directly into the fabric of how work is structured and experienced. The traditional rigid division of Labor and fixed job descriptions yield to more fluid arrangements where roles become dynamic portfolios shaped by both organisational need and individual growth aspirations. Flexible schedules, remote work options, and project-based assignments expand the latitude for employees to explore diverse responsibilities and apply their evolving competencies in real time. This situational agility serves as a hedge against disruption, enabling organisations to respond rapidly to market fluctuations without bottlenecking talent or workflow. Moreover, the voluntary nature of flexible arrangements empowers professionals to tailor their contributions around personal circumstances, which in turn fosters greater engagement, reduces burnout, and bolsters retention rates. By intertwining the principles of cross-training with flexible work models, companies build ecosystems where skill versatility and work-life harmony coexist, enhancing both performance and employee well-being.

Allys Watson

Central to the vitality of cross-training and flexible work structures is an unwavering commitment to continuous learning — a philosophy that champions perpetual growth as the heartbeat of workforce agility. In an era where technological evolution and market paradigms pivot with staggering speed, what was relevant a year ago risks rapid obsolescence. Thus, organisations must instil a culture that not only accommodates change but eagerly anticipates it through lifecycle learning initiatives that evolve alongside business strategy. Continuous learning transcends formal training sessions to include informal knowledge sharing, personalized development plans, mentorship programs, and access to digital learning platforms that democratize skill acquisition. Imagine a global financial services firm instituting a continuous learning ecosystem where employees engage monthly in curated webinars on emerging fintech trends while participating in peer-led innovation labs that challenge them to apply new concepts to ongoing projects. This perpetual cycle of learning energizes the workforce, encourages proactive upskilling, and primes the organisation for sustained adaptability.

The interplay of these three elements — cross-training, flexible work models, and continuous learning — constitutes a robust framework for workforce versatility that is both proactive and reactive to the demands of contemporary business environments. The artful integration of cross-training programs within flexible working arrangements and learning cultures is most effective when championed by visionary leadership that recognizes workforce agility as a strategic asset rather than a logistics challenge. Leaders serve as conductors in this human symphony, orchestrating intentional initiatives that align skill journeys with future organisational needs while fostering inclusive cultures where experimentation and mistakes are valued as part of the growth process. The challenge lies not merely in implementing isolated training workshops or policy changes but in embedding versatility into the organisational DNA so deeply that it becomes reflexive and self-sustaining.

Practical application of cross-training begins with a deep diagnostic assessment of core business processes and talent gaps, combined with a forward-looking perspective on evolving skills requirements. Through this lens, companies identify which roles or capabilities hold strategic significance in the near and distant future and map potential cross-functional pathways for employees. Importantly, cross-training must emphasize experiential learning through job shadowing, rotations, and collaborative projects rather than relying solely on didactic instruction. This immersive approach accelerates knowledge transfer, blends theoretical understanding with operational context, and builds confidence among employees to step into unfamiliar roles. Furthermore, recognized achievements within cross-training programs — whether certifications, project outcomes, or peer endorsements — foster motivation and create a meritocratic environment that celebrates adaptability.

Flexible work models amplify these efforts by removing structural constraints that previously limited how and when employees deploy their range of skills. Transitioning from rigid nine-to-five paradigms to more fluid time zones and remote collaborations allows individuals to engage with various projects and teams in ways that optimize both productivity and personal fulfillment. For example, in creative industries, flexible arrangements enable professionals to allocate time block segments for different disciplines such as design, client engagement, and innovation brainstorming, nurturing a multipotentiality that sparks novel solutions. Similarly, in public sector organisations, flexible work policies can facilitate cross-departmental assignments and crisis response units staffed by personnel with broad training, enhancing governmental resilience when unforeseen events occur. By removing temporal and geographic barriers, flexibility fosters an ecosystem where skill versatility can flourish unhindered by tradition.

Continuous learning undergirds and accelerates this dynamic by offering employees continuous streams of relevant, actionable knowledge that keep their competencies aligned with emerging trends and technologies. The advent of AI-powered personalized learning platforms revolutionizes this domain by tailoring educational content to individual skill gaps, learning preferences, and career trajectories in real time. These adaptive systems harness organisational data and market intelligence to forecast future skill demands, thus enabling proactive upskilling that pre-empts obsolescence. Consider a global retail chain where store managers engage in AI-curated leadership modules that address regional consumer behaviours and digital marketing techniques, continuously refining their expertise as the company expands into new digital channels. Blending these technologies with human coaching and peer learning creates a rich mosaic of development opportunities that nourish both individual fulfillment and organisational excellence.

However, the journey toward a truly versatile workforce is not without its challenges. Resistance to change often surfaces as employees confront unfamiliar responsibilities or fear dilution of expertise. Time constraints and workload pressures can inhibit participation in cross-training and learning initiatives, while inconsistent leadership support may undermine momentum. Organisations must therefore cultivate trust and psychological safety, actively communicating the strategic rationale behind versatility programs and recognizing the value of diverse skill sets in career advancement. Embedding metrics that track skill breadth, mobility, and learning outcomes into performance management systems reinforces accountability and signals institutional commitment. Success stories and role models who have thrived through cross-training and development exemplify the tangible benefits, inspiring widespread buy-in.

The return on investment in cross-training and skill development ripples far beyond immediate operational gains. A workforce steeped in versatility breeds a culture of curiosity, collaboration, and continuous improvement—qualities indispensable for innovation and resilience in volatile markets. It enables organisations not just to react but to anticipate, not just to survive disruption but to harness it as a catalyst for evolution. Employees evolve into empowered agents of change, navigating complex landscapes with confidence and adaptability. As human capital becomes more nuanced and interconnected, the ability to cultivate and leverage versatility may well define organisational success in the years to come. In essence, the mastery of workforce versatility through cross-training, flexible work models, and continuous learning is the conductor's baton that orchestrates an adaptive, harmonious, and future-ready workforce poised to play the evolving symphony of business with excellence and creativity.

Flexible Work Arrangements

In the evolving symphony of modern workforce strategy, flexible work arrangements have emerged as the gracious melody that permits organisations to adapt and harmonize with the shifting rhythms of the global market. At the heart of this melody lies a recognition that the traditional, rigid workplace model—where employees clock in at fixed hours behind a static desk—is no longer sustainable or desirable for many, especially in a world that is accelerating towards digital integration and a deeply interconnected society. Remote work, the gig economy, and other flexible models have moved far beyond mere trends; they have become fundamental pillars upon which agile and resilient organisations build their talent architectures. These models offer not only practical solutions to immediate operational challenges but also deeper cultural transformations that echo throughout an organisation's DNA, fostering innovation, inclusivity, and continuous learning.

Remote work, once viewed sceptically as an experiment or a privilege, has matured into a mainstream arrangement, redefining the very concept of the workplace. When the global health crisis accelerated this shift, it forced leaders to confront long-held assumptions about productivity and presence, inviting a more nuanced understanding of performance and engagement. Remote work unlocks opportunities for organisations to tap into talent pools that transcend geographical boundaries, allowing them to craft teams whose competencies match the strategic needs rather than the constraints of location. However, the success of remote work is not simply about displacing desks and laptops into living rooms or co-working spaces; it demands a reimagination of communication modalities, managerial practices, and trust paradigms. Companies must weave new threads of connection—digital rituals, asynchronous communication, and outcome-based evaluations—to hold the fabric of their culture tightly together even as physical proximity loosens. Crucially, remote arrangements empower employees with autonomy and flexibility, fostering job satisfaction and work-life integration, which can, in turn, spur creativity and reduce burnout. Yet, achieving this balance requires deliberate investment in technology platforms, cybersecurity, and leadership development, blending technical readiness with human empathy.

Parallel to the rise of remote work is the burgeoning gig economy, a mosaic of freelance, contract, and project-based roles that defy the permanence of traditional employment. This economy is not merely a byproduct of technological advancement but a tectonic shift in how Labor is valued and exchanged. For organisations, embracing the gig economy means cultivating a dynamic talent ecosystem that is inherently fluid, capable of swelling and contracting in response to market fluctuations without the encumbrance of long-term fixed costs. This flexibility enables companies to access niche expertise and innovative perspectives on demand, turning to specialists who bring fresh energy and insights that may not flourish within the boundaries of permanent roles. Yet this model also challenges leaders to rethink their approach to workforce identity, legal frameworks, and ethical considerations.

How does one maintain organisational coherence and loyalty when the labor force is partially composed of transient contributors? It invites a strategic balance between retaining core talent with deep institutional knowledge and integrating agile contributors who invigorate the system with new skills and ideas. Moreover, companies must craft compelling engagement strategies that honor these gig workers as valued participants rather than peripheral resources, integrating them into collaborative efforts and fostering a sense of belonging despite shorter-term tenures.

Beyond remote work and gig arrangements, the spectrum of flexible work models also encompasses practices such as compressed workweeks, job sharing, flexitime, and hybrid schedules—each a uniquely tuned note within the orchestral composition of an agile workforce. These models respond to the human need for adaptability, recognizing that employees navigate complex lives, weaving together professional responsibilities with personal aspirations and obligations. Flexible scheduling, for instance, embraces the reality that productivity is not a monolithic, clock-bound measure but often a rhythm that varies from person to person. Allowing variations in start and end times—or condensing work into fewer days—unlocks higher engagement and can reduce absenteeism. Job sharing, where two or more employees collaboratively undertake the responsibilities of a single full-time position, can create pathways for talent retention, particularly for those balancing caregiving duties or pursuing advanced education. The hybrid model, which blends remote and in-office work, offers the best of both worlds: the spontaneity and culture-building potential of face-to-face interactions alongside the concentrated focus and flexibility of remote setups. Each of these arrangements requires thoughtful customization; there is no one-size-fits-all formula but a strategic orchestration that responds to organisational goals, employee preferences, and the demands of the marketplace.

To imbue these flexible work arrangements with true effectiveness, organisations must integrate cross-training and continuous learning as structural pillars. Cross-training—the deliberate preparation of employees to handle multiple roles and responsibilities—imbues the workforce with versatility and resilience akin to multi-instrumentalists adept at switching melodies mid-performance. It mitigates risks associated with turnover, absenteeism, or sudden market pivots by ensuring that critical skills are distributed across teams rather than siloed in individuals. Employees benefit from cross-training as well; it enhances their career trajectories and engagement by offering variety and growth opportunities rather than stagnation. However, cross-training requires a supportive culture where knowledge sharing is not merely encouraged but embedded into daily routines, complementing flexible work arrangements by fostering connectivity and collective responsibility. By blending cross-training with flexible schedules and remote or gig work, organisations create a dynamic tapestry where workforce agility is not a theoretical ideal but a living, breathing reality.

Continuous learning, meanwhile, is the lubricant that keeps this complex machinery operating smoothly in an ever-changing environment. The rapid evolution of industries—be it through technological innovations, shifting consumer demands, or geopolitical upheavals—renders static skills obsolete with alarming speed. Flexible work models are fertile ground for cultivating a growth mindset, as employees must remain nimble and proactive to adjust their work patterns and expertise. Organisations championing continuous learning embed development opportunities into the workflow: virtual workshops, micro-learning modules, peer coaching, and experiential projects become routine rather than exceptional. This culture of perpetual learning sustains workforce agility by ensuring that talent pathways evolve in tandem with strategic priorities. It also reinforces employee engagement by validating growth as a cornerstone of professional identity. Leveraging emerging technologies such as AI-driven personalized learning platforms enables organisations to tailor development to individual needs and aspirations, further enhancing the synergy between flexibility and capability building.

Together, remote work, the gig economy, compressed schedules, cross-training, and continuous learning compose a rich and adaptive orchestra capable of navigating the unpredictable tempos of modern business. They dissipate the historical tension between efficiency and flexibility, illustrating that organisations can simultaneously optimize operations and honor human variability. Leaders, however, must act as skilled conductors, guiding this ensemble with intentionality and vision. They must cultivate an organisational culture that embraces change, supports psychological safety, and champions inclusive communication. Transparent articulation of flexible work policies, commitment to equitable access to opportunities irrespective of work model, and investment in robust digital infrastructures are indispensable notes in this symphony. Moreover, data analytics play a pivotal role in fine-tuning these arrangements, providing insights into employee productivity patterns, satisfaction levels, and skill gaps, informing continuous adjustments.

Challenges naturally arise—questions of maintaining cohesion, mitigating burnout among remote workers, ensuring fair treatment of gig contributors, and aligning performance metrics across diverse work formats demand ongoing attention. Yet, these challenges are not barriers but instruments inviting innovation. Organisations adopting flexible work arrangements prepare themselves not only to weather disruption but to harness it, transforming volatility into a source of competitive advantage. In this fluid landscape, the workforce transcends its traditional boundaries, becoming a living force that can be redrawn in response to shifting business goals and societal trends.

Ultimately, flexible work arrangements represent more than operational choices; they are a profound redefinition of work itself in the 21st century. They affirm the primacy of human dignity, autonomy, and collaborative spirit even as technology reshapes the contours of Labor. When embedded thoughtfully within a comprehensive strategic framework—surrounded by cross-training and continuous learning—they empower organisations to compose vibrant, resilient futures. The orchestra of human potential, conducted with care and insight, can then resound with a harmony that propels not only economic success but the enduring flourishing of people and communities in an era of relentless change.

Continuous Learning Cultures

In the ever-evolving landscape of contemporary business, where change is not a fleeting wave but a persistent tide, cultivating a culture of continuous learning is no longer a luxury but a fundamental imperative for organisational vitality. Within this dynamic milieu, the concept of lifetime learning transcends the simple acquisition of skills; it becomes the anchor of adaptability, the very heartbeat of workforce agility that enables organisations to navigate uncharted waters with both confidence and creativity. Like a river that constantly reshapes its banks to accommodate shifting currents, companies that embed a robust ethos of learning into their DNA ensure that their people do not merely react to transformation but anticipate and even shape it, sculpting new pathways in the terrain of tomorrow's work.

The foundation of this ongoing learning culture is inextricably linked to cross-training initiatives. Envision a symphony orchestra where musicians are not rigidly bound to their instruments alone but possess the ability to fluidly transition across sections—string players capable of dueting on wind instruments, or percussionists who integrate seamlessly into vocal harmonies. In workforce terms, cross-training cultivates a versatile ensemble of talent equipped with overlapping competencies, fostering depth and breadth in skill sets that safeguard against disruptions stemming from unexpected departures or emergent challenges. This cross-pollination imbues employees with a panoramic perspective of the business, breaking down departmental silos and catalyzing innovation. When team members understand the inner workings of multiple roles, they navigate collaboration with nuanced empathy and strategic insight, facilitating an environment where knowledge flourishes, and the collective repertoire expands.

Cross-training is more than duplicating functions; it is an intentional design of learning pathways that stimulate intellectual curiosity and foster psychological safety. Organisations that champion this approach embed the practice into their leadership ethos, framing it not as remedial or remedied knowledge gaps but as a rich garden for professional growth. Leaders become gardeners, tending to everyone's learning journey with nurturing patience and inspired vision. This paradigm shift reframes learning as an indispensable thread weaving itself through every workday, every project, every informal exchange—transforming the mundane into moments of discovery. When workers feel empowered to develop skills beyond their immediate job description, motivation ignites, engagement deepens, and a palpable sense of ownership emerges. Employees no longer see themselves merely as cogs in a complex machine but as vital contributors to a living, breathing organism.

Inextricably linked to cross-training is the embrace of flexible work models, which act as architectural scaffolding supporting the edifice of continuous learning. As the pillars of the traditional 9-to-5 office model taper and yield to the rising arches of remote work, hybrid schedules, and asynchronous collaboration, the contours of learning evolve in tandem. Flexible work arrangements seed fertile ground for experimentation with learning modalities that transcend geographic and temporal limitations. Employees no longer must fit their development into narrow windows carved around rigid work hours but can engage with learning experiences that accommodate their unique rhythms and personal commitments. This fluidity mirrors the ebbs and flows of creativity itself, offering fertile soil for knowledge to root and expand organically.

Moreover, flexible work models challenge the conventional top-down dissemination of learning, encouraging a decentralization of knowledge that empowers individuals to take charge of their growth trajectories. Digital platforms, virtual workshops, and on-demand microlearning become the instruments through which talent cultivates competencies, often in tandem with their real-world project demands. The asynchronous nature of much of this learning invites reflection and deeper absorption, fostering an introspective approach that is often absent in traditional instructor-led environments. The convergence of flexible schedules with innovative learning technologies crafts a learning ecosystem that is truly employee-centric, propelling a culture where curiosity is kindled not by obligation but by passion, where adaptability is harvested not under duress but through enlightened practice.

At the heart of these interconnected strategies lies a profound understanding that continuous learning is neither incidental nor episodic but a sustained journey—akin to the relentless refining of a masterpiece by an artisan who never ceases to hone his craft. Organisations that internalize this truth embed continuous learning as a strategic priority, not a mere HR checkbox. They recognize that in the theatre of workforce planning, continuous learning is the choreography that allows all performers to stay in harmony, even as the music shifts unexpectedly. This entails investing not only in formal education and training but in fostering an environment where informal learning—those serendipitous conversations, peer-to-peer mentoring, and knowledge sharing—can flourish with equal Vigor.

Leadership's role in anchoring this learning culture cannot be overstated. Leaders must model the behaviour they wish to see, embracing vulnerability by acknowledging what they do not know and publicly engaging in their own development journeys. Such transparency humanizes them, breaking down hierarchical barriers and signalling to employees that growth is a collective and ceaseless pursuit. Furthermore, astute leaders cultivate learning agility by rewarding experimentation and reframing failures as crucial feedback, not indictments of competence. This mindset transforms fear of risk into a catalyst for discovery, emboldening teams to venture beyond comfort zones with courage and resilience.

In the intricate web of workforce resilience, continuous learning acts as the sinew—the connective tissue that binds strategy to capability. It accelerates the ability to pivot in response to disruption, allowing organisations to recalibrate skill profiles ahead of market shifts, rather than scrambling to retrofit outdated talent pools. As technological advancements unfurl at an accelerated pace and market volatility becomes the norm, the capacity for rapid upskilling and reskilling emerges as a competitive differentiator. Companies that harness this dynamic position themselves not just to survive change but to sculpt their futures proactively.

Allys Watson

Yet, fostering continuous learning requires a delicate balance between providing structure and encouraging autonomy. While robust frameworks—such as learning management systems, competency models, and skill inventories—are essential to coordinate growth efforts and measure progress, they must not ossify into bureaucratic impediments that stifle creativity and self-direction. Instead, they should serve as navigational beacons, guiding learners through vast seas of knowledge without restricting their exploratory impulses. Encouraging employees to craft personalized development plans, supported by coaching and feedback loops, promotes a sense of agency that fuels engagement and intrinsic motivation.

The mechanisms to sustain a continuous learning culture often hinge on the strategic integration of technology that amplifies human potential rather than replacing it. Artificial intelligence-driven personalized learning paths, adaptive content curation, and predictive analytics offer unprecedented opportunities to tailor development experiences to individual learner profiles and career aspirations. Gamification and social learning platforms inject elements of playfulness and community, enhancing knowledge retention and fostering networks of practice that transcend organisational hierarchies. However, it is vital to temper technology's allure with a mindful approach that centres empathy and human connection, ensuring that learning remains a profoundly social and humane Endeavor.

Furthermore, continuous learning cultures act as powerful antidotes to workforce stagnation and disengagement. When employees perceive career trajectories as continually evolving rather than fixed or plateaued, their commitment to the organisation strengthens. Learning becomes an instrument for personal fulfillment as much as professional advancement, weaving meaning into daily work experiences. This cultural vitality nourishes organisational loyalty and mitigates turnover risks, creating a virtuous cycle where investment in people yields dividends in innovation, productivity, and resilience.

The ripple effects of embedding continuous learning extend beyond individual performance to sculpt organisational identity and reputation. Companies known for robust learning cultures attract high-calibre talent who seek environments where their growth is prioritized and their contributions valued. These organisations become magnets for creativity, diversity of thought, and cross-functional collaboration, thriving as ecosystems of collective intelligence. In this way, continuous learning elevates the organisation from being a static entity to a living organism, perpetually evolving in concert with the shifting demands of the external environment.

In an era where uncertainty is an elemental force shaping business realities, the imperative to cultivate continuous learning cultures assumes profound strategic significance. It is a commitment to nurturing human capital as an infinite resource, replenished and refined through curiosity, courage, and connection. By weaving cross-training, flexible work models, and sustained learning into the fabric of organisational life, leaders orchestrate a dynamic workforce poised not only to endure the maelstrom of change but to harness it as a wellspring of opportunity. Through this harmonic convergence of strategy and culture, organisations find that their most enduring competitive advantage lies not solely in technology or capital but in the relentless, vibrant, and collective pursuit of knowledge that propels them forward into an ever-unfolding future.

Metrics for Agility

In the swiftly shifting landscape of contemporary business, agility has emerged not merely as a desirable attribute but as a critical lifeline for organisational survival and success. To navigate the turbulent waters of market disruption, technological innovation, and evolving workforce dynamics, companies must measure how responsive and flexible their human capital truly is. This is where the concept of "Metrics for Agility" takes centre stage—a sophisticated yet deeply practical approach to quantifying the often-intangible qualities of workforce adaptability. Agility, in essence, is the workforce's capacity to pivot, to learn anew, and to reorient itself in alignment with fresh strategies or unforeseen challenges. But how does one go about quantifying such fluid characteristics that naturally resist rigid statistical confines? The answer lies in exploring the rich dimensions of cross-training, flexible work models, and continuous learning, each serving as a pillar upon which the fortress of workforce agility is built.

Consider first the power embedded in cross-training, a strategic investment that reimagines employees not as narrow specialists but as versatile artisans capable of weaving multiple threads of expertise into the evolving tapestry of operations. The traditional approach—where workers master a singular function— is increasingly outpaced by the demands of unpredictability. Cross-training transcends this limitation by enabling staff to acquire competencies beyond their initial roles, creating a reservoir of latent talent ready to be tapped when disruptions strike. Yet, to manage and improve this capacity, organisations must turn their attention to metrics that reliably capture the depth and breadth of cross-functional skills present in their teams. Here, the measurement extends beyond mere headcounts of trained personnel. It encompasses assessments of proficiency levels across domains, frequency of skill refreshers, and the actual deployment of cross-trained employees in scenarios requiring role fluidity. For example, tracking the ratio of multi-skilled workers to total headcount unveils the breadth of readiness, while monitoring the time it takes for an employee to shift competently between functions reflects responsiveness. Metrics also examine the organisational network effects, identifying how well knowledge flows and how cross-trained individuals facilitate communication bridges across departments. The beauty of these measures lies in their double function: they quantify the current state of agility and inform leaders where investment in skill diversification can most effectively enhance resilience.

Alongside cross-training, flexible work models stand as a transformative lever reshaping how agility is not just measured but lived. Flexibility, when framed as a metric, transcends policy checklists of remote work or fluctuating hours; it becomes a dynamic indicator of an organisation's ability to configure its workforce in ways that amplify responsiveness. The pulse of these metrics beats in patterns of scheduling adaptability, geographic dispersion, and the empowerment granted to employees to control their work modalities. Metrics for flexible work models probe the extent to which organisations accommodate diverse arrangements without compromising performance or cohesion. Quantifying this involves capturing data points such as the percentage of employees engaged in flexible or hybrid schedules, variations in work location, and the frequency with which teams successfully execute projects without physical co-location. But beyond mere incidence statistics, these metrics delve into qualitative measures of employee satisfaction and engagement linked to flexibility, underscoring the human undercurrent that sustains sustainable adaptability. Employee feedback loops, retention rates in flexible programs, and productivity benchmarks relative to traditional arrangements coalesce to form a nuanced picture. Equally significant is the measurement of technological enablement—the seamlessness with which digital tools facilitate agility—encompassing uptime, usability scores, and real-time collaboration frequencies that uphold the flexible fabric of work in motion. Thus, these metrics do not simply tally flexible policies; they animate them, exposing how integral they are to an agile rhythm that embraces change with confidence rather than resistance.

The third cornerstone of agile workforce metrics resides in the realm of continuous learning, an ongoing, iterative process that transforms employees from static repositories of knowledge into active, evolving participants in the organisation's strategic dance. Continuous learning embodies the imperative that agility is not a state to be achieved once but a perpetual motion maintained through renewal and growth. Measuring this requires a multi-dimensional approach attentive to not only the volume of learning activities but also their impact on actual workforce adaptability. Metrics here traverse participation rates in training programs, frequency of skills acquisition, and diversity of learning modalities engaged—from formal courses to informal peer knowledge sharing and immersive simulations. The true vitality of continuous learning metrics, however, pulses in gauging their penetration into performance improvements and innovation outcomes. Tracking the translation of acquired knowledge into enhanced problem-solving capabilities, reduced time-to-competency in new roles, and the generation of novel ideas or efficiency gains offers tangible insight into how learning fuels agility. Furthermore, longitudinal snapshots charting employee life cycles of learning, skill decay countermeasures, and alignment with emergent business needs provide strategic feedback loops that recalibrate developmental priorities. The discourse of continuous learning metrics also emphasizes the role of leadership support and cultural reinforcement—areas measured through surveys of learning culture perception, managerial coaching frequencies, and recognition systems that valorise growth mindsets. These indicators kindle the ongoing flame of curiosity and adaptability, securing the workforce's capacity to pivot gracefully amid evolving landscapes.

Bringing these pillars together—the cross-training breadth, flexible work arrangements, and the ceaseless growth of continuous learning—crafts a holistic matrix of agility metrics that transcends reductionist snapshots. When deployed thoughtfully, these measurements become part of a living dashboard, weaving quantitative data and qualitative insight into a coherent narrative of workforce responsiveness. They invite leaders to perceive agility not simply as a checkbox but as a dynamic capability to be nurtured, monitored, and evolved. Yet, the true art of measuring workforce agility lies in synthesizing these disparate strands into an integrative framework that reflects the organisation's unique contours. For instance, a manufacturing firm might weigh cross-training heavily, given the operational necessity of shift coverage, while a technology company might skew toward continuous learning metrics as a driver of innovation velocity. Similarly, value resides in tracking not only individual indicators but their interplay—how increased cross-training complements flexible work, or how continuous learning propels greater adaptability in scheduling or role fluidity. The subtle interplay captured through composite metrics offers predictive foresight, signalling where agility is gaining momentum or where silos and rigidity risk eroding responsiveness.

The narrative of workforce agility measurement also unfolds with an acute awareness of potential pitfalls. An overemphasis on numerical tallies risks reducing vibrant human capabilities to sterile statistics, obscuring the lived reality of adaptability. Conversely, neglecting structured measurement leaves organisations vulnerable to agility illusions—believing they are prepared for disruption when critical gaps remain hidden. The balance, therefore, shifts towards embedding metrics within a culture that values dialogic reflection and continuous improvement. For example, supplementing numerical scores with storytelling sessions where employees recount agility in action enriches understanding and cements commitment. Furthermore, integrating metrics with talent management systems and performance reviews ensures that agility is not a side conversation but a central thread in organisational DNA. By doing so, organisations cultivate a symphony where every instrument—skills, schedules, knowledge—plays in concert to produce rapid, harmonious responses to change.

In practice, the most effective organisations align their agility metrics with broader strategic objectives, reinforcing the message that workforce responsiveness directly underpins business outcomes. Metrics linked to customer satisfaction improvements following agile workforce deployment, speed to market gains attributed to flexible teams, or cost efficiencies realized through cross-trained Labor pools sharpen the bottom-line argument for investment. This alignment catalyses greater executive attention and resource allocation, embedding agility as a strategic priority rather than a tactical experiment. Moreover, the cultural implications ripple outwards; when employees see agility measured and rewarded, they internalize the value of adaptability, fostering proactive behaviours and innovation mindsets. The workforce evolves into a living organism, resilient in the face of disruption, thriving in complexity, and perpetually poised to compose the next successful movement in a rapidly changing business symphony.

Ultimately, metrics for agility form not just a measurement toolkit but a strategic compass, guiding organisations toward enhanced resilience and competitive edge. They crystallize the intelligence necessary to anticipate talent gaps, optimize workforce configurations, and inspire continuous renewal. Through meticulous attention to cross-training depths, flexible work architectures, and learning cultures, leaders gain the clarity to orchestrate their human capital with precision and creativity. In this way, they transform workforce agility from an aspirational ideal into a measurable, manageable reality—an ever-evolving melody played with both grace and power in the complex concert hall of the future of work.

Allys Watson

Measuring Success: Metrics and KPIs for Workforce Planning

Identifying Relevant KPIs

In the complex, interconnected ecosystem of workforce planning, identifying the right Key Performance Indicators (KPIs) is akin to selecting the perfect musical notes to craft a melody that resonates deeply with an audience. These KPIs do not just represent dry data points or numerical thresholds; instead, they become the vital signals, the barometers by which organisations measure their progress toward a strategic horizon. Selecting metrics that are genuinely reflective of business goals requires a thoughtful, nuanced approach—a careful alignment that transcends simplistic measurement and weaves into the very fabric of organisational purpose and ambition.

The process begins with a profound understanding of the overarching business strategy, much like how a conductor studies the score before raising the baton. It is essential to immerse oneself in the fundamental drivers of the organisation's success: what are the critical objectives that propel the business forward? Is it market expansion, innovation leadership, customer satisfaction, or cost efficiency? Each strategic imperative demands a unique lens

236

through which workforce performance should be viewed. Selecting KPIs, therefore, becomes an act of translation—converting abstract goals into concrete, measurable indices that keep every part of the workforce symphony aligned and attuned.

At the heart of KPI identification lies the balance between quantitative and qualitative data. While numbers provide a clear, often objective snapshot—such as turnover rates, average time to fill a vacancy, or employee productivity metrics—qualitative insights breathe life into these figures, offering context and texture. Metrics like employee engagement, cultural alignment, or leadership effectiveness may resist easy quantification, yet their impact ripples profoundly through organisational outcomes. These soft metrics, gathered through surveys, interviews, or 360-degree feedback mechanisms, serve as the harmonic undertones that modulate the workforce's performance, revealing nuances in motivation, collaboration, and adaptability that numbers alone could never capture.

One cannot overstate the danger of adopting KPIs that are disconnected from true business needs. The temptation to measure what is simple or convenient rather than what is meaningful leads organisations astray, directing focus to vanity metrics that shine brightly but ultimately do not illuminate the path to growth or resilience. For instance, tracking sheer headcount growth without regard for the quality or strategic value of those roles can create false optimism, masking underlying talent mismatches or skill deficits. Thus, selecting relevant KPIs requires a rigorous vetting process— engaging with business leaders, HR professionals, and line managers to ensure each metric resonates with the strategic heartbeat of the enterprise.

Amidst this collaborative Endeavor, it becomes evident that effective KPIs possess several defining qualities. They must be specific rather than generic, rooted in clear, articulate definitions that leave no room for ambiguity. For example, rather than tracking "employee satisfaction" as a broad concept, drilling down to "percentage of employees rating manager communication as effective" yields a more actionable focus. KPIs also need to be measurable with reliable data sources, ensuring that the information collected is accurate, timely, and repeatable. Equally important is their relevance across different organisational layers, enabling cascading goals that provide meaning not only at the executive level but also within teams and individual contributors' daily work.

Another dimension to consider is the temporal nature of KPIs. Some metrics serve as leading indicators—early signals forecasting future trends or risks—while others function as lagging indicators, reflecting the outcomes of past actions. For example, a leading indicator might be the percentage of the workforce enrolled in emerging skill programs, forecasting readiness for anticipated market shifts. In contrast, turnover rates present a lagging view, revealing retention challenges after they have already impacted the organisation. An astute mix of both types equips leaders with a comprehensive framework, a dynamic dashboard that balances foresight with reflection, agility with control.

In this quest, advanced analytics and technology emerge as powerful enablers. Machine learning algorithms and AI-driven platforms can sift through vast troves of workforce data to uncover hidden correlations and predictive insights that human intuition might overlook. These tools help tether KPIs not only to current business realities but also to emerging trends, offering a real-time pulse of workforce dynamics. Yet, technology is a servant, not the master; without a grounded strategic context, even the most sophisticated analytics run the risk of generating noise rather than meaningful signals.

Importantly, KPIs also serve a psychological function within an organisation. When thoughtfully chosen, they become motivators, rallying cries that unify employees around shared aspirations. Transparency in reporting and consistent communication about what is measured—and why—nurtures trust and engagement, transforming metrics from sterile statistics into shared commitments. Employees feel seen and valued when their contributions are reflected in KPIs that resonate with their experiences and ambitions, creating a virtuous cycle of accountability and empowerment.

Moreover, the identification of KPIs must anticipate change. The business environment is fluid, markets evolve, and workforce needs shift with agility, increasingly becoming the currency of success. What holds true at one moment may become obsolete in another. Therefore, KPIs are not static constructs; they require regular review and recalibration. This iterative process ensures that the workforce measurement framework remains a living, adaptive system, responsive to new strategic priorities, competitive pressures, or internal transformations such as mergers or digital disruptions.

Organisations often find the greatest value when KPIs are integrated within a broader performance management ecosystem. Rather than existing in isolation, they interlock with goal-setting processes, talent development initiatives, and reward systems. Such integration ensures that measurement, motivation, and management operate in concert, amplifying their impact. For example, if innovation speed is a strategic priority, KPIs might track not only the number of new products launched but also the diversity of teams contributing and the speed of internal decision-making cycles, each facet reinforcing the others.

Reflecting on the richly varied landscapes of industry, the choice of relevant KPIs must also respect contextual uniqueness. No two organisations share the exact same combination of culture, market position, or talent architecture. Case studies illustrate this vividly: a high-tech company aiming for rapid product iteration might prioritize KPIs around skills acquisition velocity and cross-functional collaboration, while a healthcare provider may focus more on compliance adherence and employee well-being indicators. Similarly, a global enterprise managing distributed teams will emphasize connectivity metrics and remote workforce engagement, tailoring KPIs to the realities of virtual collaboration.

The narrative of workforce KPIs is ultimately a testament to the art and science of strategic alignment. It requires creative vision to see which indicators truly capture the essence of human capital's contribution to business triumph. It demands analytical rigor to design metrics that are precise, actionable, and anchored in evidence. And it calls for empathetic leadership to translate numbers into narratives that inspire, guide, and cultivate organisational harmony. When this triad of insight converges, KPIs become more than measures—they become the guiding stars by which enterprises navigate the unpredictable seas of talent and transformation.

Drawing this expansive picture to a close, it becomes clear that identifying relevant KPIs is not a one-time selection but a continuous journey. A company's strategic aspirations evolve, technologies advance, and workforce dynamics shift in ways both subtle and seismic. Throughout, KPIs serve as the vital instruments that translate intention into insight and insight into action. They empower leaders to perceive patterns beneath the surface, anticipate talent demands, and orchestrate human potential with both precision and passion. In this way, KPIs anchor the workforce Planning firmly in reality, enabling organisations not only to measure progress but to master the art of strategic workforce planning itself.

Data Collection and Analysis

In the intricate dance of workforce planning, data is the rhythm that keeps the entire performance coherent, precise, and harmonious. To effectively craft a strategic plan for tomorrow's talent needs, organisations must first cultivate a robust baseline of information, ensuring that every decision sprouts from fertile ground nurtured by reliable insights. Gathering accurate data is not merely about numbers; it is about attaining a nuanced understanding of the workforce's composition, potential, and trajectory, embarked upon through an intricate weaving of quantitative and qualitative metrics. These twin strands form the backbone of comprehensive analysis, enabling leaders to discern patterns that might otherwise remain invisible and to anticipate future demands with a clarity born of thorough observation and inquiry.

The process of data collection begins with identifying what constitutes relevant and actionable information within the context of workforce strategy. This involves a deliberate and methodical mapping of the organisation's current human capital landscape, encompassing headcounts, skill inventories, turnover rates, and demographic diversity. Quantitative metrics such as these provide the hard framework, almost skeletal in nature, forming a visual architecture through spreadsheets, dashboards, and analytic tools. These numbers, however, are not isolated data points; they are alive and interrelated signals that reflect the underlying health and potential of the workforce ecosystem. A headcount increase, for example, might superficially suggest growth, yet when delved into alongside turnover frequency, absentee trends, or engagement scores, the narrative may uncover hidden vulnerabilities or emergent strengths critical to strategic foresight.

Yet, the power of these quantitative metrics is significantly magnified when supplemented with qualitative insights. Rather than mere figures, qualitative data provides flesh and emotion—contextual richness that captures the lived experiences, motivations, and attitudes of the workforce. Methods such as employee interviews, focus groups, exit surveys, and engagement assessments reveal layers of organisational culture and human factors that numbers alone fail to illuminate. This additional dimension provides a lens into morale shifts, leadership effectiveness, and workforce sentiment, which serve as vital predictors of talent retention and productivity. For instance, an uptick in turnover rate supported by qualitative data uncovering dissatisfaction with leadership communication can lead to targeted interventions, ultimately reducing risk and aligning workforce initiatives with authentic human needs.

The marriage of these complementary datasets is an art form requiring meticulous care in design and execution. High-calibre data collection demands rigor in ensuring accuracy and authenticity, necessitating well-calibrated tools and thoughtfully designed instruments. The sophistication of modern technology provides assets such as applicant tracking systems, HR information systems, and pulse survey platforms that streamline data harvesting at scale while maintaining fidelity. Yet, technology alone cannot guarantee insight. The human element in designing the questions, framing the analysis, and interpreting subtleties is paramount to avoid blind spots and bias. For example, an overreliance on automated sentiment analysis without contextual follow-ups risks misinterpretation or superficial understanding of complex workplace dynamics.

Beyond initial acquisition, the analysis stage is where raw numbers and narratives coalesce into clarity and foresight. Advanced statistical methods coupled with data visualization techniques transform disparate data points into coherent stories. Trend analyses reveal the rhythm of workforce flux—identifying seasonal hiring needs, skill shortages looming on the horizon, or patterns in internal mobility. Predictive analytics takes this a step further, embedding historical data within models that forecast future states, enabling proactive rather than reactive workforce planning. These predictive insights empower leaders to anticipate bottlenecks, skill gaps, or surges in Labor demands, crafting solutions before challenges manifest. A notable example lies in the technology sector, where predictive modelling of attrition and talent acquisition cycles allows firms to ramp up hiring well ahead of product launches, ensuring readiness and competitive advantage.

Central to effective analysis is the thoughtful segmentation of data to uncover nuanced insights that broad aggregates might mask. Splitting metrics across dimensions such as department, geography, tenure, or skill categories enables a granular view tailored to specific strategic questions. This segmentation fuels targeted interventions and resource allocation, ensuring that efforts are not scattered but concentrated where they yield maximal impact. An international company, for instance, may discover through segmented analysis that talent shortages are acute in certain regions or business units, prompting localized recruitment drives or investment in retraining programs aligned with local market realities and cultural factors.

Crucially, tracking progress and outcomes requires establishing clear, measurable indicators that align closely with strategic objectives. Key performance indicators in workforce planning mirror the scorecards of conductors, ensuring that organisational movements stay within tempo. These might include turnover rates, time-to-fill vacancies, employee engagement index scores, internal promotion ratios, and skill acquisition benchmarks. Regularly monitoring these metrics not only provides accountability but also fosters agility, revealing when calibrations or course corrections are necessary. In organisations with iterative planning cycles, real-time dashboards coupled with periodic reviews integrate data into decision-making processes continually, avoiding the trap of retrospective assessments that come too late to impact outcomes.

Moreover, the effective use of data in workforce strategy extends beyond internal boundaries—it also involves incorporating external environmental scanning. Benchmarking against industry standards, economic indicators, and Labor market trends enriches organisational insights with a broader contextual fabric. This external data layer enables firms to position themselves dynamically within competitive landscapes, adapting talent strategies to evolving external pressures. For example, shifts in national skill availability, demographic trends, or regulatory changes detected through market intelligence help organisations anticipate changes in supply and demand for key roles, allowing strategic pivots in recruitment, training, or outsourcing decisions.

An often underestimated yet vital aspect of data collection and analysis in workforce planning is the recognition of data's temporal dimension. Talent needs are rarely static; they are fluxing currents shaped by business cycles, technological innovation, and socio-economic fluctuations. Historical data provides a longitudinal view that reveals cyclical behaviours and the impact of prior strategies, serving both as a warning and a guide. This retrospective insight, combined with forward-looking scenarios, creates a comprehensive temporal Planning—informing not only what the organisation needs now but what it must prepare for on the horizon. This dual temporal approach is imperative for sustainable workforce resilience, ensuring that plans are not shortsighted but designed for enduring relevance.

Navigating the challenges of data quality—such as incompleteness, inconsistency, and bias—is a continuous imperative. Establishing robust governance frameworks for data stewardship ensures standards are met, fostering trust in the analytics outcomes. This governance encompasses clear protocols for data privacy, regular audits, and cross-functional collaboration between HR, IT, and business units. Transparency in data processes engenders confidence among stakeholders, breaking down silos and encouraging a culture that champions data-driven insights. The organisational shift towards data literacy also forms part of this governance, empowering managers and leaders to not only consume reports but engage critically with the underlying data narratives, thus elevating the strategic discourse across hierarchy levels.

Integrating qualitative anecdotes and quantitative data cultivates a storytelling approach that resonates on both intellectual and emotional levels, engaging stakeholders deeply in the workforce planning journey. When data speaks with the voice of lived experience, strategic plans transform from sterile documents into compelling narratives that rally leadership and employees alike. This integration is critical in change management, where data-driven storytelling builds the case for shifts in workforce strategy, illustrating challenges vividly while showcasing the pathways to opportunity and improvement.

Finally, the evolution of technology has unlocked unprecedented capabilities in real-time data collection and sophisticated analytics, propelling workforce planning into a new era. Artificial intelligence algorithms can sift through massive datasets to detect patterns imperceptible to humans, providing recommendations or flagging risks before they surface. Machine learning models enhance predictive accuracy over time, continuously refining talent forecasts. Yet, the essence of data collection and analysis remains anchored in human judgment—interpreting patterns within context, balancing quantitative assurance with qualitative nuance. When technology amplifies human insight rather than replacing it, workforce planning ascends to its highest form—an artful orchestration of facts, feelings, and foresight that converges to sculpt an agile, empowered, and future-ready human capital ensemble.

Harnessing the full potential of data collection and analysis is, therefore, an intricate, ongoing process—one that blends meticulous measurement with empathetic listening, rigorous methods with creative interpretation. The journey from raw data to strategic decision-making is neither direct nor simple; it requires patience, expertise, and a commitment to continuous learning. Yet, when successfully undertaken, it crystallizes into a powerful lens through which organisational leaders can foresee talent horizons, navigate uncertainties, and compose a workforce strategy that sings with precision, resilience, and vitality across the ever-changing tides of tomorrow.

Continuous Improvement Processes

In the intricate dance of workforce planning, continuous improvement processes serve as the unseen rhythm that keeps the entire performance harmonious and vibrant. Just as a seasoned conductor listens intently to the orchestra, noting subtle variances in tempo and timbre to fine-tune the delivery, organisational leaders must attentively monitor workforce strategies, consistently refining them through a delicate balance of quantitative and qualitative metrics. This ongoing recalibration is essential for creating a workforce Planning that remains responsive and effective amid the ceaseless evolution of economic conditions, technological advancements, and human aspirations. Harnessing metrics with a nuanced understanding transforms strategic planning from static projections into a dynamic, living process—one that embraces feedback, learns from experience, and fosters a culture of perpetual growth and adaptation.

At the heart of continuous improvement lies the delicate art of measurement—not merely to collect data, but to interpret its meaning deeply and contextually. Quantitative metrics offer the first glance: hard numbers that provide clarity and specificity yet often require the interpretive lens of qualitative insights to breathe life into their austere precision. Metrics such as turnover rates, time-to-fill positions, employee engagement scores, and productivity indices sketch the broad strokes of workforce health and performance. They create a framework within which raw figures translate into patterns of behaviour and organisational vitality. Yet metrics alone tell only part of the story. To truly discern the effectiveness of workforce planning initiatives, one must weave these figures with the rich textures of qualitative assessments—employee feedback, managerial observations, narratives of workplace culture, and the nuanced experiences of diverse departmental teams.

Consider the employee turnover rate, a commonly cited quantitative metric, which, when elevated, can trigger alarms about retention challenges. On its own, a high turnover percentage suggests instability, but without exploring the qualitative 'why', the data remains a mere symptom rather than a clue toward a remedy. Engaging with exit interviews, pulse surveys, and focus groups reveals multifaceted insights: Is dissatisfaction stemming from a lack of career progression, inadequate leadership, or misalignment with organisational values? Perhaps external factors, like competitive offers or evolving employee aspirations toward remote work, play a more significant role. These stories infuse statistics with human complexity, guiding leaders to craft targeted interventions that range from revamped development programs to cultural transformations. By marrying the quantifiable and the experiential, workforce planners gain a fuller understanding that elevates strategic decision-making beyond guesswork into informed artistry.

Embedding continuous improvement processes into workforce planning demands the establishment of clear, relevant, and actionable key performance indicators (KPIs) that evolve alongside organisational objectives. These KPIs must stretch across multiple dimensions—talent acquisition efficiency, skills development rates, leadership bench strength, diversity and inclusion metrics, and employee well-being measures—with regular intervals of review and recalibration. The cadence of these evaluations is as crucial as the data itself. Quarterly or biannual reviews create rhythm and momentum, allowing organisations to catch the first signs of imbalance and course-correct proactively.

Moreover, the flexibility to adapt these KPIs—to retire outdated ones and to introduce fresh, predictive metrics—ensures that the measurement system itself remains a driver of agility and foresight rather than rigidity.

A compelling example can be drawn from a global technology company that integrated comprehensive workforce analytics into its strategic planning. Initially, the firm tracked standard metrics such as hiring velocity and performance ratings. However, through continuous improvement, it expanded its lens to include sophisticated indicators such as the internal mobility index, innovation contribution scores, and sentiment analysis derived from natural language processing of employee communications. By combining these quantitative and qualitative insights, the company identified subtle shifts in workforce engagement before they manifested as attrition or performance dips. Leadership then implemented targeted upskilling programs and redesigned team compositions to better align with emerging business priorities. This iterative approach not only optimized workforce capabilities but fostered a culture where data-driven empathy—understanding human factors through analytics—became a hallmark of strategic planning.

Beyond internal assessments, continuous improvement also hinges on benchmarking against industry standards and best practices, weaving external perspectives into the organisational narrative. Comparing one's metrics to peers and competitors offers valuable context, revealing gaps and opportunities that may otherwise remain obscured. Yet benchmarking must be approached with discernment. Organisations operate within unique ecosystems; an innovation-driven startup's talent dynamics differ starkly from those in a regulated manufacturing firm. Hence, a critical eye is necessary to interpret benchmarking data thoughtfully extracting relevant lessons while honouring the idiosyncrasies of organisational culture, strategy, and market positioning. Such external insights, blended with internal metrics, enhance strategic foresight by situating workforce planning within a broader landscape of trends, risks, and transformative forces.

A vital dimension of continuous improvement involves cultivating a feedback-rich culture where communication flows bidirectionally across hierarchies and functions. Workplace feedback mechanisms—whether through structured performance reviews, anonymous suggestion platforms, or informal team dialogues—create a fertile ground for uncovering latent issues and recognizing emerging talents. Leadership plays an instrumental role in nurturing this environment, demonstrating openness to criticism, celebrating transparency, and embedding learning as an organisational value. This cultural foundation transforms feedback from a perfunctory chore into a vital compass for workforce refinement, empowering employees as active stakeholders in shaping the future of work. Moreover, such inclusivity enhances trust, engagement, and alignment, reinforcing the very metrics that signal workforce health.

Critical too is the integration of advanced technologies that augment continuous improvement endeavours. Artificial intelligence and machine learning technologies have revolutionized the ability to capture, analyse, and predict workforce trends with unprecedented granularity and speed. Predictive analytics models sift through complex datasets to identify correlations and patterns that elude traditional analysis—anticipating talent shortages in specific skill areas, forecasting the impact of demographic shifts, or even simulating the outcomes of various hiring scenarios. These insights equip decision-makers with scenario-based foresight, enabling the design of proactive strategies rather than reactive firefighting. However, technology adoption must be tempered with a vigilant ethical framework, safeguarding employee privacy and ensuring that algorithmic recommendations complement rather than replace human judgment.

The discipline of continuous improvement also demands a keen understanding of cause-and-effect relationships within workforce metrics—a task that can be deceptively complex. For instance, increasing employee engagement scores often correlates with improved productivity, but the underlying drivers of engagement may be multifarious: meaningful work, recognition, leadership quality, or work-life balance considerations. Thus, dissecting these causal links requires sophisticated analytical frameworks and cross-functional collaboration among HR, finance, and operations teams. Actionable insights emerge not from isolated data points, but from interconnected trends and dynamic simulations that encapsulate workforce realities in their full complexity. This integrative mindset elevates continuous improvement from mechanical monitoring to a strategic orchestra of insights, adjustments, and innovations.

Within this landscape, visualization tools play a pivotal role in translating metrics into accessible narratives that resonate across organisational levels. Dashboards, heat maps, and interactive reports transform streams of data into vivid images—much like a conductor's score transforms notes into melodies visible to the eye. These visualizations foster shared understanding among executives, line managers, and employees, aligning perspectives and facilitating rapid, evidence-based discussions. Regular analytics reviews become collaborative experiences where insights are debated, hypotheses tested, and solutions co-created. This participatory approach reinforces accountability and accelerates the translation of metrics into meaningful action, knitting measurement tightly into the fabric of workforce culture.

Reflection also forms an essential pillar of continuous improvement in workforce planning. Organisations benefit from dedicating moments for introspection—examining what has worked, what has faltered, and why. Post-implementation reviews and 'after-action' analyses provide structured opportunities to learn from successes and setbacks alike. These reflective practices encourage humility and curiosity, vital for embracing the complexity and uncertainty inherent in workforce dynamics. Leaders who foster a learning mindset openly share findings, encourage experimentation, and view failure as a stepping stone toward resilience and innovation. This psychological safety accelerates adaptation and empowers the workforce to co-create evolving strategies that anticipate future demands rather than merely respond to immediate pressures.

Importantly, continuous improvement processes must also consider the human impact of measurement initiatives. How metrics are gathered, communicated, and acted upon influences employee morale and engagement profoundly. Overemphasis on quantitative targets without regard to individual and collective well-being risks reducing people to numbers, fostering disengagement or resistance. Therefore, workforce planners must craft balanced scorecards that honour both operational efficiency and human flourishing— measuring aspects such as psychological safety, inclusivity, and empowerment alongside traditional performance indicators. By valuing the full spectrum of human experience within the workforce, organisations lay the groundwork for sustainable, ethical, and vibrant strategic growth.

Ultimately, continuous improvement in workforce planning is less about chasing perfection and more about nurturing an adaptive ecosystem. It thrives on curiosity, responsiveness, and the courage to challenge assumptions. This process resembles a living symphony—never static, always evolving—where leaders, HR professionals, and employees coalesce as instrumental voices in creating a harmonious future. As they refine their metrics and the stories these numbers tell, they do more than optimize headcounts or skill matrices. They cultivate an organisational spirit capable of anticipating change, embracing complexity, and orchestrating human talent with the grace and precision of a maestro guiding a timeless masterpiece. This ongoing journey, grounded in rigorous measurement yet elevated by empathy and vision, defines the essence of true workforce mastery—a continuous performance of growth where every note counts, and every individual contributes to a compelling collective resonance.

Embedding Strategy: Implementation and Communication

Developing Implementation Roadmaps

In the realm of strategic workforce planning, crafting a visionary plan is only the inception; the true measure of success lies in its seamless execution. Developing implementation roadmaps emerges as the vital bridge between abstract strategy and tangible organisational transformation. These roadmaps function as meticulously detailed maps, guiding stakeholders through a landscape bristling with complexities, uncertainties, and interdependencies. They act as navigational aids that align discrete actions with overarching objectives, ensuring the workforce strategy does not dissipate into lofty ideas but instead unfolds into cohesive, purpose-driven outcomes. To chart such a roadmap with efficacy demands more than a superficial timeline or a checklist; it calls for a structured approach, a deliberate orchestration of processes that involve clear articulation of milestones, stakeholder engagement, transparent communication channels, and dynamic feedback loops. Together, these elements foster a living document, flexible enough to adapt yet rigid enough to compel disciplined adherence to strategic intent.

At the heart of implementation roadmaps lies the essential task of prioritization. Not all workforce initiatives bear equal urgency or strategic weight, and the roadmap must delineate which actions warrant immediate pursuit and which can be sequenced for subsequent phases. This prioritization flows naturally from a comprehensive situational analysis, where internal capabilities, external market dynamics, and business imperatives intersect. For instance, the identification of a critical skills gap that threatens near-term operations might demand a rapid launch of targeted upskilling programs, while broader cultural transformation initiatives, despite their long-term significance, may warrant a phased rollout to allow gradual assimilation. The roadmap must, therefore, be thoughtfully segmented into time-bound phases—each with clear deliverables— crafting a cadence of achievement that propels momentum and builds stakeholder confidence.

Stakeholder engagement breathes life into implementation roadmaps. The process of translating strategy into action is too complex and often too multifaceted to be the charge of a solitary champion or a narrow team of specialists. Instead, it must be a collective enterprise where functional leaders, HR business partners, employees, and even external partners are woven into the fabric of execution. Meaningful engagement hinges upon inclusivity, inviting diverse perspectives and expertise to surface insights that sharpen the roadmap's precision. Early involvement of stakeholders also engenders ownership; when individuals and teams recognize their roles as pivotal cogs in the strategic machinery, motivation surges, and resistance to change diminishes. This inclusiveness manifests through forums, workshops, and cross-functional task groups convened to dissect the roadmap's components, articulate concerns, and contribute suggestions that refine feasibility and impact. It is through this collaborative dialogue that the roadmap evolves from a static plan into an energized rallying point around which the organisation coalesces.

Transparency is a critical companion to engagement, serving as the oxygen that fuels trust and alignment during the execution journey. Implementation roadmaps thrive when their contents—the assumptions, timelines, responsibilities, and success metrics—are openly shared with all relevant participants. This transparency demystifies decisions and exposes the rationale behind sequencing and prioritization, preventing the erosion of confidence bred by ambiguity or concealed agendas. Communication, therefore, must be both comprehensive and nuanced: detailed enough to equip teams with actionable clarity, yet framed within the strategic narrative that links daily tasks to the broader vision. Visual tools, such as Gantt charts or flow diagrams, can amplify understanding, transforming complex dependencies into easily digestible formats that invite participation rather than perplexity. Regular, transparent updates on progress, setbacks, and course corrections serve as vital feedback conduits, reinforcing a culture of accountability and continuous improvement.

Embedded within the architecture of implementation roadmaps are feedback mechanisms that elevate execution from a linear process to a dynamic, learning-oriented cycle. Rigid adherence to predetermined plans risks obsolescence in a business environment characterized by volatility; agile responsiveness can only arise when organisations actively monitor execution outcomes and glean lessons in real time. Feedback loops operate on multiple levels: quantitative data emanating from workforce analytics reveals whether hiring goals or retention thresholds are being met; qualitative inputs gathered from frontline managers and employees illuminate experiential realities that numbers alone cannot capture. These insights should feed directly into periodic roadmap reviews, enabling recalibration of priorities, reallocation of resources, or modification of tactics where necessary. Crucially, these feedback processes must be institutionalized rather than episodic; only then can adaptation become an ingrained organisational competency rather than an emergency reaction.

The carefully sculpted roadmap is inherently an instrument of change management, which heightens the imperative for meticulous communication strategies entwined with execution. Change, particularly at a systemic workforce level, often incubates apprehension and inertia; the roadmap must thus function as both a strategic plan and a narrative device that frames transformation positively. Compelling storytelling around implementation progress maintains engagement by connecting emotional and intellectual dimensions of change. Leaders and change agents within the organisation wield the roadmap as a script from which to articulate successes, acknowledge challenges, and remind all actors of the ultimate vision. To fortify this narrative, explicit links should be drawn between workforce initiatives and measurable business outcomes—whether improved productivity, innovation velocity, customer experience, or market share gains—thereby rendering abstract efforts concrete and meaningful.

Resource planning forms another cornerstone in developing effective implementation roadmaps. No matter how elegant the strategy or compelling the narrative, execution falters when requisite resources—be they financial, technological, or human capital—are inadequately allocated. The roadmap must, therefore, integrate a granular resource matrix, identifying where capacities must be amplified or newly sourced. This could involve detailed forecasting of hiring volumes, budgeting for training platforms, or upgrading HR information systems to support new talent analytics capabilities. Importantly, resources are not merely inputs but strategic enablers; mapping their deployment over time ensures that bottlenecks are pre-empted and that workforce initiatives cascade harmoniously rather than compete destructively for organisational attention.

Technology also plays an instrumental role in the execution phase, especially in visualizing, tracking, and managing the components of the roadmap. Integrated platforms that allow real-time updating, stakeholder collaboration, and alerting on deviations enhance transparency and speed responsiveness. These digital tools transform the roadmap from a static document into an interactive command centre, where project owners can rally teams, share documents, and measure progress against key performance indicators seamlessly. Additionally, leveraging data analytics embedded in workforce planning software enables predictive insights that inform decision-making throughout implementation, such as identifying early signs of talent shortages or engagement risks. The allure of technology lies not only in efficiency gains but also in its capacity to translate strategic complexity into navigable, actionable intelligence.

As an implementation roadmap evolves, attention must be paid to embedding governance structures that sustain momentum and mitigate risks. This governance encompasses clearly defined roles and responsibilities for decision-making, escalation protocols when challenges arise, and a cadence for steering committee meetings. These governance forums act as steering wheels, continuously adjusting organisational direction and smoothing the road ahead through proactive problem-solving. Furthermore, risk management processes within the roadmap identify potential execution pitfalls—like unforeseen skill gaps, budgetary overruns, or external disruptions—and prescribe mitigation strategies. Contingency planning becomes interwoven into the roadmap's DNA, ensuring readiness and resilience rather than reactive scrambling in the face of adversity.

An often-underappreciated element in crafting implementation roadmaps is the human dimension of motivation and behaviour. Achieving strategic intent depends fundamentally on influencing attitudes and habits at every organisational layer. Therefore, the roadmap must incorporate incentive alignment mechanisms that reinforce desired behaviours crucial for execution. Whether through recognition programs that spotlight workforce planning champions or performance management systems calibrated to reward contributions to plan milestones, these motivational constructs transform abstract goals into personal aspirations for individuals and teams alike. Similarly, fostering a culture that embraces experimentation and tolerates calculated risks encourages innovation within execution, essential for adaptation in a fast-changing Labor market.

To ensure the roadmap extends beyond initial posturing into sustainable practice, it must include continuous learning loops. This aspiration elevates the implementation process into a transformative journey where each phase becomes a classroom. Lessons distilled from past successes and missteps are codified, institutionalized through knowledge-sharing platforms, training sessions, and documented best practices. This living knowledge base enriches future iterations of the roadmap, creating a virtuous cycle of strategic refinement and enhanced organisational capability. The involvement of leadership is paramount here; their modelling of learning mindsets and championing of reflective practices accelerates cultural shifts that support ongoing workforce adaptability.

In practice, the power of an implementation roadmap lies in its capacity to transform a multifaceted and often intimidating strategic initiative into a coherent, actionable pathway. As it unfolds, the roadmap harmonizes diverse stakeholder energies, channels fragmented initiatives into symphonic progress, and fortifies the psychological contract between leadership and workforce. It transforms strategic workforce planning from a theoretical exercise into a practical art form—much like an orchestra conductor not only holds the score but guides every instrument to meld into a resonant masterpiece. Through deliberate emphasis on stakeholder engagement, transparency, feedback mechanisms, disciplined resource planning, and organisational culture, the implementation roadmap becomes the lifeblood of enduring transformation. It charts the journey from aspiration to achievement, ensuring that tomorrow's talent needs are met not by happenstance, but through orchestrated, strategic intentionality.

Stakeholder Engagement

In the grand symphony of workforce planning, engaging stakeholders is akin to tuning the instruments before the first note is played—a fundamental process that ensures harmony throughout the performance. Stakeholder engagement transcends the mere dissemination of information; it is a dynamic, ongoing dialogue that invites collaboration, cultivates understanding, and fosters ownership among those whose voices ripple through the organisation's ecosystem. When leadership takes the initiative to construct bridges of trust, transparency, and shared purpose, the workforce strategy becomes not just a top-down decree but a living, breathing framework shaped and strengthened by diverse perspectives. Engaging stakeholders effectively requires more than punctual updates; it demands a commitment to genuine inclusion, openness to feedback, and a meticulous orchestration of how communication flows across strategic, operational, and individual levels. This multifaceted approach not only mitigates resistance but empowers every participant to become an advocate, contributing actively to the Planning's refinement and ultimate success.

At its core, stakeholder engagement is about embracing a collective mind where different functions, seniority levels, and personal aspirations converge. This convergence is crucial because workforce planning inherently cuts across boundaries—it involves finance directors who stress budgetary prudence, HR leaders championing talent development, department heads grappling with operational demands, and frontline employees envisioning their career journeys. Each stakeholder brings a unique lens shaped by daily realities and strategic vantage points. For instance, a customer service manager's perspective on staffing needs may emphasize flexibility to handle fluctuating call volumes, while the legal team might prioritize compliance and risk management around employment contracts. Integrating these viewpoints into a coherent strategy necessitates an environment of respect and curiosity, where exploring divergent opinions is not a threat but an opportunity to deepen understanding and refine assumptions. Effective engagement, therefore, cultivates a culture where stakeholders feel safe to voice concerns and innovative ideas alike, sparking a collective intelligence that far exceeds top-down mandates.

Transparency is the linchpin that holds stakeholder engagement together, transforming it from a performative ritual into an authentic partnership. Transparency means openly sharing not only the successes but also the uncertainties and potential risks embedded in workforce projections. This candidness fosters credibility and invites stakeholders to co-navigate the complexities of forecasting and scenario-building. When organisational leaders disclose the methodologies, assumptions, and limitations underlying their plans, they demystify the process and create a reference point for ongoing dialogue. Consider the subtle yet profound difference between presenting a workforce plan as a finalized certitude versus framing it as a flexible roadmap subject to change. The latter approach nurtures an adaptable mindset among stakeholders who recognize their role in monitoring trends, providing frontline intelligence, and adjusting tactics as conditions evolve. Moreover, transparency fuels alignment, for stakeholders who grasp the rationale behind decisions can more ardently support necessary trade-offs or resource allocations—even when these spur short-term discomfort or strategic shifts.

The mechanism through which transparency materializes is communication—deliberate, multidimensional, and respectful of diverse preference and capacity. Successful stakeholder engagement thrives on well-crafted channels that blend formal updates, interactive workshops, and informal conversations. For example, periodic town halls serve as a platform for leadership to articulate broad strategic narratives and respond to questions, while targeted focus groups enable deeper dives into specific workforce challenges, engaging subject matter experts and affected teams directly. Digital platforms can amplify reach and participation, enabling real-time feedback and the democratization of input across geographical and hierarchical divides. Yet, the rhythm and tone of communication matter profoundly. Overwhelming stakeholders with dense reports or jargon-heavy presentations breeds disengagement, while a one-size-fits-all approach neglects the nuances of audience needs. Tailoring messages to resonate emotionally and cognitively—linking abstract data to real-life impacts on careers, workloads, and team dynamics—sparks genuine interest and connection. Active listening further enriches this communication ecosystem; it is not enough to hear words but to understand underlying sentiments, hesitations, or aspirations that influence how messages are received and acted upon.

Feedback mechanisms emerge as vital instruments in this dialogue, closing the loop between planners and stakeholders and enriching the strategic process with iterative insights. Constructing avenues for two-way feedback requires intent and design, embedding opportunities to critique, question, and co-create. Surveys structured to test assumptions about skills shortages, hiring timelines, or training efficacy provide quantitative gauges, while open forums and narrative accounts reveal qualitative nuances often missed by data alone. Importantly, feedback should transcend tokenism; it demands transparent acknowledgment of contributions and visible incorporation into subsequent plan iterations. When stakeholders witness how their input shapes decisions, it reinforces trust and motivates sustained engagement, transforming participants into true collaborators rather than passive recipients. Additionally, leveraging feedback fosters agility—timely course corrections can mitigate risks before they magnify, harnessing collective foresight to navigate uncertain business environments with greater confidence.

Stakeholder engagement is not static; it evolves alongside the lifecycle of the workforce plan and shifts within the organisational context. Initial enthusiasm can wane without nurturing, and emerging concerns or new stakeholders may surface, necessitating ongoing recalibration. Recognizing this dynamic nature, leaders adept in engagement approach it as a continuous relationship-building exercise rather than a checklist item. This mindset encourages embedding engagement milestones into the overall planning cadence—pre-launch consultations, mid-cycle reviews, and post-implementation retrospectives—each designed to reaffirm commitments, share learnings, and surface newly emergent issues. At the same time, organisations must remain vigilant against engagement fatigue, balancing the frequency and depth of interactions to maintain energy and focus. Effective leaders discern when to convene broad meetings for shared understanding and when targeted groups can deliver more focused contributions. This deliberate orchestration optimizes stakeholder time and respects their competing demands, further cementing goodwill and cooperation.

The role of leadership as the architect of stakeholder engagement cannot be overstated. Authentic leaders personify transparency and inclusiveness, setting the tone by modelling open communication and valuing dissenting perspectives. They champion workforce planning as a collective Endeavor that transcends silos, breaking down hierarchies that barrier the free flow of ideas. Moreover, leadership commitment signals priority—when executives visibly participate in engagement forums and respond to stakeholder concerns, it communicates that workforce planning is not an administrative chore, but a strategic imperative intertwined with organisational destiny. Leaders also bear the responsibility for cultivating a culture where psychological safety flourishes, enabling employees and managers alike to contribute boldly without fear of reprisal or marginalization. This cultural foundation shifts engagement from transactional 'check-the-box' dynamics to transformative partnerships that underpin sustainable change.

Building support through stakeholder engagement also extends to forging alliances beyond internal boundaries. External stakeholders—such as labour unions, educational institutions, industry associations, and even regulatory bodies—play a pivotal role in shaping the talent ecosystem. Engaging these actors requires strategic diplomacy blended with an understanding of mutual dependencies. For instance, closer collaboration with universities can inform pipeline development and influence curricular adjustments that better prepare future hires. Dialogue with unions may ease transitions during restructuring, aligning workforce plans with shared concerns about job security and working conditions. Regulatory agencies' involvement can anticipate compliance requirements and emerging labour standards, pre-empting operational disruptions. This external engagement adds richness and realism to the workforce planning canvas, rooting it in broader socioeconomic realities and expanding the horizon of possibilities and constraints.

Amidst the complexity of orchestrating stakeholder engagement, the use of technology offers powerful enablers to streamline and enrich interactions. Digital platforms facilitate asynchronous collaboration, allowing stakeholders spread across locations and time zones to contribute on their schedule while preserving institutional memory of discussions and decisions. Advanced analytics integrated into engagement tools can synthesize feedback patterns, highlight emerging concerns, and identify stakeholder sentiment trends, providing planners with real-time intelligence to adapt approaches. Emerging technologies such as artificial intelligence can even simulate stakeholder dynamics, testing how proposed changes might resonate across different groups before actual implementation. However, technology must serve as an enabler rather than a substitute for human empathy and nuanced judgment. The most effective stakeholder engagement blends digital efficiency with personal connection, sustaining trust and solidarity essential for collective action.

The benefits of robust stakeholder engagement ripple through every phase of the workforce planning process. When stakeholders are engaged early and meaningfully, plans are imbued with richer data, diverse expertise, and realistic assumptions, enhancing their robustness. This inclusivity also builds a shared commitment to execution—when stakeholders see themselves reflected in the strategy, their willingness to champion its implementation increases markedly. In times of disruption, this social capital becomes invaluable; a well-engaged network mobilizes swiftly, collaborating across boundaries to address talent shortages, pivot to new skill requirements, or manage workforce transitions with agility. Moreover, the process cultivates organisational learning as stakeholders develop a deeper appreciation of systemic interdependencies influencing workforce health. This continuous learning loop strengthens future planning cycles and contributes to a resilient organisational culture attuned to both risk and opportunity.

Yet, embedding effective stakeholder engagement faces challenges that organisations must intentionally address. Competing priorities and time constraints often limit participation, especially among senior leaders who juggle myriad responsibilities. Overcoming this requires demonstrating the tangible value of engagement—how it can reduce costly misalignments, prevent talent gaps, or unlock innovation. Additionally, power dynamics can skew whose voices are heard, marginalizing critical insights from less visible groups or frontline staff. Leaders must consciously democratize participation, creating inclusive forums that empower diverse contributions and confront unconscious biases. Communication barriers—whether linguistic, cultural, or technological—also pose risks of misunderstanding. Employing multiple communication modalities, fostering cultural competence, and ensuring accessibility are necessary countermeasures. Finally, sustaining momentum over the long planning horizon calls for dedicated facilitation resources and continuous monitoring of engagement quality, reinforcing accountability and responsiveness.

In essence, stakeholder engagement is the lifeblood that animates workforce planning from a static, abstract schema into a vibrant, living strategy that breathes with the organisation's collective will and wisdom. It embodies the art of building support through authentic connection, transparent dialogue, and shared ownership. Without it, even the most visionary workforce plan risks faltering as a disconnected plan; with it, the plan becomes a resonant symphony, harmonizing disparate voices into a powerful ensemble capable of navigating the unpredictable rhythms of tomorrow's talent needs. Engaging stakeholders is not a singular event but a continuous dance—one that invites patience, creativity, and steadfast commitment—but its rewards manifest in strategies that are resilient, inclusive, and primed for sustained success.

Transparent Communication Strategies

In the delicate art of orchestrating a workforce strategy that resonates with precision and purpose, transparent communication emerges not merely as a facilitator but as the lifeblood sustaining trust and cultivating an environment where openness flourishes. Imagine the organisation as an intricate fabric, each thread representing a unique individual or team, woven together by the deliberate and artful exchange of information. Without transparency, the fabric weakens, its threads fraying and unravelling beneath unseen tensions and mistrust. For strategic workforce planning to be effective, it must rest upon foundations of honest dialogue, inclusive engagement, and iterative feedback that breathe life into the plans and inspire collective ownership.

At its core, maintaining openness within any organisation requires a culture that not only permits but champions the free flow of information — a culture where every voice, from the highest executive suites to the frontline employees, is heard and valued. This culture transcends mere policy or protocols; it is a living ethos cultivated through consistent, authentic interactions. The unvarnished sharing of intentions, challenges, successes, and uncertainties frames workforce planning as a shared journey rather than a top-down mandate. Leaders who embrace transparency set a resonant tone by deliberately—and vulnerably—communicating not just the what, but the why behind decisions, thus demystifying the motivations that drive strategic choices. This openness seeds credibility, transforming stakeholders from passive recipients into active participants engaged in co-creating the workforce Planning.

Engagement of stakeholders in workforce planning is an iterative dance choreographed through dialogues that extend beyond formal meetings and memos. It involves weaving engagement into the daily fabric of organisational life—an ongoing conversation about needs, capacities, and aspirations. To foster this depth of connection, communication strategies must employ rich, multidimensional approaches tailored to the nuances of diverse stakeholder groups. For instance, executives may prefer high-level summaries supported by predictive analytics and trend insights, while frontline managers and employees often crave concrete implications and opportunities for personal growth. Employing storytelling techniques grounded in real data, framed as compelling narratives rather than cold statistics, bridges these varying needs.

Such narratives allow individuals to see themselves within the strategic vision, crystallizing abstract workforce plans into tangible, relatable experiences.

Yet, transparency is not achieved simply by broadcasting information broadly; it demands a sophisticated exchange where listening holds equal weight to speaking. Feedback mechanisms become critical in this endeavour, evolving into channels through which the organisation absorbs collective wisdom and recalibrates its planning efforts in real time. The true measure of transparency lies not in the frequency of updates, but in the responsiveness and adaptability that feedback enables. Creating safe, accessible arenas for honest dialogue encourages stakeholders to voice concerns, propose innovations, and challenge assumptions without fear of reprisal. When employees witness that their perspectives materially influence strategic adjustments, trust deepens, and commitment intensifies. It is through this iterative loop of dialogue— communicate, listen, respond—that workforce strategies adapt fluidly to shifting realities, ensuring relevance and resilience.

Moreover, the architecture of transparent communication must be deliberately inclusive to prevent information silos and parity gaps that undermine trust. This inclusivity manifests in thoughtful timing and sequencing of communications, ensuring that all pertinent parties receive information simultaneously and in contexts appropriate to their roles and decision-making power. Transparency falters when some groups access critical insights before others, breeding perceptions of favouritism or exclusion. Hence, deterministic dissemination—strategically planned and executed—reinforces a unified organisational narrative. It also sets the stage for collaborative problem-solving, as stakeholders equipped with shared understanding can more effectively align their efforts and leverage collective intelligence to anticipate potential obstacles or opportunities within workforce planning.

Trust, the elusive but indispensable currency of transparent communication, demands consistency over time. It cannot be conjured through isolated bursts of candour but must be nurtured through persistent integrity—communicating not only triumphs but also setbacks with unflinching honesty. When workforce plans necessitate difficult choices, such as restructuring or role eliminations, transparent communication becomes both a balm and a beacon. It humanizes complex processes by acknowledging the real impact on individuals and communities within the organisation. Leaders who articulate these realities with empathy and clarity help mitigate anxiety and speculation, thereby preserving organisational cohesion. Furthermore, transparency paired with genuine opportunities for dialogue cultivates a climate where resilience thrives; employees are motivated not by blind optimism but by informed confidence in the organisation's direction and their role within it.

Intersecting with the behavioural dimension, transparent communication also plays a crucial part in simplifying complex data inherent in strategic workforce planning into accessible insights. The rising sophistication of analytics, artificial intelligence, and predictive modelling provides organisations with unprecedented foresight, yet these tools risk alienating stakeholders unfamiliar with their technical underpinnings. To avoid the opacity of jargon or the intimidation of data overload, transparent communication embraces the educator's role—translating numbers into narratives rich with context, implications, and actionable steps. Visual storytelling tools, interactive dashboards, and scenario simulations democratize strategic understanding, inviting participants to explore "what if" scenarios and witness how workforce models respond to variables such as market shifts, talent shortages, or technological disruption. This democratization fosters ownership by transforming stakeholders from passive audiences into competent navigators of the workforce journey.

Recognizing the dynamic nature of modern workplaces, transparent communication strategies must also be agile and multilayered, leveraging multiple channels to reach audiences effectively. In an era where digital platforms coexist with traditional face-to-face interactions, a blended communication ecosystem is indispensable. For example, town halls and workshops provide direct human connection and emotional resonance, while intranet portals and mobile apps ensure immediacy and accessibility of up-to-date information. Transparent organisations carefully curate the cadence of these channels, balancing frequency to avoid fatigue with the necessity for timely updates. They also create spaces—virtual or physical—for informal exchanges where questions and clarifications can flow organically, reinforcing formal communication streams. The interplay between structured messaging and spontaneous dialogue enriches understanding and underscores that transparency is not a static declaration but an evolving conversation.

In embracing these communication practices, organisations encounter inevitable challenges that must be navigated with intentional leadership. Resistance often emerges from entrenched cultures where information was traditionally siloed or managed restrictively to maintain control. Shifting such mindsets requires more than directives; it calls for modelling transparent behaviours at all leadership levels and incentivizing openness. It also demands patience and persistence, recognizing that transparency matures gradually as trust compounds through repeated positive interactions. Leaders must confront the discomfort of uncertainty, be willing to share incomplete information while inviting collaborative problem-solving. This humility, paradoxically, strengthens authority by demonstrating confidence in the collective capacity to adapt. Additionally, transparent communication must safeguard against inadvertent breaches of confidentiality or over-disclosure that might jeopardize legal or competitive standing. This balance embodies the nuanced skill of mounting the stage as an open orchestra conductor—inviting harmony without chaos.

Ultimately, transparent communication strategies are not ends in themselves but pivotal enablers of a workforce Planning that is vibrant, adaptive, and resilient. They transform abstract workforce plans into living documents animated by human connection and shared purpose. They create a cultural symphony where openness composes trust, engagement sustains momentum, and feedback fine-tunes the collective cadence. Through this dynamic interplay, organisations transcend transactional workforce planning to establish enduring partnerships with the very people who constitute their greatest asset—their talent. The result is not only alignment with tomorrow's business needs but also the empowerment of a workforce prepared to innovate, collaborate, and thrive amid uncertainty. Transparent communication thus stands as the beacon illuminating the path from strategic vision to realized potential—a guiding light that invites every stakeholder to participate in the masterpiece of organisational evolution.

Feedback and Adjustment Cycles

In the orchestral performance of strategic workforce planning, the concept of feedback and adjustment cycles plays a role akin to the tuner's continuous atonement of every instrument, ensuring harmony remains intact despite ever-shifting conditions. This iterative process, far from a mere administrative chore, stands as a dynamic, living mechanism that breathes adaptability and resilience into the entire workforce Planning. In an environment as volatile as the contemporary business world, the assumption that a single, rigid plan will flawlessly navigate future uncertainties is not only naive but profoundly risky. Instead, the plan must be conceived as a malleable structure, one that regularly invites critique, insight, and recalibration from a diverse array of voices – stakeholders who collectively hold the keys to both foresight and practical execution.

At the heart of effective feedback and adjustment cycles lies engagement—engagement that transcends funnelling decisions top-down and instead fosters a culture where transparency is not an afterthought but a foundational value. Transparency dismantles the ivory towers that so often alienate employees and leaders alike, opening the doors to dialogues that integrate frontline insights with strategic visions. Without this openness, feedback risks becoming an exercise in vanity or box-ticking, rather than a creative exegesis of truth. It necessitates an environment where stakeholders, including business unit leaders, HR professionals, frontline employees, and even external partners, feel empowered and motivated to share observations, concerns, and innovative ideas. This collective intelligence, when harvested correctly, infuses the workforce plan with a robustness that outpaces any top-down forecasting model.

Initiating this cycle requires first building trust. Stakeholders must believe their input will be acknowledged and valued, and crucially, will effect change. Feedback mechanisms, therefore, require thoughtful design: anonymous surveys may capture candid opinions where fear of repercussion lurks, while structured dialogues, town halls, and interactive workshops facilitate collaboration and co-creation. It is within these spaces that raw data transforms into a nuanced understanding. For instance, a midmarket technology firm might discover through an internal feedback workshop that its workforce agility is hampered not by lack of skills but by rigid middle management practices. Such insight, invisible in traditional KPI reports, becomes a critical inflection point for adjustment.

A potent feedback loop also integrates technological enablers. Advances in people analytics platforms and real-time data dashboards provide the scaffolding on which transparent and actionable feedback can flourish. These tools enable continuous monitoring of workforce metrics aligned with strategic goals and trigger alerts when deviations or emerging trends occur. Yet, raw metrics alone cannot capture the texture of human experience, reinforcing why qualitative feedback remains indispensable. Integrating structured data points with narrative accounts crafts a holistic picture—one that can pinpoint not only what adjustments are necessary, but why they are needed. This synergy elevates feedback from reactionary firefighting to proactive strategic refinement.

The cadence of these adjustment cycles must balance responsiveness with thoughtful deliberation. Too rapid a pace risks oscillations born of overreaction to transient issues; too sluggish a rhythm risks ossification, allowing misalignments to crystallize into systemic dysfunction. Many leading organisations adopt quarterly or semi-annual formal review intervals, augmented by continuous informal checkpoints. During these reviews, the workforce Planning is revisited through the prism of new business priorities, external environmental shifts, and the latest talent market signals. These gatherings become crucibles for strategic conversation, where assumptions are challenged, and new hypotheses are tested. They also serve to recalibrate expectations and reaffirm collective commitments, crucial for maintaining momentum and avoiding feedback fatigue.

Equally important is the language through which feedback and adjustments are communicated. Clear, candid, and empathetic communication reinforces the perception of legitimacy and equity. Leaders who transparently share how insights have shaped modifications reinforce the value of stakeholder contributions and enhance future engagement. Conversely, when feedback appears to vanish into a black hole, cynicism quickly germinates. To counter this, many organisations embrace storytelling as a powerful vehicle, narrating 'before and after' scenarios that make the impact of feedback tangible. For example, recounting how employee insights led to redesigned role descriptions that improved engagement and output transforms abstract strategy into a relatable human experience.

Beyond communication, embedding feedback and adaptation into the organisational psyche demands structural enablers. Cross-functional task forces or workforce strategy councils can institutionalize this iterative mindset. These bodies act as custodians of the workforce Planning's health, ensuring stakeholder viewpoints from talent acquisition, operations, finance, and technology continually inform planning. Their cross-pollination of perspectives averts siloed thinking and aligns workforce strategies seamlessly with complex, intersecting business objectives. Moreover, by distributing ownership of adjustments, these councils foster accountability and a shared sense of stewardship vital in volatile markets.

Adjustment cycles are not without challenges, however. They often confront cognitive biases such as confirmation bias, where decision-makers favor information that reinforces existing beliefs, or recency bias, where disproportionate weight is given to recent events at the expense of longer-term trends. Overcoming these requires deliberate practices such as scenario analysis and devil's advocacy, facilitating the surfacing of divergent views to enrich the dialogue. Additionally, psychological safety must underpin these interactions, encouraging dissenting voices and risk-taking without fear of reprisal. Only then does feedback elevate from perfunctory to transformative.

Another potential pitfall lies in the complexity of balancing competing priorities across stakeholder groups. For instance, operations may advocate for hiring to sustain production targets, HR might champion upskilling investments for future needs, while finance demands cost containment. The iterative cycle becomes a negotiation arena where these tensions are surfaced and trade-offs transparently assessed. This balancing act necessitates a strategic compass that keeps the workforce plan tethered to overarching business goals, preventing fragmentation. Feedback mechanisms thus serve not only as inputs for adjustment but also as forums for clarifying ambitions and constraints.

The iterative nature of feedback and adjustment cycles also reinforces the imperative of agility and resilience within the workforce itself. As market realities pivot unexpectedly, so too must the human capital strategy flex, whether through redeployment of talent, accelerating learning pathways, or recalibrating succession plans. Feedback loops function as early warning systems, revealing cracks before they widen into chasms. For example, a retail chain might learn through frequent employee pulse surveys that seasonal staffing demands are undermined by burnout and turnover intentions. Responding promptly, they could test flexible scheduling pilots or introduce digital scheduling tools—a clear embodiment of iterative learning in action.

Finally, feedback and adjustment cycles enrich the long-term sustainability of workforce plans by embedding a continuous learning ethos. Each iteration becomes a repository of knowledge, capturing past missteps and successes, evolving methodologies accordingly. These cycles transform workforce planning from a periodic exercise into a perpetual dialogue with reality, enhancing organisational intelligence. Leaders who champion this approach cultivate a culture that views change not as disruption but as opportunity, thereby transforming human resources into a strategic asset poised for future growth.

Through these myriad dimensions—engagement, transparency, technological integration, communication, governance, cognitive rigor, and cultural alignment—feedback and adjustment cycles emerge as the lifeblood of strategic workforce planning. They ensure the Planning remains neither brittle nor static, but a vibrant composition attuned to the shifting rhythm of business and talent landscapes. In embracing this iterative dance, organisations unlock the power to orchestrate their human capital with the finesse of a maestro, navigating uncertainty with confidence and creativity.

Embracing the Future: Trends Shaping Workforce Planning

Remote and Hybrid Workforces

In the grand concert of organisational dynamics, the traditional office, once the central stage where talent gathered in synchronous rhythms, is no longer the sole locus of performance. The emergence and rapid adoption of remote and hybrid workforces have transformed this stage into an expansive, multifaceted arena where the boundaries between physical and digital spaces blur seamlessly like the overlapping harmonies of a complex symphony. This seismic shift compels leaders and workforce strategists to reimagine not only where work happens but how it is orchestrated, coordinated, and ultimately aligned with the evolving business objectives. To truly master strategic workforce planning for tomorrow's talent needs, it is vital to embrace these changing workplace dynamics with a nuanced understanding that captures their implications, challenges, and immense opportunities for innovation.

The narrative of work's metamorphosis is rooted in broader societal transformations that have been years in the making but accelerated dramatically by global events such as the COVID-19 pandemic. Suddenly, organisations worldwide experienced an involuntary yet powerful experiment in remote work, pushing employees out from the familiar confines of office buildings into living rooms, kitchen tables, cafes, and far-flung corners of the globe. This forced reconfiguration revealed striking truths about our collective ability to adapt, communicate, and deliver results beyond traditional frameworks. Many organisations, initially sceptical, discovered that productivity did not taper off as feared; rather, it often flourished under these new conditions as workers gained autonomy over their time, environment, and work styles. However, this newfound freedom introduced fresh complexities; questions about maintaining engagement, collaboration, and culture became urgent as the physical proximity that once anchored teams dissolved into pixels on a screen.

Remote and hybrid workforces are not merely logistical contingencies; they represent fundamental changes in how human capital interacts with organisational design and strategy. Remote work denotes a fully distributed model wherein employees operate wholly apart from office spaces, connected primarily through digital means. Hybrid models offer more fluidity—a blend of remote and on-site work that attempts to balance flexibility with in-person interaction. Both approaches demand an intricate weaving of policies, technologies, cultural norms, and leadership styles to function optimally. From a strategic perspective, planning for such distributed ecosystems requires envisioning a workforce that transcends geography, accommodating diverse needs and preferences while aligning with business imperatives that continue to evolve in a volatile, uncertain world.

One of the most profound implications of this transition is the redefinition of workforce boundaries. Geographic barriers that once restricted talent searches now increasingly dissolve, presenting organisations with an unprecedented talent pool that spans cities, countries, and continents. This democratization of hiring can be a competitive advantage when harnessed thoughtfully. However, it also means planning must account for disparate labour laws, cultural expectations, tax codes, time zones, and communication norms that complicate traditional workforce models. Strategic planners must cultivate a cultural dexterity that allows the organisation to not only navigate this multiplicity but also incorporate it as a source of strength and innovation. Diversity in location often brings diversity in thought, skills, and perspectives, which are critical for creativity and resilience in today's shifting markets.

Yet, to leverage this opportunity, there must be a rigorous foundation of infrastructure—technological, managerial, and cultural—that supports remote collaboration without sacrificing cohesion or clarity of purpose. The rapid deployment of digital collaboration tools, video conferencing platforms, cloud-based project management systems, and AI-driven workflows has been instrumental in enabling these dispersed teams to function. However, technology is merely the scaffold; culture is the architecture that sustains these structures. Planning efforts must foreground culture-building mechanisms that retain connection and belonging among employees dispersed across physical spaces. Intentional rituals—virtual coffee breaks, remote town halls, peer recognition programs—can replicate some of the social glue lost in physical separation. Leadership styles must evolve from command-and-control to trust-and-empower, empowering leaders at every level to nurture autonomy while ensuring alignment with organisational goals.

Moreover, workforce planners need to account for the psychological and emotional dimensions of remote and hybrid work arrangements. The freedom from commute, the ability to balance personal and professional demands more fluidly, and the reduction of workplace distractions can positively impact well-being and job satisfaction. Conversely, the risk of isolation, burnout, blurred boundaries between home and work life, and reduced spontaneous interaction are genuine challenges that can erode motivation and productivity over time if left unaddressed. Strategic planning must therefore incorporate policies and support systems that promote mental health and work-life balance as core components of workforce design, recognizing that a sustainable talent ecosystem depends on nurturing the whole person, not just their output.

The hybrid model introduces unique complexities as organisations navigate dual modes of work. Scheduling, meeting design, communication protocols, and performance evaluation all demand recalibration to ensure fairness and inclusion. For instance, meetings must be structured to enable equal participation from in-office and remote attendees, shifting reliance from physical cues to explicit facilitation techniques. Performance metrics need to transcend mere seated presence, anchoring instead on deliverables, impact, and collaboration effectiveness in distributed contexts. Workforce planners must lead the charge in crafting policies that bridge these divides, embedding flexibility and equity at the core of talent strategies rather than treating remote or hybrid work as peripheral or reactive accommodations.

Furthermore, the spatial reimagination of work calls for a re-examination of office spaces themselves. No longer purely hubs for routine tasks, offices can transform into dynamic centres for creativity, social bonding, mentorship, and critical synchronous activities that benefit from in-person interaction. From a planning standpoint, investments in real estate must be justified not merely on square footage but on the value they add to a blended workforce. This requires data-driven insights and employee input to design environments that foster engagement and innovation while complementing the digital workflows that support remote work. Hence, strategic planners must weave together physical and virtual touchpoints into a cohesive ecosystem that honours the unique affordances of each and maximizes workforce potential.

Leadership in this reshaped landscape assumes heightened significance. Leaders become conductors not just of processes but of connection, culture, and empathy across dispersed ensembles. Their ability to create a shared vision, build trust remotely, champion continuous learning, and model adaptive behaviours will determine the success of workforce strategies grounded in distributed models. Planning must thus include leadership development programs tailored to remote and hybrid contexts, instilling skills in digital fluency, emotional intelligence, and inclusive communication. Successful organisations invest deliberately in equipping their leaders to navigate the intricacies of distributed team dynamics as a critical strategic asset.

Incorporating remote and hybrid workforce models also demands a reevaluation of talent development and career progression pathways. Traditional paradigms based heavily on physical visibility and proximity to power centres risk marginalizing remote workers if not adapted thoughtfully. Workforce planning must ensure that development opportunities, mentorship, performance feedback, and succession planning processes are equitable and accessible regardless of location. Designing virtual leadership programs, digital learning platforms, and transparent career frameworks that recognize both outputs and potential across diverse working modes becomes essential for retaining and advancing top talent in these new ecosystems.

Another dimension to consider is the impact on organisational agility and resilience. Remote and hybrid configurations can enhance an organisation's ability to pivot rapidly in response to market disruptions or unforeseen crises by dispersing risk and fostering decentralized decision-making. However, agility depends on underlying frameworks of communication, data transparency, and trust that must be intentionally engineered. Strategic workforce planners need to embed agility principles within remote and hybrid work policies to ensure that flexibility does not devolve into fragmentation or loss of coherence. By cultivating adaptive cultures that celebrate experimentation and learning, organisations can harness the full potential of these models for sustainable growth.

The metrics and analytics used to measure workforce effectiveness must evolve accordingly. Traditional indicators such as time spent at a desk or physical presence lose relevance, while new dimensions such as digital collaboration patterns, employee engagement scores, innovation contributions, and well-being indicators acquire prominence. Workforce analytics tools leveraging AI and machine learning provide powerful means to capture these nuanced insights, enabling planners to fine-tune strategies in near real time. However, ethical considerations around data privacy and surveillance must be carefully balanced to maintain trust and respect employee autonomy. Cloud-based platforms can integrate workforce data holistically, presenting leadership with dashboards that illuminate both human and operational dynamics within these dispersed models, informing more agile and informed decision-making.

Legal and compliance issues also take centre stage with remote and hybrid workforces transcending jurisdictions. Labor standards, tax implications, data protection laws, and occupational health regulations vary widely across geography, necessitating robust frameworks to manage risk while enabling flexibility. Workforce planning must collaborate closely with legal, finance, and compliance functions to develop policies and contracts that accommodate these complexities. This often involves creating repositories of compliant practices, training for managers on cross-border regulations, and ongoing monitoring systems to mitigate risks proactively. The ability to navigate this labyrinth of legalities becomes a competitive advantage, ensuring workforce strategies are not only innovative but sustainable and compliant.

Reflection on the future trajectory of remote and hybrid workforce models reveals that these are not simply transient adaptations but enduring shifts in how work integrates with life, technology, and organisational purpose. The blend of human connection and digital facilitation invites continuous innovation in collaboration technologies, virtual reality environments, and AI-enabled productivity tools that reshape the contours of work itself. Workforce planners must remain vigilant to emerging trends, anticipating how next-generation innovations will further alter talent ecosystems and preparing their organisations to harness these advances dynamically.

Ultimately, strategic workforce planning that embraces remote and hybrid workforces can orchestrate human capital with a visionary precision akin to a master conductor leading a globally dispersed orchestra. It requires an astute blend of technology integration, cultural stewardship, leadership evolution, and policy innovation—all underpinned by empathy, trust, and adaptability. For leaders and planners willing to engage with these profound workplace dynamics proactively, the opportunities are vast: not just in accessing unparalleled talent and fostering flexibility, but in building resilient, motivated, and future-ready workforces that can thrive amid uncertainty and change. By anticipating and integrating the diverse dimensions of remote and hybrid work into their planning, organisations can compose a workforce symphony that harmonizes individual potential with strategic aspirations, creating enduring value and innovation in the concert hall of tomorrow's business landscape.

Automation and AI Impact

In the sweeping symphony of workforce strategy, the crescendo of automation and artificial intelligence emerges not merely as a background rhythm but as a transformative movement, reshaping the very fabric of talent needs across industries. Technology, once a supporting instrument, now conducts whole sections of the orchestra, altering the score that organisational leaders and HR professionals must interpret and integrate with precision. To truly master strategic planning for tomorrow's talent, one must navigate this technological odyssey with acute awareness and foresight, anticipating not only what roles may fade but what novel capacities will emerge, demanding a recalibration of skills, mindsets, and workforce structures.

The impact of automation and AI on talent needs is multifaceted, weaving together threads of opportunity and disruption, creativity and efficiency, uncertainty and innovation. At the most visible level, automation threatens to displace routine, repetitive tasks—those once considered the backbone of many operational functions. Manufacturing lines hum with robotic efficiency; customer service queries are triaged by AI-driven chatbots; data entry is no longer the domain of humans but of algorithms parsing and organizing information with relentless, error-free consistency. This evolution prompts a fundamental inquiry: which jobs are vulnerable, and which will triumph in the era of intelligent machines? The answer, however, resists simplistic categorization. Talent planning must transcend fear of obsolescence to embrace a nuanced understanding that automation redefines roles rather than abolishes them outright.

Indeed, as machines assume transactional and process-driven responsibilities, the premium shifts to skills that technology cannot replicate: emotional intelligence, strategic thinking, complex problem-solving, and creative innovation. This shift compels organisational leaders to rethink their talent acquisition and development planning, fostering a workforce adept at collaborating with AI systems rather than competing against them. The human-machine partnership becomes a focal point—one where employees are empowered to leverage AI as a tool for enhanced decision-making, productivity, and innovation. For instance, data scientists transform raw data into actionable business insights, not merely by crunching numbers, but by interpreting AI-generated analytics to inform strategy. Similarly, marketing professionals use AI to predict consumer trends and personalize outreach, but rely on their instinct and narrative skill to craft compelling campaigns that resonate on a human level.

Looking deeper, automation and AI introduce complexities into talent strategies by enabling new types of work and altering the scale and pace at which organisations operate. The expansion of AI capabilities is driving the proliferation of "hybrid" roles, where employees must blend technical proficiency with domain-specific expertise. A healthcare professional might integrate AI diagnostic tools into patient care, requiring an understanding of algorithmic outputs alongside empathetic patient interactions. In finance, risk managers analyse AI-generated predictive models while maintaining judgment over nuanced market forces. Thus, workforce planners must not only assess the immediate tasks automation can replace but also anticipate the emergence of roles that blend human intuition with technological augmentation. This requires a dynamic competency framework, flexible enough to evolve as AI capabilities advance, and training programs that emphasize lifelong learning and adaptability over fixed skill sets.

Moreover, the diffusion of AI and automation reshapes organisational hierarchies and collaboration paradigms. Traditional chains of command give way to more decentralized, agile structures where cross-functional teams coalesce around AI-enabled projects. Talent planning must evolve to identify not just individual skill gaps but collective capabilities—how teams, equipped with diverse expertise and AI tools, achieve synergistic outcomes. The leadership challenge becomes one of cultivating a culture that embraces technology as an enabler rather than a threat, fostering psychological safety that encourages experimentation and iterative learning in adopting AI solutions. Leaders must therefore possess technological savvy alongside emotional intelligence, guiding their organisations through complex transitions with clarity and empathy.

In confronting the accelerating pace of technological change, businesses also confront ethical considerations that impact talent strategies. AI systems, inherently designed by humans, risk perpetuating biases and inequities if not carefully managed. Talent planning thus must incorporate skills in ethical AI governance, data privacy, and inclusive design to ensure that workforce augmentation does not inadvertently undermine diversity or fairness. This anticipatory labour shapes recruitment priorities, emphasizing capabilities around critical thinking, ethical reasoning, and interdisciplinary collaboration. Organisations that embed these values at the heart of their AI integration signal a commitment not only to innovation but to responsible stewardship—a message that resonates profoundly with socially conscious talent pools and modern consumers alike.

The ripple effects of automation and AI extend to the very nature of work arrangements and employment models. The gig economy, empowered by technological platforms, flourishes with flexible, project-based engagements that challenge traditional notions of long-term employment. AI algorithms facilitate matching between specialized freelancers and corporate needs at scale, fostering a fluid talent ecosystem. Strategic workforce planning must incorporate this growing contingent workforce—not merely as a tactical stopgap but as a strategic asset—requiring new approaches to onboarding, engagement, performance monitoring, and integration with core teams. Leaders must cultivate capabilities in managing distributed workforces, harnessing digital collaboration tools, and aligning diverse contributors toward coherent, agile outcomes.

Furthermore, AI-driven automation introduces novel metrics and analytics into talent management, revolutionizing how organisations monitor workforce effectiveness and predict future needs. Advanced analytics provide granular insights into employee performance, potential burnout, skills development trajectories, and turnover risks—enabling strategic interventions well before challenges escalate. AI-powered predictive models assist in scenario planning, simulating the impact of technological adoption on talent requirements across varied market conditions. This data-driven foresight represents a paradigm shift from reactive human resource management to proactive, anticipatory workforce orchestration. Yet, to harness this power fully, leaders and HR professionals must develop fluency not only in interpreting AI insights but in integrating them with qualitative, contextual understanding—a synergy where technology informs but human judgment directs.

Training and reskilling initiatives emerge as critical levers in adapting to AI-enhanced realities. Organisations invest heavily in continuous learning platforms, often AI-enabled themselves, that tailor training programs to individual employee profiles, accelerating skill acquisition with personalized content and real-time feedback. Yet, effective workforce planning demands a strategic approach beyond technology adoption; it requires fostering a learning culture where individuals embrace change with curiosity and resilience. Such cultural transformation is as crucial as any technical upgrade, ensuring that talent pipelines remain robust amid shifting demands. Leaders play a pivotal role here, modelling growth mindsets and providing psychological incentives that embolden employees to engage in lifelong learning as a core professional norm.

Looking forward, the interdependence between human talent and intelligent machines invites radical reimagining's of workforce composition. Some foresee roles where human creativity and judgment operate in tandem with AI's relentless precision, crafting hybrid workflows that optimize outcomes on scales hitherto unimagined. Others emphasize the emergence of entirely new professions cantered on AI governance, algorithmic auditing, and human-centric technology design—domains demanding not only specialized knowledge but broad system thinking and ethical stewardship. Workforce planners must therefore cultivate an expansive vision, peering beyond immediate disruptions to map pathways for sustainable human-AI collaboration that amplify human potential rather than diminish it.

Allys Watson

The challenge for today's strategists is to avoid succumbing to the dichotomy of dystopian anxiety versus utopian fantasy that often surrounds automation discourse. Instead, they must anchor their approach in pragmatic optimism: recognizing that, while AI and automation redefine roles, they also create unprecedented opportunities for innovation, efficiency, and value creation. This balanced perspective shapes workforce planning into a proactive discipline—one that anticipates change, identifies emergent capabilities, and orchestrates talent ecosystems that remain resilient in the face of dramatic technology-driven transformations.

To integrate these technological trends effectively, workforce planners need frameworks that incorporate technology assessment as a fundamental component of talent forecasting. This means establishing processes where emerging technologies are continuously evaluated against organisational goals and talent capabilities, feeding insights into workforce design and development cycles. Collaboration across functions—IT, HR, strategy—is vital to ensure that technology adoption is aligned with human capital strategies, creating feedback loops that adapt plans as AI evolves. The agility embedded in such frameworks is essential to navigating the fluid technological landscape without losing sight of enduring human values and business imperatives.

Ultimately, the impact of automation and AI on talent needs is less about replacement and more about orchestration—creating a

304

harmonious interplay between human ingenuity and machine efficiency that drives organisational excellence. Strategic workforce planning, informed by this perspective, becomes an artful endeavour where leaders, much like conductors, guide diverse instruments— human and technological alike—to perform a symphony of innovation, adaptability, and sustainable growth. Embracing technology as a transformative partner rather than a disruptive adversary empowers organisations to build future-ready workforces that not only survive but thrive amid the relentless tides of change. In this unfolding narrative, the Planning for workforce success demands vision, courage, and an unwavering commitment to human potential amplified through intelligent design.

Demographic and Social Shifts

In the vast, dynamic landscape of workforce planning, demographic and social shifts serve as the subtle undercurrents that shape the rivers of organisational talent. They represent nuanced, transformative forces that ripple through employee bases, influence labour market availability, and ultimately define the contours within which strategic human capital decisions unfold. The recognition of these shifts is not merely a nod to changing headcounts but a profound engagement with the fundamental patterns that govern who is available to work, how they engage with employment, and what the evolving social fabric demands from workplaces. As we peer into the kaleidoscopic evolution of populations and social structures, we begin to see that anticipating these changes is akin to reading the subtle cues of an orchestra tuning before a grand performance—each voice, each instrument, vital to the harmony the organisation hopes to achieve.

Population changes, with their inexorable ebb and flow, compel strategic planners to think beyond immediate hiring needs and navigate the deeper currents of age, migration, generation, and diversity. The global population, for instance, is not static; it is a living organism morphing through birth rates, aging waves, migrations, and shifting social norms. The aging of the workforce in many developed economies constitutes one of the most pressing demographic considerations. As baby boomers steadily approach retirement, organisations find themselves facing a dual challenge: the looming departure of a significant portion of their experienced workforce and the necessity to fill those knowledge gaps with new talent whose skills may differ dramatically from their predecessors. This transition is not a straightforward replacement but a transformation, where the rhythm of experience adapts to the cadence of fresh perspectives.

Simultaneously, in many parts of the world, younger generations—often characterized by distinct attitudes towards work, technology, flexibility, and purpose—are entering the labour market in unprecedented numbers. Millennials have already reshaped workplace expectations, and Gen Z promises to deepen this evolution with a profound digital native fluency coupled with a strong inclination toward social responsibility and authenticity in the workplace. Understanding the interests, aspirations, and concerns of these emerging generations is crucial for workforce planners who seek to construct a responsive and resilient talent pipeline. This means shifting from traditional attract-and-retain models toward a more fluid engagement framework that values continuous learning, diversity of thought, and adaptability.

Migration and mobility also exert powerful influences on workforce demographics, inflecting patterns of skill availability and cultural composition. Global migration trends are increasingly complex, driven by economic disparities, geopolitical shifts, climate change, and evolving immigration policies. Talent flows from one region to another, sometimes in surges triggered by technological booms, conflicts, or natural disasters, creating new hotspots of expertise as well as unexpected talent shortages. Organisations must cultivate a keen eye not only on their immediate labour pools but also on afar horizons, where untapped skills await discovery. This demands that global workforce strategies incorporate cultural intelligence, legal compliance, and a welcoming organisational culture that harnesses the richness inherent in diversity.

Diversity itself transcends simple demographic categorization. It envelopes a wider spectrum, encompassing gender, ethnicity, cognitive styles, educational backgrounds, disabilities, and a diverse set of lived experiences. The social expectations of inclusivity and equity have reshaped the very tenets of talent management. Companies now recognize that diverse teams are not just a beacon of social responsibility but a strategic imperative linked to innovation, market relevance, and competitive advantage. The plethora of perspectives brought forth by diverse employees enables organisations to better understand and serve increasingly diverse customer bases, solve complex problems with creativity, and build cultures of belonging that retain talent through resonance and respect.

Importantly, integrating considerations around diversity and inclusion into workforce planning is not a passive checkbox exercise; it is an active, thoughtful process that weaves these values into every stage—from recruitment through to development, assessment, and retention. For planners, this involves dissecting existing demographic data and social trends, conducting rigorous gap analyses on representation, and crafting targeted interventions that recognize systemic barriers and seek to dismantle them. These efforts must be backed by an organisational commitment expressed through transparent leadership, training programs that cultivate empathy and cultural competence, and policies that uphold fairness and accessibility. The true measure of progress lies not in the optics of diverse headcounts but in the lived experiences of employees who feel empowered, respected, and enabled to contribute fully.

Layered on top of demographic realities are social shifts in attitudes toward work itself. The rise of gig economies shifts toward remote and hybrid work modalities, and evolving expectations around work-life integration illustrate how social evolutions influence workforce dynamics. People increasingly seek meaning, flexibility, and continuous growth rather than static roles confined within rigid structures. This social movement impacts how talent is sourced, how careers are managed, and what organisational loyalty looks like. For workforce planners, this means expanding the traditional talent Planning to accommodate contingent workers, freelancers, and digital nomads, while also reimagining organisational structures to foster collaboration across flexible geographical and temporal boundaries.

These social currents also reflect a broader generational recalibration of values where sustainability, transparency, and ethical leadership gain prominence. Organisations that fail to recognize the voice of these currents risk alienating emerging talent pools and limiting their future competitive edge. For example, younger workers often prioritize not just remuneration but environmental stewardship, corporate social responsibility, and authentic engagement with societal issues. Workforce planning must therefore incorporate these intangibles, yet critical, elements by embedding corporate social purpose into talent attraction and retention strategies, ensuring the organisation remains a beacon for those seeking not just jobs, but meaningful careers.

Forecasting talent needs through a demographic and social lens requires a blend of quantitative and qualitative approaches grounded in robust data and empathetic understanding. Traditional statistical models must be enriched with ethnographic insights, market trend analyses, and ongoing dialogue with workforce participants to capture the human nuances behind the numbers. This ongoing assessment enables planners to anticipate shifts such as declining labour participation rates in certain groups, rising multiculturalism in urban centres, or new educational trends influencing skill pipelines. Armed with this intelligence, organisations can architect workforce strategies that are not only reactive but proactively sculpted to nurture resilience and agility in the face of uncertainty.

An illustrative example comes from the healthcare sector, where aging populations globally intensify demand for services while the pool of qualified care providers shrinks due to retirement and burnout. Forward-thinking healthcare organisations have responded by reimagining recruiting strategies—actively targeting younger generations, migrants, and traditionally underrepresented groups while investing heavily in training and technology to augment human capacity. This multidimensional response shows the power of integrating demographic and social insights into tangible, strategic actions that safeguard organisational vitality.

Similarly, the technology industry, often perceived as young and fast-moving, confronts its own challenges related to diversity and inclusion. Historically, it has struggled with gender imbalances and limited ethnic representation. Recognizing the innovation-stifling effects of homogeneity, many firms have implemented ambitious diversity hiring programs, mentorship networks, and inclusive culture-building practices that are documented to improve both creativity and employee satisfaction. Such efforts are not just moral initiatives but strategic manoeuvres ensuring these organisations remain competitive in a global talent war.

Moreover, demographic shifts can vary dramatically based on geographic, economic, and cultural contexts, demanding hyper-localized workforce strategies. A global multinational, for instance, must navigate aging workforces in some countries, burgeoning youth populations in others, and varied social norms that shape work styles and expectations. This complexity reinforces that workforce planning cannot be a one-size-fits-all exercise but rather a sophisticated act of orchestration blending local knowledge with global vision.

Effective anticipation and integration of demographic and social trends into workforce plans also hinge on cultivating partnerships—not only internally across business units and HR but externally with educational institutions, government bodies, and community organisations. These collaborations allow organisations to influence talent pipelines upstream and contribute to social infrastructure that supports a sustainable talent ecosystem. Programs that support STEM education in underrepresented communities, apprenticeships that build skills aligned with future needs, or immigration initiatives facilitating talent mobility are all vital threads in the broader fabric of strategic workforce planning.

As demographic and social landscapes continue their relentless transformation, a workforce plan anchored in these insights transforms from a static document into a living, breathing roadmap. It becomes a testament to organisational foresight, inclusivity, and agility, one that deftly balances the scales of tradition and innovation, experience and novelty, local realities and global trends. It encourages leaders not only to react to change but to shape it thoughtfully, crafting workplaces that resonate with the rich diversity and evolving aspirations of the human capital they steward.

Ultimately, the recognition and incorporation of demographic and social shifts into workforce planning is both an art and a science. It demands analytical rigor and narrative sensitivity, quantitative precision and empathetic leadership. When executed with intentionality, it enables organisations to transcend the uncertainties of workforce dynamics and instead embrace a future filled with opportunity—a vibrant symphony composed of diverse talents, harmonized through strategic vision and persistent adaptability. Through this lens, we understand that demographic and social realities are far more than statistical trends; they are living stories informing how we build, sustain, and inspire the workforce of tomorrow.

Allys Watson

The Final Movement: Crafting Your Workforce Planning

Framework Overview

In the vast and intricate tapestry of organisational success, strategic workforce planning emerges as both an art and a science, demanding a framework that is simultaneously robust and fluid—a Planning that melds precision with imagination. At its core, the framework for strategic workforce planning is the conductor's score, the unseen guide that orchestrates every note the human capital ensemble must play. It is the synthesis of foresight, alignment, and execution, purposefully designed to bridge today's operational realities with tomorrow's aspirational horizons.

To begin, this framework rests on the foundational principle that workforce planning cannot exist in isolation; it is tethered tightly to the overarching business strategy. There is a profound necessity to translate an organisation's vision, mission, and goals into tangible workforce imperatives. This means leaders must first understand their business context intimately—not just the current market conditions, but the trajectory and evolution of their industry landscape. It calls for a disciplined approach to environmental scanning, not as a peripheral exercise but as the heartbeat that vibrates through every decision. This scanning involves interpreting signals from technological advances, demographic trends, economic forces, and cultural shifts—all of which influence the demand for talent and the skills that will be prized in the future workplace. The organisation must gaze beyond the present, cultivating a panoramic lens that captures emerging disruptions and opportunities with equal clarity.

Once the business context is illuminated, the framework advances to workforce demand analysis—the deliberate process of forecasting the quantity and quality of talent required to execute strategic objectives. This step is akin to charting a complex constellation, where each star represents a skill, role, or competency critical to success. This is not merely speculation, but a methodical synthesis of data drawn from multiple internal and external sources—historical performance metrics, industry benchmarks, turnover rates, and succession pipelines. Harnessing predictive analytics here is transformative, empowering leaders to anticipate surges in demand, identify critical talent gaps, and prepare for varying scenarios with agility and confidence. Embedded in this process is a nuanced understanding that precision in forecasting is sculpted over time; it thrives on iterative learning and continuous refinement.

Parallel to demand forecasting is the examination of supply—the analysis of current workforce capabilities, availability, and potential. This involves a deep dive into the internal talent ecosystem: assessing not only who is currently employed but also their readiness, mobility, and development trajectories. Like a master chemist blending elements, strategic workforce planners evaluate the mix of skills, experience, diversity, and potential across teams and departments. They consider retention risks, succession readiness, and the latent talents that may be unlocked through targeted development programs. Importantly, this supply assessment acknowledges the external talent market dynamics, recognizing that the workforce extends beyond organisational borders. The availability of contingent workers, freelancers, and gig-economy professionals is scrutinized as an integral facet of a comprehensive talent ecosystem.

Bridging demand and supply, the framework embraces gap analysis—a diagnostic lens that reveals disparities between future requirements and current capabilities. This is the crucible where strategic decisions are forged. It exposes vulnerabilities that may compromise strategic execution if left unaddressed, yet it also uncovers untapped strengths ripe for amplification. This truth-telling process demands candour and creativity, encouraging leaders to confront discomfort with a problem-solving mindset. Gap analysis forms the foundation upon which workforce strategies are built—whether that means upskilling existing employees, redesigning roles, restructuring teams, or expanding recruitment channels to attract scarce talent.

Crucially, this framework does not stop at diagnosis; it propels toward action through talent strategy formulation and implementation planning. Strategies become the instruments through which gaps are closed, and alignment is secured. These tactical approaches range from developing robust learning and development programs that cultivate critical capabilities internally to forging strategic partnerships with educational institutions and technology providers to secure pipelines of future-ready talent. The integration of technology here becomes paramount, as workforce planning increasingly harnesses AI-driven tools and data analytics to personalize career paths, optimize workforce deployment, and simulate outcome scenarios with remarkable granularity. Execution plans are designed with thoughtful consideration of timelines, resource allocation, and governance structures, ensuring accountability and momentum across all organisational layers.

Oversight and continuous evaluation form the framework's reinforcing feedback loop. Strategic workforce planning is not a static, annual exercise but an ongoing rhythm embedded into the organisational culture and operations. Key performance indicators and workforce metrics serve as vital sign monitors—tracking progress against objectives, measuring the efficacy of interventions, and illuminating areas for course correction. Leaders engaged in this iterative process foster a learning environment that embraces agility, adaptability, and responsiveness, qualities essential in an era marked by volatility and complexity.

Beyond the structural elements, the framework incorporates critical enablers of success, beginning with leadership engagement. The most sophisticated plans falter without authentic commitment from senior leaders who champion workforce initiatives as strategic imperatives. These leaders model the mindset of workforce stewardship, investing in the development of talent as a core organisational asset. They cultivate a culture that values transparency, inclusivity, and open dialogue, recognizing that workforce planning is a collective endeavour influenced by diverse perspectives across hierarchy and function. Communication strategies are embedded thoughtfully within the framework to ensure that workforce plans resonate through the organisation, galvanizing alignment and shared ownership.

Risk management is woven integrally into every phase of the planning cycle. Leaders must identify potential challenges from labour market fluctuations, technological disruptions, socioeconomic shifts, and regulatory changes, then proactively design mitigation tactics. This anticipation transforms risks into resilience-building opportunities, allowing organisations to pivot swiftly and maintain continuity under pressure.

In practical application, this framework offers a suite of tools and methodologies designed to accelerate momentum. Interactive talent dashboards provide real-time visibility into workforce metrics, scenario planning workshops encourage visionary thinking alongside pragmatic contingency preparedness, and workforce segmentation techniques allow for targeted interventions tailored to high-priority groups. These tools empower practitioners not only to visualize complexity but also to translate insight into decisive, exemplary action.

Most importantly, the framework's architecture nurtures a mindset shift—from reactive firefighting to deliberate orchestration—transforming workforce planning from a bureaucratic task into a dynamic, empowering strategic capability. It invites organisations to envision their workforce as a living ecosystem—interconnected, adaptive, and thriving—where human potential is nurtured continually in harmony with business aspirations. By grounding themselves in this framework, leaders are equipped not only to anticipate future talent needs with clarity but to mobilize their organisations swiftly and confidently toward success.

Every element of the framework, from environmental scanning to strategy execution and evaluation, works symbiotically. It encourages organisations to start where they are, building incremental progress fuelled by learning and sustained by commitment. With reflection questions and practical templates embedded within the framework, readers are guided to translate theory into practice immediately, crafting their own workforce planning with clarity and conviction. This approach fosters ownership and adaptability, ensuring that workforce planning becomes not just a process, but a continuous journey of growth and renewal.

Through embracing this comprehensive yet flexible framework, organisational leaders and HR professionals are handed the baton—ready to conduct their workforce like a finely tuned orchestra, aligning every note and rhythm to the evolving melody of business success. It is a call to action as much as a guide, urging readers to step confidently into the role of visionary strategists, crafting a future workforce that is resilient, agile, and deeply attuned to the needs of tomorrow's dynamic markets. The framework is not merely a plan; it is a promise—a promise to transform human potential into extraordinary outcomes, and to harmonize talent with strategy in a symphony of sustained organisational excellence.

Action Planning Tools

In the intricate tapestry of strategic workforce planning, moving from insight to action is where many organisations find themselves at a crossroads. The journey from understanding future talent needs to effectively implementing solutions demands a reliable set of tools that transform abstract strategies into concrete, executable plans. It is within this vital transition that action planning tools become not just helpful, but indispensable. These templates and checklists are more than static instruments; they serve as dynamic frameworks that empower leaders, HR professionals, and strategists to drill down into the complexities of workforce planning and emerge with clear, manageable pathways toward measurable outcomes.

At the heart of these tools lies the notion that effective implementation hinges on clarity, structure, and continual reflection. A well-crafted template acts as a Planning tool, enabling organisations to dissect grand ambitions into manageable steps, assign responsibilities, anticipate obstacles, and align timelines with both strategic milestones and operational realities. One such cornerstone is the workforce action plan template — an adaptive framework designed to map out each phase of planning with meticulous attention to detail and a focus on alignment. Imagine this template as a conductor's score, where every instrument—be it recruitment, training, succession, or performance management—has its precise entrance, crescendo, and exit, allowing the entire composition to resonate harmoniously within the organisation's goals.

Within this template, three vital dimensions invite continuous engagement: objectives, resources, and evaluation. By articulating crystal-clear objectives, each segment of the action plan secures a north star, preventing drift and fostering synchronized effort across departments. Resources are catalogued not only in terms of budget or personnel but also extend to technological tools, external partnerships, and tacit knowledge, providing a holistic view of what must be harnessed to bring the plan to life. Evaluation mechanisms embedded within the template offer checkpoints for progress and pivot points for course corrections; they transform the plan from a static document to a living roadmap, responsive to evolving circumstances and emerging insights.

Parallel to templates, checklists serve as grounding instruments for everyday operational rigor. Often underestimated, a checklist becomes the guardian of consistency and accountability, ensuring that critical tasks don't slip through the cracks amid the whirlwind of workforce transitions and change management initiatives. It is a tool that democratizes responsibility, enabling teams at all levels to engage with, contribute to, and own the plan's execution. Take, for instance, a recruitment readiness checklist, which goes beyond verifying job descriptions or candidate pools— it outlines the alignment of hiring goals with projected talent gaps, the integration of diversity and inclusion metrics, screening processes adapted to future skills requirements, and timelines synchronized with broader business cycles. Such a checklist elevates recruitment from a transactional activity to a strategic endeavour deeply embedded in workforce foresight.

Moreover, action planning tools foster a culture of transparency and collaboration, weaving these values into the fabric of workforce orchestration. When action plans and checklists are shared openly across teams, they forge a common understanding, breaking silos and encouraging dialogue. This not only enhances buy-in but also surfaces innovative ideas from unexpected quarters, enriching the planning process with diverse perspectives. Transparency creates a shared sense of ownership that drives momentum and cultivates resilience in the face of inevitable challenges.

Integral to these tools is the balance they strike between specificity and flexibility. While detailed enough to offer clear guidance, they are intentionally designed to be adaptable across industries, organisational sizes, and maturity levels in workforce planning practices. This versatility means that whether a global manufacturing firm is expanding robotic automation or a fintech startup is racing to scale its customer support teams, the templates and checklists remain relevant, customizable, and scalable. Their modular nature allows organisations to tailor action steps according to their unique talent ecosystems, development priorities, and risk appetites, making these tools foundational yet fluid instruments in strategic execution.

Complementing this adaptability is the infusion of iterative cycles into action planning tools, reinforcing the principle that workforce planning is not a one-off project but an evolving discipline. Built-in reflection points encourage leaders to pause, assess progress against key performance indicators, and recalibrate actions as external environments shift and internal realities evolve. This cyclical approach cultivates agility and embeds continuous learning into the rhythm of workforce management. Tools that merely dictate steps without inviting reflection limit efficacy; those that invite questions such as "What assumptions have changed?" or "How have emerging trends altered our talent landscape?" prompt adaptive responses essential for long-term success.

Technology integration plays an increasingly pivotal role here, seamlessly interfacing with these templates and checklists to amplify their impact. Cloud-based platforms facilitate real-time updates, scenario simulations, and stakeholder notifications, transforming static documents into vibrant collaborative hubs. Artificial intelligence enhances predictive insights embedded within templates, suggesting optimal resource allocations based on historical data and projected market changes. Interactive dashboards aligned with checklists provide visual cues of progress, risk, and opportunities, serving as motivational feedback loops that keep teams aligned and focused. When workforce strategists harness these technological enablers alongside foundational tools, the orchestrated effort reaches a new level of precision and responsiveness.

Beyond structural and technical attributes, effective action planning tools embody a mindset shift—moving from reactive problem-solving to proactive talent shaping. They encourage leaders to anticipate bottlenecks before they materialize, identify critical skill adjacencies, and pilot innovative workforce models in low-risk environments. By laying out scenarios and contingency steps, these tools transform uncertainty from a source of paralysis into a domain of calculated exploration and creative problem-solving. This shift marks a departure from traditional notions of workforce planning as static headcount exercises to a dynamic, strategy-aligned dialogue with the organisation's future.

Use cases further illustrate the transformative power of these tools. Consider a retail giant facing rapid digitization of its sales channels, grappling with the need to reskill frontline employees while simultaneously expanding e-commerce expertise. Implementing the action planning template allowed their HR leadership to break down the strategy into targeted interventions: massive digital literacy programs, revamped hiring criteria focusing on hybrid skill sets, and redesigned career pathways to encourage lateral moves between store operations and online functions. Checklists tracked milestone completions, such as vendor trainings contracted, learning management system launches, and talent pipeline diversifications. Crucially, embedded review points facilitated agile adjustments when pandemic-related market disruptions accelerated the shift to online, ensuring workforce readiness kept pace with business imperatives.

Another vivid example emerges from a high-tech engineering firm that leveraged customized checklists to refine succession planning amid looming retirements of critical senior engineers. Their approach involved mapping competencies, identifying potential internal successors, outlining development programmes, and monitoring leadership bench strength continuously. The discipline instilled by checklist adherence not only mitigated risk but also enhanced organisational transparency and morale, reassuring employees that future leadership was in capable hands. This translated not only into smooth knowledge transfer but also into a culture that valued preparedness and foresight.

Embedded reflection questions within the templates further enrich the planning experience. Questions such as "Which workforce segments present the highest risk if left unaddressed?" or "How does this action align with our five-year innovation roadmap?" invite critical thinking and self-assessment beyond mere task completion. These inquiries prompt teams to connect operational activities with strategic aspirations, fostering deeper engagement and more insightful decision-making. The invitation to continually question assumptions transforms workforce planning into an evolving dialogue rather than a static checklist exercise.

The practical benefits of these tools extend to measurability as well. Frameworks that integrate key performance indicators at each step enable organisations to quantify progress, identify early warning signals, and communicate results effectively to stakeholders. This metric-driven approach addresses a frequent stumbling block in workforce initiatives: translating success into tangible business impact. By linking actions to outcomes with clear data points, planning tools reinforce accountability and justify ongoing investment, creating a virtuous cycle where demonstrated value fuels further innovation and dedication.

Similarly, communication protocols embedded within action planning templates facilitate clear messaging both vertically and horizontally. They delineate who is responsible for updates, how frequently progress should be communicated, and channels for feedback and escalation. This embedded communication architecture ensures that workforce plans do not languish in isolated silos but become living conversations energizing the entire organisation. A well-informed team feels empowered, reducing resistance to change and fostering a culture of trust.

Moreover, these tools foster alignment not only within HR functions but also across business units, finance, operations, and technology teams. By creating shared artifacts that transcend departmental languages and priorities, action planning templates and checklists act as a lingua franca, bridging diverse stakeholders. The resulting alignment increases the likelihood that workforce strategies will receive the resources, attention, and strategic support needed for success, ensuring plans shift from idealized concepts into executable realities.

In practice, introducing these tools requires thoughtful change management itself. Organisational leaders must champion the adoption of templates and checklists, modelling their use and incentivizing compliance through recognition and reward mechanisms. Training sessions with interactive workshops help demystify the tools' application, turning initial scepticism into enthusiasm. Showcasing quick wins from early implementations creates momentum and embeds tools organically into planning rhythms. Over time, these action planning tools evolve from novel interventions into standard operating procedures embedded within corporate culture and workflows.

Crucially, these instruments also serve as repositories for institutional knowledge, capturing lessons learned and best practices over successive planning cycles. When properly maintained, they form a rich library of organisational intelligence, preventing the reinventing of wheels and enabling quicker responses to emerging challenges. As the business context shifts, historical comparisons provide essential perspective, informing scenario planning and enriching strategy discussions.

In sum, the power of action planning tools lies not merely in their design but in their capacity to activate intention into motion, to translate the vision of future-ready workforces into pragmatic steps capable of tangible progress. They bridge the intangible with the concrete, the strategic with the operational, fostering disciplined creativity in workforce orchestration. By embracing these templates and checklists, leaders and practitioners empower their organisations to move beyond aspirational talent management rhetoric, equipping themselves with the instruments to compose and conduct a workforce composition that thrives in the uncertainties of tomorrow's business symphony. The ultimate reward is a plan that doesn't gather dust but dances dynamically through changing market rhythms, delivering talent resonance and innovation harmonies that drive sustainable success.

Sustaining Momentum

The journey of workforce planning, much like conducting a grand orchestra, demands more than a momentary burst of enthusiasm or a transient grasp of strategy. Instead, it requires a sustained, deliberate momentum—a continuous, evolving pulse that propels the organisation forward, rhythmically adapting to shifting landscapes while maintaining a clear, unwavering vision. Sustaining momentum in strategic workforce planning is no easy feat; it calls for a profound commitment embedded within every layer of an organisation. It begins by recognizing that workforce planning is not a project with a definitive end date but a dynamic, living process that undergoes constant refinement. This perspective alone transforms how leaders engage with the task. No longer is it a task to be checked off a list but a vital, ongoing symphony that must be rehearsed and tuned incessantly.

To sustain this driving force over the long haul, leaders must anchor their strategies in authentic purpose and a compelling vision that resonates deeply with their teams and stakeholders. It is the vivid clarity of this vision that fuels engagement and sets the tone for persistent effort. When organisations articulate how workforce planning connects to their overarching mission—in shaping not just productivity but the very future of the company—they imbue the process with meaning that transcends mundane administrative duties. This emotional and strategic anchoring transforms workforce planning into a shared cause, a collective enterprise in which each individual feels ownership and pride. When the vision is compelling enough to inspire hearts and minds, the inevitable challenges and setbacks encountered along the way become surmountable hurdles instead of debilitating roadblocks.

Crucially, sustaining momentum hinges on embedding workforce planning deeply within the organisational culture, transforming it from a sporadic exercise into a core organisational rhythm. This cultural embedding requires more than just lip service; it demands visible, genuine commitment from senior leadership who actively champion the cause. Leaders must consistently communicate the importance of workforce planning, celebrate milestones, and recognize the efforts of individuals and teams who contribute to the process. This ongoing advocacy weaves workforce planning into the very fabric of day-to-day operations, making it an integral element of decision-making and strategic dialogue. By fostering a culture where continuous learning, adaptability, and proactive talent management are valued norms, organisations build resilience that sustains momentum even when external conditions fluctuate unpredictably.

But culture alone is insufficient without the scaffolding of precise, actionable processes that turn vision into reality. Establishing routine cycles of review and recalibration is essential. Just as a conductor periodically revisits scores and rehearses sections to perfect timing and harmony, organisations must implement regular workforce strategy sessions that reflect on progress, analyse new data, and realign priorities. These feedback loops function as vital gears in maintaining forward thrust, enabling swift identification of emerging gaps, risk areas, or opportunities that require immediate attention. Integrating key performance indicators and workforce analytics into these sessions converts abstract insights into tangible actions, providing leaders with measurable evidence of success and areas for adjustment. This balance of rigor and responsiveness ensures workforce planning remains a vibrant, evolving discipline rather than a static document gathering dust.

Equally important is the empowerment of mid-level managers and HR professionals who operate as the frontline conductors of workforce initiatives. By equipping these individuals with the right tools, knowledge, and authority to own segments of workforce planning, organisations build distributed leadership, which is critical for sustaining momentum. Empowerment catalyses local innovation and responsiveness, accelerating problem-solving and adaptation in ways centralized leadership often cannot achieve alone. When managers are trained to interpret workforce data, engage in scenario planning, and implement targeted talent development strategies, they become active contributors to the organisational symphony rather than passive observers. This diffusion of responsibility fosters accountability and enthusiasm, essential ingredients that keep machinery well-oiled and moving consistently forward.

Another powerful strategy for sustaining momentum revolves around leveraging technology as an enabler rather than a mere adjunct. Today's rapid technological advancements—artificial intelligence, predictive analytics, and real-time data dashboards—offer unprecedented capabilities for constantly scanning the talent horizon and fine-tuning workforce strategies. However, technology's true value is realized only when embedded deliberately into the workflow with clear user adoption practices. Investing in intuitive, accessible platforms that integrate data across recruitment, learning, and performance systems ensures that workforce insights are timely, relevant, and actionable across various organisational levels. Furthermore, ongoing training to deepen digital fluency empowers personnel to harness these tools confidently, transforming data from a static resource into a strategic asset that fuels ongoing innovation and pre-emptive action. This seamless integration of technology fortifies the momentum by delivering clarity and precision to workforce decision-making.

Consider, for example, an organisation that implemented an enterprise-wide workforce analytics system coupled with a culture of continuous improvement. The leadership consistently held quarterly strategic reviews, including diverse stakeholders from HR, finance, and operations, to interpret emerging trends and adjust workforce priorities in real time. Mid-level managers were provided access to customized dashboards and empowered to pilot talent development initiatives aligned with future skill demands. Over time, these practices became habitual rhythms, a pulse that sustained the workforce strategy's vitality despite fluctuating economic climates and market disruptions. Employees at all levels began to see workforce planning not simply as a corporate directive but as an adaptive mechanism embedded within their daily work lives. This enduring momentum translated into a highly agile and engaged workforce prepared to meet challenges head-on.

Even as these tactical levers drive ongoing movement, organisations must guard against the twin dangers of complacency and burnout—silent momentum killers. The ebb and flow of organisational priorities and human energy naturally introduce periods of fatigue or distraction, which can disrupt even the most disciplined efforts. Addressing this requires embedding strategies for resilience and reinvigoration within the workforce Planning. Regularly celebrating achievements, no matter how incremental, nurtures a positive feedback cycle that energizes participants. Encouraging reflection sessions where teams share lessons learned and acknowledge hurdles fosters psychological safety and continuous learning. Additionally, rotating leadership roles or injecting fresh perspectives through cross-functional teams can revitalize discussions, preventing stagnation. By consciously managing the human dimension of momentum—emotions, motivation, and well-being—organisations sustain not just the mechanics but the spirit of workforce planning.

Simultaneously, clear and consistent communication emerges as a lifeblood for sustaining momentum over time. Workforce planning involves complex, multi-stakeholder processes where clarity about goals, changes, and expectations is paramount. When communication is transparent, frequent, and bidirectional, it cultivates trust and alignment. This ensures that all participants—from C-suite executives to front-line employees—understand how their contributions impact the broader organisational journey and are empowered to adjust their behaviours accordingly. Storytelling, vivid metaphors, and tangible examples breathe life into otherwise abstract concepts, making workforce plans relatable and compelling. This narrative approach keeps the workforce strategy top of mind, transforming it from a technical document into a living story that everyone feels a part of. For instance, framing workforce agility as a collective dance or a navigated voyage turns strategic objectives into vivid shared experiences that inspire commitment.

At the heart of sustaining momentum lies the imperative of agility—the ability to pivot gracefully in response to unforeseen disruptions or opportunities without losing stride. The business landscape is a shifting kaleidoscope influenced by technological innovation, economic uncertainty, demographic shifts, and global crises. Organisations that embed agility into their workforce planning processes become adept navigators, continuously scanning the environment, experimenting with new talent models, and iterating on strategies. This requires fostering a mindset where change is embraced as an opportunity rather than a threat, supported by robust scenario planning exercises that anticipate multiple futures. When workforce plans are formulated with flexibility, including built-in contingencies and modular approaches to talent deployment, organisations maintain forward propulsion regardless of external flux. Such resilience is evidenced by companies that rapidly redeployed teams or reskilled employees amidst abrupt market changes, maintaining operational continuity and seizing emergent prospects.

One transformative approach that sustains workforce planning momentum is creating learning ecosystems— environments prioritizing continuous upskilling and knowledge sharing that keep human capital fresh and aligned with evolving demands. Organisations committed to lifelong learning build structures where formal training, mentoring, stretch assignments, and informal peer learning coalesce into a holistic talent ecosystem. This culture of development encourages employees to take ownership of their growth journey, reinforcing their engagement and adaptability. Leaders who model lifelong learning and allocate resources strategically create fertile soil where workforce plans thrive, as skills dynamically evolve alongside business needs. The workforce transforms from a static resource to a dynamic reservoir of potential, continuously replenished and optimized, providing an endless source of momentum for talent strategies.

Moreover, securing sustainable momentum necessitates the alignment of incentives with long-term workforce goals. When rewards and recognition systems reinforce behaviours that advance strategic talent objectives—such as collaboration, innovation, and agility—the workforce Planning gains gravitational pull. Incentive structures need not be limited to financial rewards but can include career progression opportunities, public acknowledgment, and meaningful work assignments. These mechanisms nurture a culture where workforce planning is viewed as an integrated path to individual and organisational success. By aligning personal aspirations with organisational ambitions, incentives create positive feedback loops, perpetuating drive and dedication. Employees become active architects of the workforce vision rather than passive recipients, contributing their creativity and energy to ensure the momentum never wanes.

Finally, to jumpstart actionable planning immediately and sustain it indefinitely, organisations must develop accessible tools and templates that demystify workforce planning and lower barriers to entry. Practical resources—step-by-step guides, scenario worksheets, talent segment mapping, risk assessment frameworks, and communication playbooks—transform abstract principles into implementable tasks. These tools serve as a shared language uniting diverse stakeholders, clarifying roles and responsibilities, and facilitating consistent execution. Importantly, accessible planning instruments empower organisations of all sizes and maturity levels to initiate or enhance their workforce strategies with confidence. Embedding these resources within digital collaboration platforms further accelerates adoption and continuity, ensuring that momentum gains traction quickly and perpetuates effortlessly.

In essence, sustaining momentum in workforce planning is an artful orchestration of vision, culture, leadership, process rigor, empowerment, technology, communication, agility, and continuous learning. It requires tireless nurturing of the intangible energies that motivate participation, balanced with robust structures that translate enthusiasm into measurable progress. With deliberate strategy and unwavering dedication, organisations transform workforce planning from a sporadic endeavour into an enduring strategic symphony—one that resonates powerfully across time to shape resilient, adaptable, and thriving talent ecosystems. This sustained rhythm becomes an invaluable asset, empowering organisations not simply to react to future challenges but to compose their own destiny with confidence and creativity, harnessing human capital as the ultimate instrument in the evolving business concerto.

Workforce Planning Information Gathering Form

This form is designed to facilitate the collection of key information necessary for effective workforce planning. It provides a structured framework to help organisations of all sizes initiate or enhance their workforce strategies by transforming abstract principles into practical, implementable tasks. The form serves as a shared language to unite stakeholders, clarify responsibilities, and enable consistent execution across diverse teams.

Section 1: Organisational Context

- Organisation Name: _____
- Industry/Sector: _____
- Location(s): _____
- Workforce Size: _____
- Stage of Workforce Planning: (Initiation, Enhancement, Review, Other) _____

Section 2: Current Workforce Profile

- List of Key Talent Segments/Roles:
- Current Headcount by Segment/Role:
- Geographically Dispersed Teams: (Yes/No; Details if Yes) _____
- Workforce Diversity and Inclusion Initiatives: _____

Section 3: Workforce Planning Objectives

- Primary Goals for Workforce Planning: (e.g., address skill gaps, support business growth, manage change)
- Key Performance Indicators (KPIs):
- Desired Cultural or Operational Outcomes:

Section 4: Risk Assessment and Scenario Planning

- Potential Workforce Risks Identified: (e.g., skills shortages, compliance issues, high turnover)
- Risk Assessment Approach Used: _____
- Scenarios Considered: (e.g., organisational change, market shifts, regulatory updates)

Section 5: Tools, Resources, and Communication

- Existing Tools and Templates in Use: (e.g., guides, worksheets, playbooks)
- Preferred Collaboration Platforms: _____
- Stakeholder Roles and Responsibilities: (List key personnel and their roles in workforce planning)
- Communication Strategies Employed: (e.g., regular updates, workshops, digital channels)

Section 6: Continuous Improvement and Learning

- Processes for Continuous Learning and Feedback:
- Mechanisms for Reviewing and Updating Workforce Plans:
- Recent Lessons Learnt or Best Practices:

Section 7: Additional Notes

- _____
- _____
- _____

This form should be embedded within your digital collaboration platform to ensure accessibility, accelerate adoption, and support ongoing workforce planning efforts. By standardising information gathering, organisations can better empower teams, sustain momentum, and drive strategic HR outcomes.

About The Author

Throughout my career as a human resource professional, I have amassed more than two decades of diverse experience spanning both the private and public sectors. My professional journey has not been confined to Australia; I have also worked internationally in regions including the Caribbean, the United States, Africa, the Middle East, and the Asia Pacific. These experiences have provided me with hands-on exposure to complex, culturally diverse HR environments, establishing greenfield operations, managing large-scale organisational change, and leading HR teams through the intricate processes of mergers and acquisitions.

My work is grounded in advanced qualifications, including a master's degree in human resource management, and certifications in workplace health and safety, alternative dispute resolution, and ISO 9000 auditing. Leveraging these credentials, I have guided organisations in developing and implementing robust HR strategies. My approach is characterised by a blend of strategic planning and pragmatic solutions, ensuring that outcomes are not only compliant and data-driven but also tailored to the unique culture and operational needs of each organisation.

On the international stage, I have adapted best-practice HR principles across a variety of industries, such as healthcare, defence, engineering, and hospitality. Working in these diverse sectors has deepened my appreciation for cultural nuances and the different regulatory landscapes impacting people management across borders. My experience includes collaborating with geographically dispersed teams, managing compliance across multiple countries, and championing diversity and inclusion initiatives that help create positive and productive workplaces.

My expertise in human resources extends beyond daily practice into thought leadership, particularly through my role as an author on HR management topics. By documenting and sharing my professional experiences, I aim to provide readers with valuable insights shaped by navigating real-world challenges and developing effective solutions in varied organisational contexts. My publications offer practical frameworks designed to support strategic HR leadership and policy development, equipping practitioners at all levels to address both immediate and long-term workforce requirements. These works also explore the integration of technology and analytics into people operations, demonstrating how data-driven approaches can enhance decision-making and drive organisational success.

Driven by a passion for continuous learning and a commitment to sharing knowledge, my career reflects a dedication to advancing the HR profession globally. Through a series of comprehensive human resources guides, I invite readers to deepen their understanding of the field and further develop their skills by drawing on proven strategies and insights gained across a wide range of contexts and industries.